SHE CAPTAINS

Heroines and Hellions of the Sea

JOAN DRUETT

A Touchstone Book

PUBLISHED BY SIMON & SCHUSTER

New York London Toronto Sydney Singapore

INTRODUCTION

One morning in 529 B.C., in an encampment on the Volga River, north of the Caspian Sea, Tomyris, Queen of the Massagetae, woke up to find herself a widow, a tricky situation. The Massagetae, a mighty tribe of watermen and warriors, were under siege by Persian forces led by Cyrus the Great, a tyrant whose ambition to control the whole of Asia from the Hindu Kush to the Mediterranean was almost fulfilled. Cyrus's conquests stretched from Greece to India and from Babylon to Lydia (now Turkey), and it was just the Massagetae that barred his path to the north.

Queen Tomyris was probably not at all surprised when the news of her husband's death led to a prompt proposal of marriage from the Persian monarch. Obviously, to Cyrus the Great a convenient wedding would seem an easy path to domination of the tribe. She flatly refused, understanding his reasons, so Cyrus ordered that the mighty Volga River be bridged with boats, while his marines and cavalry prepared for battle. Seeing this, Tomyris decided to negotiate, offering terms to which Cyrus pretended to agree. Before he withdrew his forces, however, he gave orders for a great feast of roasted meat and unwatered wine to be left in his abandoned encampment. The Massagetae warriors fell for the trick, eat-

An Amazon in battle.
Detail from a wall slab, mausoleum, Halikarnassos.

ing and drinking so heavily that they became stupefied, and easy victims for the Persians, who stealthily returned in the night.

Furious at this treachery, Tomyris sent Cyrus a message in which she vowed "by the sun, the lord of the Massagetae, that for all you are so insatiate of blood, I will give you your fill thereof." And she was as good as her word. They met on another battleground, and this time her forces prevailed. Cyrus was killed. As soon as the dust had settled Queen Tomyris personally searched the battlefield for his corpse. Then she chopped off the Persian king's head and triumphantly plunged it into a bag of human blood.

Thus runs just one of the ancient lost tales of the powerful women of the rivers and seas—the female maritime heroes. Nowadays, "hero" is an unequivocally masculine noun meaning "a man distinguished for bold enterprise." Yet Hero was a legendary priestess whose lover, Leander, swam across the Hellespont to join her every night, guided by a beacon in her window. One night, a storm blew the lantern out, and Leander drowned. Distraught, Hero cast herself into the sea, the first in the long line of women who star in the old magic legends of maritime lore.

They are stories that span the world. Like the siren sea nymphs of Greek mythology who would have lured the Greek pirate-hero Odysseus to destruction on the rocks if he had not been forewarned by the sorceress

Circe, the fox fairies of Chinese folk-lore were dangerously seductive to susceptible seafarers. The Greeks also told stories of the Amazons—a race of tough and beautiful battlers who were allied with Troy in the Trojan War—while the Norse bards sang of the Valkyria, the warrior-handmaidens of Valhalla. In Japan, they used to tell of a beautiful pearl fisher named Tokoyo who saved her father from a long and cruel exile in the Oki Islands. Single-handedly, she sailed a coracle to find him, and then as ransom for his freedom she killed the evil god Yofune-Nushi. Like Beowulf, the Icelandic hero, she dived into the roaring deep to meet and murder her foe—an impressive sea monster with writhing, serpentine shape, phosphorescent scales, fiery eyes, and many tiny, waving legs—and at the same time retrieved a statue of the emperor that Yofune-Nushi was holding hostage. She did not wait for a man to do it; Tokoyo did it all by herself.

Head of an Amazon.
Detail from a wall slab, mausoleum, Halikarnassos.

In the third century B.C., another kind of maritime heroine flowered in the East. The beautiful Princess Sanghamitta boarded a ship to sail from her homeland to meet the king of a deeply forested and very mountainous island. She was the daughter of the great King Dharmasoka of In-

Princess and lady-in-waiting. The Princess has a parasol above her head—a mark of her status.
Relief, Temple of Borobudur, Indonesia.

dia, and the island was Sri Lanka, which in times to come was occasionally known as Ceylon.

Princess Sanghamitta was following in the footsteps of her brother, Prince Mahinda. King Dharmasoka was a fervent Buddhist who felt a great desire to share his faith. When the king of Sri Lanka had heard of this, he decided it would be diplomatic to ask for a missionary to come to the people of his island. As the request came from a fellow ruler, King Dharmasoka sent Prince Mahinda. Princess Sanghamitta's brother did

such a good job that the women of Sri Lanka wanted a female to teach them this new philosophy, so, of course, the appropriate emissary was Princess Sanghamitta.

Men hoisting sails, readying for departure, while the King (center) studies a portrait of a beautiful woman. Relief, Temple of Borobudur, Indonesia.

She carried a precious gift, a rooted sapling of the tree that had sheltered the Buddha when he had experienced his great enlightenment. This made a wonderful impression on the waiting crowd, the Sri Lankan king himself wading waist-deep to carry the sapling ashore on his head. Indeed, it was so solemn and marvelous that Princess Sanghamitta's ship was turned into a shrine. The men lifted up the entire craft and carried it to shore, then built three temples about it, focused on the stem, mast, and rudder. And so, because of a pretty princess with a persuasive gesture, Buddhism is the national religion of Sri Lanka.

Seagoing ship with tiller, similar to Princess Sanghamitta's vessel. Relief, Borobudur.

Thus it can be seen that women were as distinguished for bold enterprise as their male equivalents. The rivers and beaches and seas were equal-opportunity spheres back then. It was not until the Victorians rewrote the old legends that women became pictured as weak and frail and witless, in great need of the gallantry of bearded sailors and the kisses of handsome princes, and it was not until the time of Disney that pirates became jolly, and nymphs and mermaids were guarded by smiling dolphins. Before that, all over the world, maritime women were proper heroines—heroines who are now almost forgotten. Their stories, at one time passed down from generation to generation, ritually related by bards and old grandmothers, now need rescuing, and that is the intent of this book. Their narratives need investigation as well as retelling. How true are the tales of heroines like Tokoyo, Queen Tomyris, and Princess Sanghamitta? The perception of female roles in folklore has changed so much that disbelief is the rule. The tendency is to dismiss such yarns as exaggerations, fairy stories, superstitions, and allegories handed down in the unverifiable ramblings of old men and women, at one with the legends of Olympus and Valhalla. Yet, that is how the recording of events began—in the spoken word. What is required is not blanket disbelief, but a sifting of myth from reality, and that is the intention here, too.

Ship in a heavy sea. Relief, Borobudur.

For example, while the evil god Yofune-Nushi is unlikely to have existed, it is quite plausible that a woman who dived every day for pearls could have retrieved a precious artifact from deep in the sea and used it to ransom her father. Documentary evidence can be very persuasive, too, even if just in the form of pictures. Although the actuality of Amazons is doubted by some, their images appear so often in classical Greek sculpture and earthenware that it seems very likely that they did indeed exist. Some scholars have even pinpointed their territory, beside the Black Sea and just to the westward of Massagetae lands where Queen Tomyris ruled.

Princess Sanghamitta was real. While the three shrines that were built about her ship have been crumbled away by time, the tree she carried still stands, the oldest historically documented tree in the world. Indeed, it has its own military guard. Her story remained oral history until the first century B.C., when the Buddhist monks of Sri Lanka included it in a historical preface to the Buddha's teachings, called "the Mahavamsa of the ancients." And vengeful Queen Tomyris, who sank the head of Cyrus the Great in a bag of human blood, was an actual person, too. We know this because her story was documented by the father of history, Herodotus.

Herodotus was a Greek, born about 484 B.C. in Halikarnassos on the Aegean Sea, now Bodrum, in Turkey. For some reason, perhaps because he was banished for political machinations, he became a well-heeled and leisured wanderer, traveling throughout Greece and the Aegean, Egypt, Syria, Mesopotamia, and the northern coast of the Black Sea. Everywhere

The father of history, Herodotus.
Artist: Ron Druett.

he went, he studied the people, observed their habits and customs, and made note of the tales they told. Then, in the middle of the century, he settled down to write a record of "astonishing and heroic achievements," in particular an account of the conflicts of the Greeks with the Persians. It is the earliest known creative work in prose.

Herodotus was more than a mere raconteur, for not only did he make an effort to get the facts right if he could, but he wrote without preconceptions or bias. "Many stories are related of Cyrus' death," he wrote at the end of his recounting of Queen Tomyris's story; "this, that I have told, is the worthiest of credence." Herodotus called this collection of plain, unvarnished facts *History,* which in Greek means "inquiry," and so written history was born. And, in the spirit of the first historian, this book sets out to relate, investigate, and document the stories of the "she captains"—the women distinguished for bold enterprise in the history of the sea.

Chapter One

THE WARRIOR-QUEENS

Had Cleopatra's nose been shorter, the whole face
of the world would have changed.
                                        —Blaise Pascal

After the time of Queen Tomyris, the Persian kings who succeeded Cyrus the Great—first his son Cambyses and then Darius the Great—were still determined to conquer the known world. Since about 545 B.C—perhaps two decades before Queen Tomyris chopped off King Cyrus's head—the Greek city-states on the coast of modern Turkey had been under Persian rule, and the Persian target was now Athens, their aim complete domination of the Greek mainland. It was a war of politics and stealth as well as open battle, and women played a part in it all. Thargelia of Miletus could well have been partly responsible for the sack of her city by Darius in 494 B.C., for she was rumored to be a Persian spy. At the same time, another woman from Miletus, Aspasia, the mistress of the great Athenian statesman Pericles, was scheming for the other side.

Then, in 490 B.C., six years before Herodotus was born, the Persians suffered a severe setback. Their forces were soundly beaten by a Greek regiment that marched out of Athens to meet them in a pitched battle on the Plain of Marathon. Burning to avenge this defeat, Darius sent messengers throughout the empire in order to raise a huge army, a project that was continued after his death by his son, King Xerxes. It was the most colossal invasion force in ancient history, commanded by Xerxes himself. His engineers made a bridge across the Hellespont by lashing three hundred boats together, and dug a canal across the peninsula of Athos that was wide enough for two galleys to row side by side. Thus, his army marched across water, and his navy sailed over the land. It was a highly successful operation, culminating in the seizure of the Acropolis, where desperate Athenians jumped to their deaths while the victorious Persians laid about with their swords. And this is where another powerful woman comes onto the stage.

Although the Athenians' army had been defeated, they still had a 380-strong fleet of highly maneuverable biremes and triremes—125-foot-long galleys propelled by two or three banks of oars and armed with bronze-sheathed rams in the bows. Obviously, this force had to be destroyed if the Athenians were to be completely beaten and mainland Greece added to the Persian Empire—quite a proposition, for the Persians, whose capital, Susa, was eight hundred miles from the sea, had no experience in water warfare. Their navy was made up of ships and crews commandeered from subject nations—nations like Halikarnassos, Herodotus's home city, which at the time was ruled by the widow of its king, Queen Artemisia. Accordingly, Xerxes hesitated, even though his fleet was more than twice the size of the Athenian force. Then, he learned that an escaped slave had brought information that the Athenian fleet was trapped in a narrow channel.

The strait where the Greek triremes were ensnared separates the island of Salamis from the western coast of Attica, where the modern port of Piraeus lies. To Xerxes, it looked like a god-sent chance. He immediately prepared for a naval engagement—and so did Queen Artemisia. She had contributed five ships to the Persian effort—reputedly five of the best ships, at that—and was in command of her flagship herself.

As Herodotus remarked in his recounting of her tale, it was impossible not to "marvel greatly that a woman should have gone with the armament against Hellas. For, her husband being dead, she herself had his sovereignty and a young son withal, and followed the host under no stress of necessity, but of mere high-hearted valor." Nonetheless, he knew for sure that it was right, for he heard the story of the great battle repeated throughout his childhood, and would have known some of the participants. Artemisia was a veteran commander, too. When she sent words of advice to King Xerxes on the eve of the battle, she pointed out that she had every right to give an opinion, for in the past she had "not been the hindmost in courage or feats of arms in the fights near Euboea."

*Bireme, with warriors, as pictured
on a water jar in 500 B.C.*

And forthwith, the queen counseled Xerxes against sending his fleet into the narrows. "Spare your ships, and offer no battle at sea," she advised, according to Herodotus—and very wisely so, for the situation was a carefully laid trap. The "escaped" slave who had passed the tidings that the Athenian navy was ensnared and lying at their mercy was an intelligence agent, a key player in a plot devised by the Athenians' admiral, Themistokles. However, it is hard to tell if Artemisia suspected this, for Herodotus recorded that she gave other reasons for caution. First, she announced that she didn't think much of Xerxes' so-called allies—"men of Egypt and Cyprus and Cilicia and Pamphylia, in whom there is no usefulness"—and, what's more, she added demurely, the Greek navy was a lot more resourceful than Xerxes had been led to believe, "for their men are as much stronger by sea than yours, as men are stronger than women."

Xerxes should have listened to her. At dawn on September 23, 480 B.C., when he settled in a golden armchair on a hill overlooking the Straits of

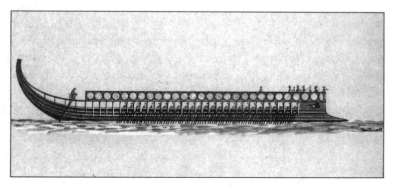

Trireme rowing into battle. Artist: Ron Druett.

Salamis, though, the scene looked promising enough. Xerxes saw a narrow stretch of water, the Athenian fleet bottled up inside it, and the Persian allies stationed at the mouth. Then the dawn breeze puffed up, involuntarily impelling the Persian allies into the maw of the straits. And, to draw them still farther into the snare, the Athenian admiral ordered his ships to back up, to give the appearance of a panicked retreat.

The unsuspecting Persian galleys eagerly pressed forward. Then suddenly, as the channel narrowed and cliffs rose around them, they found themselves running afoul of each other. Oars snagged oars and ships collided, crunching and tangling because there was no room to move. Ahead, the way was blocked by the suddenly stilled Athenians. Astern, retreat was blocked by the Persians' own forces.

And Themistokles gave the signal. According to some tales, his order was sung out by a woman. And the Athenian ships charged. They shattered the Persian allies as their galleys fought for space to maneuver in the crowded strait. The sea ran with blood as floundering seamen and marines were speared like fish, and panic and dire confusion prevailed. Artemisia, like many others, found to her horror that she was on the verge of attack by an Athenian trireme. For her, the only way out was blocked by one of the Persian allies, a Calyndian craft.

Without hesitation—friend or not—she rammed at full speed. The Calyndian vessel sank with all hands, opening up a way of escape. And out of the ambush Artemisia stormed, pursued by her other four ships. She was doubly lucky, for "when the Attic captain saw her charge a ship of foreigners, he supposed that Artemisia's ship was Greek or a deserter from the foreigners fighting for the Greeks, and he turned aside to deal with others. By this happy chance," Herodotus remarked, "it came about that she escaped and avoided destruction."

Watching from the shore, Xerxes did not suspect a thing. In fact, "one of the bystanders said, 'Sire, see you Artemisia, how well she fights, and how she has sunk an enemy ship?' Xerxes then asking if it were truly Artemisia that had done the deed, they affirmed it, knowing well the ensign of her ship; and they supposed that the ship she had sunk was an enemy." And not a single man had survived the ramming of the Calyndian ship to wade ashore and correct their mistake.

Indeed, Xerxes asked Artemisia's advice about what to do next— whether to try to turn defeat into victory by attacking the Peloponnese, or wait to recruit his strength. Queen Artemisia advised him to give up and go home to boast about the burning of Athens instead—"which thing was the whole purpose of your expedition"—and this time he listened. Xerxes slunk away, the remnants of his land forces were soundly defeated at Plataea the following year, and the Golden Age of Greece commenced.

Two hundred fifty years passed. The might of Greece burgeoned, peaked, and then diminished, as the shadow of Rome fell over the eastern Mediterranean, helped not a little by the piratical activities of another warrior-queen, this one documented by another Greek historian, Polybius.

A citizen of Megalopolis on the shores of the Ionian Sea, in 168 B.C., Polybius was captured by the Romans and sent to Rome as a hostage. There he became the tutor of the sons of a Roman general and accompanied one of them, Scipio, on African military campaigns. Therefore Polybius was present at the fall of Carthage, in 146 B.C. Back in Rome, he devoted the rest of his life to writing a forty-volume work called *Universal History,* recording the rise of the Roman Empire. And, for reasons that will soon become obvious, the story of Queen Teuta of Illyria was featured as part of the tale.

Illyria was a country on the eastern coast of the Adriatic, and Teuta was the second wife of King Agron, who died after a drunken binge. In 232 B.C. his forces returned from a great battle weighed down with loot, and Agron celebrated their victory both unwisely and too well, with the result that he dropped dead of pleurisy. "His wife Teuta succeeded him on the throne," wrote Polybius,

> and managed the various details of administration by means of friends whom she could trust. . . . Her first measure was to grant letters of marque to privateers, authorizing them to plunder all whom they fell in with; and she next collected a fleet and military forces . . . and dispatched them with general instructions to the leaders to regard every land as belonging to an enemy.

In effect, Teuta had declared war on the rest of the world, and turned the Illyrian navy into a privateer fleet. Her seamen had royal leave to sally forth in their small, extremely fast, single-banked galleys called *lembi* to attack whatever ship or settlement they liked, and bring back as much loot as they could carry.

They did have priorities. Although Teuta's corsairs would not disdain a heavily laden, plodding, unarmed merchant vessel, they much preferred to ransack coastal settlements for valuables, provisions, and slaves. Sneaking in after dusk, they would attack without warning and leave plunder-

Illyrian galley. Artist: Ron Druett.

laden after hours or days of mayhem and murder. These raids were so persistent and devastating that they affected the settlement of the Mediterranean. Coastal villages were plundered so often that major centers were moved inland to escape the ravages of the raiders, but this simply worsened the situation. The city troops had so far to march that by the time they arrived at the scene of the action the pirates had long since departed. And so, within a remarkably short time, the Illyrian raiders were in virtual control of the coasts.

And it seems that Queen Teuta did more than sit back on her throne and enjoy this wonderful source of public revenue, for she personally accompanied her Illyrian mariners on some of their raids, even taking command. According to one testimony to her cold-bloodedness, she and her raiders landed at the city of Epidamnos and approached the walls with water jars on their shoulders, crying out that they were dying of thirst and desperate for water. Then, the instant the city gates were opened, they snatched out the swords that were hidden in the jars and massacred the guards. The Epidamnosian troops rallied and eventually drove the Illyrians off, but it was more usual for such treacherous tactics to succeed.

By 230 B.C. the Illyrian captains had turned their attention to committing "acts of piracy on a number of Italian merchants; some they merely plundered, others they murdered, and a great many they carried off alive into captivity." The Romans sent a delegation to Illyria to lodge a strong protest with the queen. The envoys, the brothers Gaius and Lucius Coruncanius, were diplomatic at first, but when she imperiously informed them that "it was not the custom for the sovereigns of Illyria to hinder private persons from taking booty at sea," one of them lost his temper and made a few pointed remarks. Again, Teuta listened, outwardly calm. After they had gone, however, she instructed a band of men "to kill the one who had used this plainness" in speaking to Her Majesty. On the way back to Rome the envoys were attacked by pirates, and the offending brother was killed.

Unsurprisingly, as Polybius went on to recount, when the people of Rome heard about this injury and insult they felt incensed enough to "set about preparations for war, enrolling legions and collecting a fleet" of two hundred ships. Meanwhile, Teuta's galleys were still terrorizing the coast and bringing in huge troves of loot, with the result that one state after another turned to Rome for help, "believing that this was their only security in the future against the piratical incursions of the Illyrians." Understandably, they were happy to get any kind of military assistance, even if the soldiers and marines who marched and sailed to their aid happened to have been ordered there by power-hungry senators. Thus, as the Roman army marched toward Illyrian territory its leaders were greeted "by envoys from many tribes," offering unconditional surrender in return for Roman protection.

The Roman fleet was meeting equal success on the water, taking several Illyrian coastal cities by storm and capturing Illyrian galleys as they sailed home laden with plunder. The Illyrian forces scattered, and Teuta escaped to the fortified town of Rhizon. The following year, 228 B.C., she caved in completely, sending envoys to Rome to conclude a treaty, "in virtue of which she consented to pay a fixed tribute, and to abandon all Illyricum, with the exception of some few districts."

Most importantly of all, she agreed not to send out more than two galleys at a time, "and those unarmed"—and so ended the career of this notably bloodthirsty warrior-queen.

In 163 B.C., Greece was finally conquered by Roman forces, and by the 40s only one great Mediterranean kingdom was still independent of the Roman Empire. This was Egypt, ruled by Cleopatra VII, a gifted and ruthless politician who is popularly remembered as the famous "Queen of Kings"—a beautiful woman who gained, retained, and then increased her power by sexual attraction and stealth.

Born about 47 B.C., Cleopatra ascended the throne at the age of sixteen, to rule jointly with her twelve-year-old brother, Ptolemy XII, who was also her husband. This kind of incestuous dynastic marriage arrangement was characteristic of the Egyptian monarchy, and Cleopatra was by no means the first woman to gain power in this way. A distant predecessor, Princess Hatshepsut, had used the system to usurp the Egyptian crown and become the first great queen of history, in 1498 B.C.

When Hatshepsut's father, Pharaoh Thutmose I, died in 1501 B.C., Hatshepsut married her half brother, Thutmose II, to make sure of control of the throne. After just three years, however, her husband–half brother died, which left Hatshepsut with no claim to power at all. She

Cleopatra VII. Artist: Ron Druett.

was determined not to lose it, so she promptly married another half brother (though he may also have been her son) and imprisoned him in luxury while she kept hold of the reins. This took the Egyptian people by surprise, for it was perfectly unknown for a woman to seize power in this way. Accordingly, Hatshepsut decreed that all statues and paintings should depict her as a man, with a beard and without breasts. By this means she remained in control until the day of her death, in 1480 B.C.

Fourteen centuries later, Cleopatra was not so lucky. After three years of joint rule with her brother, she was deposed and sent into exile. Instead of taking this tamely, she assembled an army and turned to the most accessible powerful Roman for help. This was Julius Caesar, who had arrived in Egypt with four thousand men in pursuit of his rival, Pompey, and taken charge of the Roman garrison. And here the legends about Cleopatra begin. According to one version of the yarn, she arrived at the foot of his throne wrapped up in a carpet, to be revealed in a dramatic state of nudity when the rug was rolled out, while other stories have her tucked inside a bedroll. What-

Queen Hatshepsut, who commanded that she be pictured without breasts and with a beard, to stave off public outrage that she had seized the throne of Egypt.
Artist: Ron Druett.

22

ever, her sudden and unexpected appearance was well calculated to impress Julius Caesar, who was a notoriously sensual man. Instantly intrigued, he was easily seduced, and easily persuaded, too, to mount a campaign against her treacherous little brother. After five months of warfare that included setting the Egyptian fleet on fire, the boy Ptolemy was drowned, and Cleopatra's ardent lover set her on the throne as the rightful queen of Egypt.

Protocol, however, forced her to marry yet another brother—Ptolemy XIII, an eleven-year-old boy. Some stories have her also married to Julius Caesar, adding bigamy as well as incest to her colorful career. What is incontestably true is that Caesar dallied an extra four months in Egypt, even though he had been declared Dictator of Rome for the second time, making it imperative that he return there to take over the helm. Instead of paying heed to political sense, he sailed down the Nile to the southernmost borders of the country with his mistress, on a voyage of unbridled pleasure.

Then, reluctantly, Caesar returned to duty, but within two years he had sent for Cleopatra—and the son, Caesarion, she had borne in the meantime, who was probably his—to come live with him as his consort. Without doubt he was bewitched. Like other besotted lovers who populate the folklore of the sea, Caesar made a fool of himself over her. He erected a shrine and dedicated it to Cleopatra, "Queen and Goddess." The citizens of Rome were both scandalized and disgusted. Cleopatra was sent packing, and Julius Caesar was assassinated on the Ides of March, 44 B.C.

The role of hero in the Cleopatra saga then passed to Mark Antony, the passionate and magnetic young man Caesar had appointed Master of the Horse about the same time that he had restored Cleopatra to the Egyptian throne. According to the legend, Antony had been captivated from the time of that first encounter, but the spark that led to one of the most famous love affairs in history did not catch fire until the midsummer of 41 B.C. Meantime, he had been fighting a vicious civil war, which resulted in a division of territory. Antony was given control of the Eastern Roman Empire, while Caesar's great-nephew and adoptive heir, Octavian, ruled the Western sphere.

Antony set up his palace at Tarsus, and Cleopatra voyaged to meet him. She sailed up the Cydnus River in a marvelous golden barge with silver oars and and royal purple sails, and arrived in splendor, attired in flimsy draperies as the goddess of love, surrounded by nymphs and cupids, while seductive music filled the air. It was a carefully choreographed scene, her motives blatantly political. Cleopatra was an astute and hard-headed administrator who had broken the monopolies of banking, oil, and salt, restored freedom of trade, and reformed the money market in Egypt. With this list of triumphs behind her, she saw no reason she should not extend her territories to tempting lands in the East—Syria, for instance—and she needed Antony's military strength for that. This must have been obvious; nevertheless Antony became as intoxicated with her as Caesar had been. When she left for Alexandria, he helplessly followed.

It was a tempestuous affair. For two years they lived together in luxury and passion while Fulvia, Antony's furiously jealous wife, made trouble back home. The lovers parted, Fulvia died, and Antony married Octavian's sister in a political alliance, then three years later returned to Cleopatra's arms. According to the legend, he married her too, bigamously, in 34 B.C. Foolishly, he gave her Jericho, taking the city-state away from his friend King Herod of Judaea. Cleopatra visited this new property, sold it back to Herod, and then tried to seduce him, a favor that he spurned. Stung, she got her revenge by cultivating Herod's wife, Mariamne. Then Cleopatra returned to Antony, who proceeded to make the same blunder as his predecessor, Julius Caesar. In a triumphal parade in Alexandria, he posed as the god Osiris with Cleopatra at his side as the goddess Isis, and directed that her head should appear alongside his on coins.

Backed by Roman outrage, Octavian declared war on Egypt. A fleet assembled under the command of Agrippa, Octavian's admiral, sailing in the fall of 31 B.C. The ships of the two nations met off the west coast of the Balkans, just north of the western end of the Gulf of Corinth, in the famous Battle of Actium. Both Antony and Cleopatra were there, each in command of his or her own part of the fleet. Antony was at a disadvantage right from the beginning, for Agrippa's ships had been raiding the Egyptian grain ships that carried provisions to the fleet. Because of an outbreak of plague, there was a shortage of oarsmen. Altogether, his men were hungry, sick, and discouraged. Nevertheless, against the advice of his generals, and reputedly because Cleopatra recommended it, Antony attacked first.

It was no minor engagement. Antony commanded five hundred ships, brightly painted in warlike colors. They were heavy, powerful galleys encompassing every rank from one row of oars up to the great ten that carried his flag. His battle plan was to plow into clusters of smaller craft, with catapults hurling a barrage of rocks and pots of hot coals and pitch on the enemy, some creative gunners theorizing that firing off pots of live snakes and scorpions might have an even more interesting effect on the enemy.

Meantime, while ranks of archers were shooting a hail of arrows, boarding parties of marines would be standing at the ready.

Agrippa, on the other hand, had only four hundred craft, but in addition to the same armory that Antony's fleet carried, many of his ships were fitted with a *harpex*, or catapult grapnel, which he had already employed with huge success in a sea battle against his patron's rival, Sextus, the previous year. This was a timber fitted with ringbolts and an iron hook that was made fast with a length of line. Fired by catapult, it went a lot farther than a grapnel thrown by hand. Once it was lodged into the deck of the enemy boat, the rope was drawn in, jamming the two galleys together, so the heavily armed marines could easily rush across to attack the opposing crew. By legend, Agrippa declared it was such a terrible weapon it would bring an end to warfare. Obviously, he was wrong, but it did, perhaps, bring an end to the Battle of Actium.

The conflict ended in anticlimax. For no apparent reason, Cleopatra took fright. Though it seems so out of character, the story goes that she gave the order to retreat, and her squadron of sixty ships hoisted sail to make a run for it. Antony, seeing his mistress sail away, followed with about forty more. His men fought on until they were persuaded to surrender with the promise of honorable treatment. And Octavian, as Augustus Caesar, was proclaimed Emperor of Rome.

Myriad tales persist about the next eleven months. Some say that Cleopatra plotted an escape east of Suez, while others describe her secret efforts to negotiate with Octavian. An enduring legend is that she shut herself up in her mausoleum and sent false news of her suicide to Antony. Desperate, he stabbed himself, learning about her deceit as his lifeblood ebbed away. Friends carried him to the foot of the crypt, and when he begged for the "poor last" of the "many thousand kisses" that Shakespeare later described, she repented and had him hauled up by cords to her hiding place, where he expired in her embrace.

Then it was Cleopatra's turn. It seems plausible that she hoped to make a conquest of yet another Roman, but after meeting the austere Octavian she realized she had no hope of mercy. Accordingly, she planned to put an end to herself, too, to avoid the humiliation of being dragged through the streets of Rome in chains. Octavian, who very shrewdly suspected her grim solution, kept her under guard within her apartments to prevent such an outcome. However, Cleopatra managed to arrange for a poisonous snake to be smuggled to her in a basket of fruit, and after bathing in milk and enrobing in ceremonial garments, she lay down and enticed the asp to sting. Or so runs the popular tale. Scholars believe that it is much

Detail of Queen Hatshepsut's voyage to Punt. Wall relief, Temple at Deir el-Bahri.

more likely that she simply poisoned herself, but the asp is so persuasively romantic and exotic that the fable lives on—just like a great deal of the rest of the Cleopatra legend. The hard part is deciding which parts are the truth.

No one doubts that Cleopatra VII existed. There is plenty of formal testament to her regime, just as there is to what her distant predecessor, Queen Hatshepsut, accomplished. Hatshepsut built a grand temple at Deir el-Bahri, complete with wonderful bas-reliefs which illustrate and document one of her greatest achievements, a trading voyage to Punt, a country on the African coast below the Red Sea. Intricately captioned, the carved vignettes detail not just what the people said ("Watch your step!" is carved over the stevedores in a loading scene) but what was carried. Those earliest Egyptian envoys traded manufactured goods—necklaces, hatchets, daggers—for incense, ivory, ebony, myrrh, gold, and exotic animals, including "a southern panther alive, captured for Her Majesty." Thus, we know that Her Majesty Queen Hatshepsut and her trailblazing voyage were real, just as coins, temple reliefs, papyrus scrolls, and financial accounts testify to Cleopatra's reign. However, Cleopatra's undoubted genius as an administrator has been largely forgotten, while the wildly colorful myths endure, distorting our perceptions so it has become virtually impossible to sort out exaggeration from veracity and fable from truth.

And that leads to the most intriguing question of all: Why did Cleopatra become such an enduringly popular icon, while women like Teuta,

Tomyris, Artemisia, and Hatshepsut have been largely overlooked? For two thousand years Cleopatra's story has fascinated generations and provided inspiration for great artists. Dryden, Shakespeare, and George Bernard Shaw created famous plays about her. Grand poetry has been written, stately music composed, noteworthy films made, all devoted to her tale. Today, Cleopatra's name is familiar to millions of people. We read it constantly—on perfume bottles, in fashionable stores, in glossy magazines—often accompanied by unlikely pictures. And, just like her physical image, her story has been blurred and colored by romantic retelling. It is as if the advertising agencies have taken over the job of preserving her story for the masses.

It is not just our generation that is so susceptible. When two ancient Egyptian obelisks were taken from Alexandria in Victorian times, one to become a London landmark, the other to find a place in Central Park, in New York, both were named Cleopatra's Needle, yet Cleopatra had no connection with them whatsoever, quite apart from the fact that they were part of her hometown scenery. Built by some unknown monarch in Heliopolis, and reerected in Alexandria by Rameses II about 1200 B.C., they predate her by many centuries. That such concrete male symbols should take on her name without any damage to her femininity is eloquent evidence of Cleopatra's potent sexuality—and a good reason for the durability of her legend, too. Throughout history this queen of ancient Egypt has been viewed as the essence of female mystery and romance. The Cleopatra legend has lived so long because it is an exotic testament to the power of beautiful women.

Cleopatra's passing also marked the passing of the era of warrior-queens, for the aggressively masculine Roman armies were now in complete control of Europe, Asia Minor, and the Mediterranean world. But, over the centuries, inevitably even the stalwart Romans lost their grip. By the third century A.D. the Goths had ravaged Greece, the Franks had overtaken Gaul (modern France) and moved into Spain, and the Saxons were raiding the coasts of both Britain and Gaul. Rome was sacked, and coastal North Africa conquered. By the end of the fifth century A.D., the Franks held almost the whole of Gaul, and in Britain the Romans had packed up and gone, leaving the native Celtic peoples to war with each other and the invading Anglo-Saxons.

All these barbarians, whether Goth, Frank, Celt, or Saxon, had something in common besides land hunger and aggressiveness. They all had been acquainted with classical traditions and Christianity by the people who had been their overlords—the Romans. But then, in the eighth century A.D., a pagan, unromanized people stormed in from the north to terrorize the coasts of the West. And a new era in maritime history commenced.

Chapter Two

THE VALKYRIA

*Even the females of the North caught the epidemic
spirit, and proudly betook themselves to the
dangers of sea-life.*

—Charles Ellms

They arrived at night, screaming and berserk, like a mad vision from the Book of Revelations. Attacking with savage ferocity, they razed whole villages, slaughtered babies for sport, dissected captured leaders alive— *from the back*—and spread their entrails in an eagle pattern on the ground. They rapidly became known as the dreaded Vikings, "sons of the fjords."

Their fine-lined oaken boats, called longships, were very different from the biremes and triremes that Artemisia and Cleopatra knew. Between seventy and one hundred feet in length, the Viking longship was a double-ended, clinker-built craft of overlapped planks, iron-fastened and tightly caulked, yet flexible. The sweeping bow was decorated with a snarling figurehead, often of a dragon or serpent. There was only one bank of oars, for the sail was the important means of propulsion. This was square, strongly sewn, and beautifully decorated with bright silks and gold embroidery by Viking women. The masts were often covered in gilt, and the rigging dyed red, and at the masthead there was a pedestal for a lantern. The oarsmen were also the warriors, and while voyaging they hung their circular shields along the ship's side for additional protection against wind and spray, thereby enhancing the ferociously businesslike appearance of the craft. When placed at the masthead, shields were used as signals, too. Breasting the rough northern seas, these ships harassed the coasts of the British Isles and France. It was no use for terrified people to flee into the interior, for the ships with their shallow draft could penetrate hundreds of miles upriver. Paris was plundered several times by Viking fleets.

Each longship was capable of carrying ten tons of loot back to Scandinavia, to be ceremoniously dumped at the feet of some king in his feast hall. These halls, often called mead halls (though mead was despised as a foreign luxury), and the celebratory feasts staged therein, formed an important element of Viking society. The food was plain, just bread and ungarnished boiled meat accompanied by ale that was served in horns from a butt, but the etiquette was punctilious.

Viking longship. From *Girl's Own Paper*, September 1885.

Despite the general drunkenness, shouting, fighting, and bone-throwing, men were seated with care, according to importance, and tales were told on an epic scale. While the diners listened raptly, their scops—or bards—retold the traditional sagas, adding and amending as they went, though keeping to a long-held pattern.

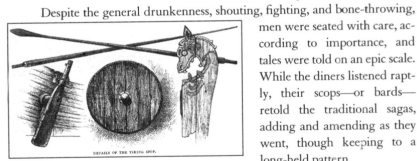

Details of Viking ship, to show the tiller, a shield, spears, and dragon figurehead. From *Girl's Own Paper*, September 1885.

The narrative poem always began with a tribal history of the protagonist, often linking him to the great god Woden (Odin). This was followed by a stirring yarn in which the king or hero was praised. Kings were inevitably brave, generous, and just, while heroes could be recognized by their "fierce falcon eyes." Heroines, on the other hand, kept their eyes demurely lowered at all times, for it was well known that a beautiful woman could seduce the strongest of heroes with one languishing glance. And such a heroine was Alfhild, otherwise variously known as Alvild, or Alwilda the Danish Female Pirate.

The Alfhild saga was first written down in the twelfth century by the Danish historian Saxo Grammaticus. Very little is known about the author, save that he was a Dane, probably from Zealand, and that his family name—a common one—was Saxo. The second name, Grammaticus, simply means "lettered," and was endowed to him by a later biographer. Written in Latin and finished shortly after the year 1200, Saxo's *Gesta Danorum* ("Deeds of the Danes") totals sixteen volumes. Alfhild's narrative is in Book Seven. Then, in 1555, an exiled Swedish scholar and prelate, Olaus Magnus ("Olaf the Great"), included the story of

Alwilda the Danish Female Pirate.
From Ellms, *Pirates Own Book*, Boston, 1837.

Alvild in his massive *Historia de Gentibus Septentrionalibus* ("History of the Northern Peoples"), which was mostly culled from ancient authorities such as Saxo. Almost three centuries later a Boston stationer, Charles Ellms, included an inaccurate summary of Olaus Magnus's version in the first chapter of his 1837 *Pirates Own Book*, which purported to be a collection of "Authentic Narratives of the Lives, Exploits, and Executions of the Most Celebrated Sea Robbers." It was illustrated with a remarkable picture of Alwilda most unconvincingly attired in a version of eighteenth-century dress—and that is all the evidence of the saga of this maritime warrior-princess.

This tardy documentation is not at all unusual. Bards were responsible for preserving traditional lore, handing it down from generation to generation by word of mouth, until the advent of Christian scholars, who had the means to write it down and ensure its survival. Beowulf, the hero of the greatest saga of the literature, performed his great feats during the reign of his kinsman, Hygelac the Geat, about A.D. 400, but his story was not written down for another five hundred years, when an anonymous

Anglian scholar composed an epic poem that infused his pagan tale with Christian elements.

Such editing was also typical, but makes it difficult to tell how much was revised. Saxo Grammaticus might have been the Herodotus of Scandinavia, but he lacked the Greek historian's laudable lack of bias, for, just like many other church-educated documenters, he could not resist the opportunity to point out moral lessons and encourage Christian principles and values.

Book publisher Ellms, on the other hand, wrote his 1837 account for mercenary reasons, so he turned the story into a mere yarn designed to appeal to as many people as possible. Thus, his work is even less reliable and, in fact, has led to a common mistake. Because of his racy style and superficial research, his rendition of the Alfhild story is linked to the situation in fifth-century Britain, when Vortigern invited the Saxons to help him fight the Picts. This timing is completely wrong. According to the genealogy of Scandinavian kings, Alfhild—a *Danish* princess—lived at least four hundred years after that, at the height of the Viking depredations, when the northern seas were prowled by longships and the rafters of the feast halls vibrated with wondrous tales.

"Hwæt!"—"Listen!"—was the conventional announcement that a stirring recital was about to begin. It has an imperative sound, so one can easily imagine the drunken diners in the feasting hall obediently focusing on the scop. Then, as silence fell over the great room, the bard shouted, *"We Gardena in geardagum þeodcyinga þrym gefrunon, hu ða æþelingas ellen fremedon!"*—"We Danes have heard of the glorious deeds of the princes of yore!"—and thus launched himself into the obligatory description of the genealogy and appearance of the saga's hero. In this instance, it was Prince Alf, son of King Sigar.

Sigar reigned over Denmark about the middle of the ninth century. According to Saxo, his son, Alf, "excelled the rest in spirit and beauty"—as was only natural with heroes. Like many princes, he "devoted himself to the business of a rover," which meant that he was one of the many longship captains who ravaged the coasts of western Europe. In other words, he was just another pirate. As was common in the epic form, his hair had such "a wonderful dazzling glow, that his locks seemed to shine silvery."

The hero described, the saga promptly shifts to the heroine of the tale, who also adhered to convention—at the start, at any rate. "At the same time," wrote Saxo,

Siward, King of the Goths, is said to have had . . . a daughter, Alfhild, who showed almost from her cradle such faithfulness to modesty, that she continually kept her face muffled in her robe, lest she should cause her beauty to provoke the passion of another. Her father banished her into very close-keeping, and gave her a viper and a snake to rear, wishing to defend her chastity by the protection of these reptiles when they came to grow up. For it would have been hard to penetrate her chamber when it was barred by so dangerous a bolt. He also decreed that if any man tried to enter it, and failed, he must straight away yield his head to be taken off and impaled on a stake.

Apart from the fanciful addition of the viper and snake, this was usual enough, heads on stakes featuring a lot in Viking literature. Because capture-marriage happened so often—being part of the blood-feud ritual—kings' daughters were very closely guarded. Fathers and brothers would fight hand to hand for them, for princesses were important property, carefully kept to one side to be given as a reward to a hero or to cement a political alliance. It did not matter if the hero or the other king was already married, for polygamy was commonplace. It was common, too, for the virtue of the heroine to be featured so prominently, for chastity was held in high regard. If there was any doubt, the test of virtue was the pressing of the breasts until the nipples bled. If no milk was admixed with the blood, the woman was considered falsely accused. If someone imagined a trickle of milk, her nose was chopped off.

It seems that quite a few young men were willing to dodge the snake and the viper to court the undoubtedly virginal Alfhild, for there were a number of heads on stakes by the time Prince Alf took an interest. Or, as Saxo phrased it, "Then Alf, son of Sigar, thinking that the peril of the attempt only made it the nobler, declared himself a wooer, and was told to subdue the beasts that kept watch beside the room of the maiden; inasmuch as, according to the decree, the embraces of the maiden were the prize of the subduer."

At this stage of the story, Alf takes on some personality, demonstrating the stuff of which resourceful rovers were made. He prepared himself by covering "his body with a blood-stained hide," to work the serpents up into a mindless frenzy. In one hand he held a pair of tongs that gripped "a piece of red-hot steel," which he plunged "into the yawning throat of the viper." In the other, more conventionally, he had a spear, which he thrust "full into the gaping mouth of the snake as it wound and writhed forward."

And so, in theory, Alf had gained the maiden's hand. However, though her father, Siward, approved of the match, he had added the proviso that

Alfhild should be happy about it—"he would accept that man only for his daughter's husband of whom she made a free and decided choice." This is perfectly plausible, for in Viking society free women did have the right of veto, and sometimes even the liberty to find a fiancé on their own. In sagas, however, it was as traditional for a woman to be complaisant about marrying the hero who had fought a strange battle for her sake as it was for unsuccessful suitors to perish in nasty ways. If affairs had moved the way they usually did, the princess would have smiled shyly and assented to the match. Prince Alf's personal hygiene might not have been the best, for it was usual for Vikings to be flea- and lice-ridden, probably because of their furs—one lover bidding his love, "Maiden, comb my hair and catch the skipping fleas, and remove what stings my skin"—but, as we know, Alf's fluorescent hair would have made the search tolerable. And so, it is reasonable for the bard's audience to have expected that Alfhild would present Alf with the usual maiden's betrothal gift of a sword, and that a ceremonious wedding would be followed by the usual noisy, drunken feast, complete with lots of bone-throwing.

A shock was in store for them, however. Alfhild did not conform to tradition. In fact, she demonstrated a rather startling character change. Rather than agree to marry Prince Alf, she "exchanged woman's for man's attire, and, no longer the most modest of maidens, began the life of a warlike rover." Or, as Olaus Magnus (who was inclined to blame her mother for this strange metamorphosis) phrased it:

Viking ship. Artist: Ron Druett.

For she so much preferred a life of valour to one of ease that, when she might have enjoyed the pleasure of royalty, drawn by a woman's madness she suddenly plunged into the hazards of war. Her determination to stay chaste was so steadfast that she began to reject all men and firmly resolved with herself never to have intercourse with any, but from then on to equal, or even to surpass, male courage in the practice of piracy.

Somehow, miraculously, not only did she acquire the necessary seafaring skills, but she also managed to recruit a crew of like-minded females. A ship was gained by a stroke of luck; Saxo recorded that Alfhild and her companions "happened to come to a spot where a band of rovers were lamenting the death of their captain who had been lost in war," and the mariners "made her their rover-captain for her beauty." Olaus, on the other hand, claimed it was "on account of her beauty and spirit." However, it is much more likely that she simply commandeered their ship—which, as it happens, was in accordance with Danish civil law at the time, one of the statutes declaring, "Seafarers may use what gear they find, including boat or tackle."

Thus Alfhild launched herself on the career of a raider, and "did deeds beyond the valor of women"—a most undomestic vocation. Saxo Grammaticus, who had a remarkably Victorian approach to the different spheres of the sexes, certainly did not approve of it, breaking into his narrative to inveigh against women who, "just as if they had forgotten their natural es-

Valkyrie. In battle, she would wear a great horned helmet and carry a shield. Artist: Ron Druett.

tate," preferred making war to making love, and "devoted those hands to the lance which they should rather have applied to the loom." This is a prime example of the kind of biased reporting that church-educated historians believed respectable, a true testament to the fact that in the 250 years that had elapsed before Saxo recorded this saga, Scandinavian men had not just been Christianized, but had become opinionated as well.

Vikings were not nearly so narrow-minded. Their mythology includes valkyria—the great god Woden's handmaidens, who rode to battle in marvelous armor to decide who should live and who should die, and to escort the souls of heroes to his feasting hall, Valhalla. Woden himself did not jib at dressing up as a woman to get into the boudoir of a lass who had taken his fancy, and heroes were perfectly happy to accept the help of female warriors. About A.D. 870, just one generation after Alfhild's time, Frey, the king of Sweden, slew the king of the Norwegians (another Siward) and put all his womenfolk into a brothel. When Ragnar, the current overlord of Denmark, heard of this insult to his relatives, he went to Norway on a mission of vengeance. When they heard that he was coming, the women dressed up as men, broke out of the brothel, and came to his camp to join his army. As Saxo himself recorded:

> Among them was Ladgerda, a famous valkyrie, who, though a maiden, had the courage of a man, and fought in front among the bravest with her hair loose over her shoulders. All marveled at her matchless deeds, for her locks flying down her back betrayed that she was a woman.

Incidentally, this saga follows convention. Ragnar, understandably impressed, took to courting Ladgerda. She set two beasts about her door in the usual obstacle course. He speared one with one hand, strangled the second with the other, and caught her up in his arms.

Viking men did not mind boasting about beating women warriors, either. Another early female raider was Sela, "a skilled warrior and experienced in roving." Sela entered the literature when a fleet commanded by her brother Koll, who was king of Norway, was confronted by the longships of a hero named Horwendil, who wanted to formalize his ownership of Jutland. Instead of commencing a naval engagement, the two admirals decided to fight it out in single combat on the beach of a nearby island—a thoroughly laudable arrangement that saved a lot of unnecessary bloodshed. After a lot of chat in which they set the rules, they went at it. Horwendil won, by the unexpected ploy of dropping his shield and wielding his sword with both hands. First he chopped up Koll's shield, then chopped off his opponent's foot, rendering him helpless. Finishing off Koll was not enough to satisfy his bloodlust, however, so he challenged Sela next, managing to defeat and kill her, too.

Other longship captains who had "bodies of women and souls of men" were Hetha, Wisna, and Webiorg. Like Sela, this trio was perfectly happy to fight on land as well as sea. Being strong and brave enough to fight on one's feet was, indeed, a prerequisite, for the design of Viking longships meant that naval battles could not be staged in the open water. Though perfectly capable of breasting the stormy North Sea, the boats were rather too delicately built for rams or catapults to be fitted, and they stove in somewhat easily, too, so all combat had to be hand to hand, apart from some archery and short-range throwing of spears and axes.

The battle was a ritual affair. When two enemy longships came face-to-face, the warriors would hold the boats still with their oars while the two captains leapt onto the forecastles and screamed insults at each other. This was part of the "bear-sark" tradition, where warriors—men and valkyria alike—worked themselves up for the fight by bellowing, barking, and biting the upper rims of their shields until they foamed at the mouth. Then, slavering with bloodlust, they would paddle alongside the enemy craft, grapple, and leap up and rush at each other with swords, axes, and clubs. One famous hero, Arrow-Odd, went on record as grabbing up the tiller for use as a bludgeon. The trick was not to stave in one's boat while doing this, something that was impossible to avoid out in an open seaway. So naval engagements had to happen in sheltered waters, or else, as with Horwendil and Sela, the dueling was relocated to a beach.

Obviously, in opting to abandon a soft, snake-guarded life at the palace to take on this kind of existence, Alfhild and her companions had accepted quite a challenge. The Norsemen were consummate seamen, navigating by the sun, the stars, the tides, the ocean currents, and the migratory patterns of birds and whales, so the women had a great deal to learn. Viking rovers were hardy, too, sleeping in leather sleeping bags with their weapons close to their hands. This was usually on some deserted beach, after their ships had been drawn up on the sand and lashed together for safety, because longships were not well designed for stretching out full-length. It was very difficult to cook in longships, too, so "strand-hewing"—or victualing with raw meat—was the rule. Watches had to be kept around the clock, *uht*—the watch immediately after midnight—being considered the most dangerous. There were dangers other than enemies, too, dragons being particularly feared, such as Beowulf's *eald uhtsceaða, sede byrnende*—"ancient twilight foe, that vomits fire."

Somehow, Alfhild managed. For weapons she would have had swords, axes, bows and arrows, and spears, and in battle she would have worn a horned helmet and perhaps an iron breastplate. She must have had a feasting hall somewhere, even if it was some humble and secluded hut made of mud and wattle, for she and her companion valkyria would have needed a place to recruit their strength, bury their treasure, and brag about their deeds. Perhaps Alfhild even retained her own scop. Like Viking men, she would have made light of all but the most serious wounds, keeping a faithful dog to lick cuts and gashes clean. She and her followers would have gone through some kind of blood "brotherhood" ceremony, pricking their hands until the blood flowed and then pressing the bloody palms together. This ensured loyalty, for blood revenge was a serious duty, and *were-gild* would be extracted from foes who killed any of their number. And she would have had her chief officers—her thanes—created by ceremoniously holding out a sword by the blade, so that the new thane could take it by the hilt. Without a doubt, Alfhild and her force would have created terror and havoc wherever they landed, and the villagers and monks who fled from their ravening screams and slashing weapons would have had no idea they were women.

So—did Alfhild exist? The genealogy of Scandinavian kings confirms the reality of most of the other participants in the saga, so there is no reason to believe that the heroine is completely fictional. Did she really take up the life of a roving warrior? That, too, is possible. About the same time, other well-documented valkyria were exhibiting bold enterprise, both on land and at sea. Queen Aud, widow of Olaf the White, the proclaimed king of Dublin, led a navy from the Western Isles of Scotland to colonize Iceland. Hers was an extremely well-organized expedition, each longship towing another ship laden with livestock such as cattle. An English princess, Æðelflæd, "Lady of the Mercias," was prominent enough in battle to merit admiring inclusion in *The Anglo-Saxon Chronicle*, a year-by-year accounting of great events of English history. Daughter of Alfred the Great and wife of Æðered, the Alderman of Mercia and Governor of London, Æðelflæd was famous as a brilliant commander. After her father's death she joined forces with her brother, Edward the Elder, to carry on the campaign against the Danes, proving herself to be one of the most capable generals of her age. And so Alfhild and Æðelflæd were on opposite sides. If they ever encountered each other, however, it has not been recorded. In fact, both Saxo and Olaus neglect to tell us anything at all about Alfhild's roving. She did very well, for by the end of the tale she had a whole fleet at her command. It is what she did with her ships that is a mystery.

It seems she did more than run-of-the-mill raiding. Perhaps she contracted herself out as a mercenary to some tribe in opposition to the Danes, or perhaps she had ambitions for a territory of her own. She could have been a true pirate, preying on merchant shipping, for not all Norse ships were battleships. Peaceful sea trade, in fact, was the Scandinavians' major activity. Furs, timber, amber, and Slavic slaves were carried to market in cargo carriers called *knorrs,* to be exchanged for corn and foreign luxuries. Whatever Alfhild did, we do know it annoyed the Danes greatly, for a number of expeditions were sent out to put a stop to this female nuisance.

One of the parties was commanded by none other than Prince Alf. According to Saxo, after "many toilsome voyages in pursuit of her," he finally tracked down Alfhild's fleet in a "rather narrow gulf" in Finland. Alfhild, who held the philosophy that attack was better than defense, immediately "rowed in swift haste forward." Alf's men, on the other hand, believed that caution was the wiser part of valor and "were against his attacking so many ships with so few." He, mindful of his reputation as a hero, paid no attention, meeting the charge head-on and seizing one ship after another.

Coincidentally, he was the one who boarded Alfhild's ship "and advanced towards the stern, slaughtering all that withstood him." Instead of losing her life, however, the Viking princess merely lost her anonymity, for Alf's lieutenant, Borgar, struck off her helmet. And, forthwith, "seeing the smoothness of her chin, [Alf] saw that he must fight with kisses and not with arms; that the cruel spears must be put away, and the enemy handled with gentler dealings." Or, as Olaus puts it in his more sinewy style, "as soon as he saw the delicacy of her countenance, [Alf] realized that they should be going to work with kisses, not with weapons."

How plausible this is, is open to debate, for Viking helmets did not have the face-concealing visors common to suits of armor in Saxo's time, dreadful grimacing and scowling being part of the battle ritual. Perhaps her long hair fell down like Ladgerda's, betraying her sex. Whatever, the upshot was that Alfhild lost her virginity, for Alf claimed what had been due to him ever since he had slaughtered her serpents. According to Saxo, "he took hold of her eagerly, and made her change her man's apparel to a woman's; and afterwards begot on her a daughter, Gurid." In the meantime, presumably, he carried her onto his ship, and they forthwith set sail for Denmark—her last voyage, and without doubt an emotional one, for her probable fate was to be shut up in a palace to get on with being a proper woman, away from the sight of the sea.

> *þa wæs be mæste   merehrægla sum,*
> *segl sale fæst;   sundwudu þunede;*
> *no þær wegflotan   wind ofer yðum*
> *siðes get wæfde; sægenga for,*
> *fleat famigheals   forðofer yðe**

---

*Roughly, this translates: "Then to the mast a sail, a great sea garment, was hoisted with ropes; the longship groaned as she breasted the waves, was not blown off her course by contrary gales, but lustily, foaming at the bows, skimmed forth."

Chapter Three

MISTRESS COWTIE
AND THE PIRATES

Afore the wind, afore the wind,
God send, God send,
Fair weather, fair weather,
Many prizes, many prizes.
   —Fifteenth-century chantey

On a blowy day in May 1582, a middle-aged woman named Agnes Cowtie stood at the quayside in Dundee, Scotland, watching the merchant ship *Grace of God* readying for departure.

Mistress Cowtie would have been dressed plainly, in a loose garment of linsey-woolsey—a cloth woven of linen and wool—belted over a petticoat, but that particular summer was cool, so she might have worn a cloak as well, which would have been richly lined. She would also have worn shoes, another sign that she was well-to-do. For most people, shoes were a luxury worn only to kirk (church), even though leather was a major export. Mistress Agnes Cowtie, however, was an affluent and influential woman in her own right, for she was the owner of

Carrack Grace of God. Artist: Ron Druett.

the ship that was weighing anchor. The *Grace of God* was her property.

It must have been a stirring scene. A Scots writer of the previous century printed an evocative description of the chanteying that accompanied work at the windlass:

> Vayra, veyra, vayra, veyra,
> Gentil gallantis veynde;
> I see hym, veynde, I see hym
> Pourbossa, pourbossa.
> Hail all and ane, hail all and ane;
> Hail him up til us, hail him up til us—
> (Ane marynal cryit, and all the laif follouit in that same tune)—
> Caupon, caupona, caupon, capona,
> Coupon hola, caupon hola
> Caupon holt, caupon holt,
> Sarrabossa, sarabossa.*

The *Grace of God* was most probably a carrack, a sturdy vessel entirely driven by sails. Merchant galleys had become very rare, as the rowers and the food they ate took up room that was better devoted to cargoes. Carracks often carried three decks, and were heavily built with lofty, overhanging bow- and stern-castles. The *Grace of God* would have been well armed, too, for a mariner who was worth his salt had to know his gunnery. However, Mistress Cowtie could have been feeling deeply uneasy. The *Grace of God* represented a substantial investment in both ship and cargo, the nature of which is unknown but was probably wool. The men of the crew were long-trusted employees, and two of her sons were on the *Grace of God* as well. All of this was precious to her. Nervous as Agnes might have been, however, she could not possibly have anticipated the scale of the disaster that was looming.

Though Cowtie was her birth name, Agnes was married, being the "spouse of George Blak." As the men on the deck of the *Grace of God* labored to weigh the anchor, George was probably standing beside her, looking as solidly affluent as she did, for Agnes Cowtie and her husband,

---

*The fourteenth-century chantey, translated freely, runs: "Weigh, weigh, gentle gallants, weigh [the anchor]; I see him [the anchor rising], verily I see him. Pull and haul, haul all and one, haul one and all. (And now one mariner sings out, and the rest follow in the same tune)—Clap on, clap on, clap on tight, secure, secure." "Than," the narrator continues, "thai maid fast the shank of the ankyr." (*Complaynt of Scotland,* c. 1450.)

George Black, were known through-out the Royal Burgh of Dundee as a "wealthy and honourable" couple. That she was running her shipping business under her maiden name was not particularly noteworthy, for Scotswomen kept their birth names after marriage so that they would not lose hereditary links with their clan. What was exceptional was that she was doing it at all.

Mistress Cowtie. Adapted from a sixteenth-century manuscript. Artist: Ron Druett.

First, Mistress Cowtie had to be one of a very privileged class, for only members of the merchant guilds were allowed to export hides, fish, or wool, import wine, sell dyed cloth, or hold fairs. All foreign trade was in their hands. Even the lairds had to trade through the guild brethren, and landowners could buy and sell only at the fairs in the burghs. While this system might seem unfair, it recognized the extreme difficulties, for the countryside, particularly in the north, was in a rough-and-ready feudal condition. Roads were shocking, and highwaymen lurked, while clan feuds abounded. Mainland Europeans regarded Scotland as a poor and infertile country, populated by near-barbarians who were hostile to foreigners and obsessed with honor and revenge. A nuncio from the Vatican City called it "the arse of the world." This reputation for aggressiveness could have been inspired by the many young Scotsmen who hired themselves out as mercenary soldiers abroad because there were no jobs at home.

Seafaring was no safer than traveling by horse or foot. Where there were vagabonds on the land, there were pirates on the water. No ship was safe from attack, for the seas around Britain swarmed with rovers. There was even a pirate enclave in the Firth of Forth, and sometimes ships from certain Scottish burghs despoiled ships belonging to others. In 1557 the Town Council of Aberdeen applied to Edinburgh for remission of taxation on account of the "damages and skaiths" that piracy had wreaked on "this poor town of Aberdeen," along with a sly hint that they were inclined to blame the burgh of Dundee. However, the worst of the pirates were the English rovers, who despoiled Scottish shipping "as if there were neither God in Heaven, nor we had a King on earth to complain to"—as the Convention of Royal Burghs protested to James VI of Scotland.

There were all kinds of reasons for men (and women) to turn to piracy. Times were very hard, for the year 1560 marked the start of a great change in the weather of the British Isles. The winters became exceptionally severe, particularly that of 1563–64, with great loss of livestock. Summers were wet and stormy, with a terrible harvest in 1565 and then again in 1567, and many people were driven to violence and theft to feed their families. The usual seasonal shoals of herring and haddock did not arrive, and wrecking, smuggling, and piracy became a natural recourse for out-of-work fishermen.

Pirate chasing a prize. Artist: Ron Druett.

More important, though, was that piracy was such an excellent investment. When Elizabeth ascended the throne of England and Ireland in 1558, she inherited a situation where nobility and gentry sent out ships on pirate cruises and provided financial backing for others. It was called "gentlemanly piracy," and in Agnes Cowtie's day a great deal of it was going on. In England, many of the port admirals were in league with the pirates, investing in their voyages, hiding their loot and then selling it for them, their only official charge being to "avoid the appearance of conniving with piracy."

One of these was Sir Walter Raleigh's father, the Vice-Admiral of Devon, who was a pirate himself, just like the men who succeeded to the job. In Lincolnshire, the Lord Admiral's representative owned a private harbor where the freebooters could haul in their plunder. The imports inspector in Arundel, Sussex, was cooperative enough to hide booty in the customshouse. At Aldeburgh, in Suffolk, a pirates' fence named Peter Lambert was so blatantly contemptuous of the law that the authorities were forced to lock him up, but his wife merely received loot in his place. Then she sent her husband a file baked in a pie, and he sawed through the bars of his cell and escaped off to sea unimpeded.

A Cornishman, Captain John Piers, delivered much of his plunder to his mother. He would arrive at Padstow after dark, where she would be waiting on the wharf. He could be sure that no one would be around to witness the unloading of the loot, for his mother was a notorious witch. On the southern coast, Pendennis Castle at the entrance to Falmouth Harbour was a hub of pirate and smuggling activity. The hereditary captains of the castle were the Killigrew family, headed by Lady Killigrew. She took charge of booty that was brought ashore, parceling it out among fiefs and relatives to be buried and hidden, and once she led a boarding party to plunder an anchored German vessel. Reputedly, the ship had a trove of pieces of eight on board, and she was determined to lay hands on this treasure herself. Some tales say that she murdered two men to get at the spoils. Officialdom came to hear of it, and she was hauled up before the bench at Launceston. Her husband, Sir John, had most officials in his pocket, however, and he secured her acquittal quite easily. Killigrew was notorious for his adeptness with bribes. A freebooter once towed a prize into Falmouth Harbour, to find to his horror that there were Queen's ships anchored there already. Sir John simply rowed out to the naval vessels to present his compliments and a hundred pounds in coin, and the pirate slipped away unhindered.

The Isle of Purbeck, in Dorset, was the premier place for young men to find berths on pirate ships, and Poole the most notorious seaport. Pirate captains strutted openly about the streets, and careened their ships on Branksea Island in the harbor. However, they preferred to anchor their ships out in Studland Bay, which was better suited for a quick getaway if Queen's ships were raised. The shore was lined with taverns where pirate crews caroused, none of them legally licensed, and the bay had a wide reputation as a market where people could buy curiosities and valuables from the four corners of the world, all remarkably well priced.

The pirates felt so confident of their continued immunity that they would even extend credit to cus-

Elizabethan pirate. Engraving by de Ram.

tomers who could not pay on the spot. A certain Captain Clinton Atkinson (otherwise known as Clinton or Clynton) had the sauce to sue a shipowner, James Covenant, who owed him two hundred pounds. Clinton went all the way to the High Court of Admiralty in London to bring the action, in spite of being one of England's half-dozen most wanted men. He was recognized, of course, and even for a time held in custody in Marshalsea Prison, but was soon allowed to return to Dorset without hindrance.

The rovers' impunity was a scandal. They swaggered freely about the towns of southeast England, all decked out in the kind of flamboyant dress that ever since has been associated with the breed. Their sword hilts were decorated with jewels, their short cloaks lined with silk, their hats large and fantastic, their doublets and breeches made of taffeta, silk, or velvet. Crowds came to gape at their magnificence and traded tales of their daring deeds, while officialdom looked on tolerantly. The chance of their being caught and punished was remarkably slight, withal, and so piracy was a booming business.

Accordingly, it would be strange indeed if Agnes Cowtie did not feel a few pangs of apprehension as she watched her carrack *Grace of God* scud off on the rippling, misted waters of the Firth of Tay. At first, however, all went well. The *Grace of God* steered for Campveere (now the holiday town of Veere) in the Netherlands, the staple port where Scots merchants had carried out their trade since the treaty of 1541. According to the agreement, in return for trading solely at that port, Scots mariners and merchants enjoyed rights and privileges there. From 1568 there had been a hiatus during the struggle for independence from Spain, but the arrangement had been reestablished in 1578. Thus, Agnes Cowtie's sons would have had free accommodation in a commodious house with a garden and piped plumbing while they were on shore doing business, along with the services of a Scottish conservator.

The Cowtie boys were excellent businessmen. In exchange for the freight they had carried to Campveere, they took on goods that were in short supply back home, guaranteeing their mother a good profit. First, they loaded "6 cast pieces and 16 small pieces of ordnance," which would have come from the foundries and manufactories of Flanders. Cannon and other ordnance were in great demand, partly because all owners were forced to arm their vessels for defense. Then the boys speculated in timber, another very desirable item in forest-scarce Scotland. First, they filled the holds with "40 masts for ships," and finished off with a deck cargo of "1000 deal boards." In July, the *Grace of God* left the protected waters of Campveere. It is unknown whether they were steering home, or had the intention of making a detour to Bordeaux, to top up their lading with wine. In any event, this makes no difference, for the ship was attacked off "Camernesse" by a fleet of English pirates headed by "Captain Clynton, Hancocke, Purser, and Newman, of Poole." This was the same Clinton Atkinson who had swaggered so insolently out of the Marshalsea, and the others were his associates.

After a savage battle in which Agnes's sons were killed, the *Grace of God* struck her flag and surrendered. That was not enough satisfaction for the pirates, however, who set to torturing the surviving crew. "Towis [were] thrawin about thair heides, quhat be licht luntis [lighted splinters] bound in betwixt thair fingers" to extract information about any store of money the Cowtie boys had been "keeping for some better hap."

These were two forms of torture remarkable even in the age of the Inquisition and the rack. The "towis thrawin about thair heides" would have been the agonizing process known as woolding, where knotted strings were bound about the head and pulled so tightly that a man's eyes would bulge out of the sockets like eggs. This maimed some of the Dundee men for life, for they lost their sight and hearing. The lighted splinters stuck up their fingernails was a new kind of torment, allegedly the inspiration of Stephen Heynes of Purbeck, who was so notoriously brutal that it is said his own crew once petitioned him to show more mercy to his miserable captives. In the case of Mistress Cowtie's men, no one was there to intercede, and several lost their thumbs and fingers.

Clinton and Purser—the latter's true name was William Walton— had been notorious for years. At one time Queen Elizabeth had offered them a free pardon if they would mend their evil ways. After due thought their answer was that though they thanked Her Majesty

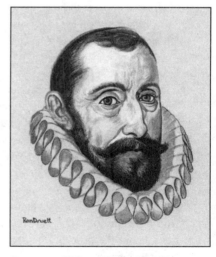

Sir Francis Walsingham.
Artist: Ron Druett.

"for so great a grace and mercy," they preferred "to hazard their fortunes bravely abroad." And so they had continued upon their merry way, and had every expectation of getting away with this attack just the way they had got away with all the rest. However, they had not allowed for the redoubtable Mistress Cowtie.

The fact that she was a woman made a difference here, perhaps. The loss of ship and cargo struck at the very foundations of her business, and the death of her sons was a deeply personal tragedy. What really stirred her up, though, was the deliberate torture and maiming of men she considered her "especial mariners." So she commenced an unflagging campaign of lobbying the authorities for redress.

First, Agnes appealed to the bailies (town magistrates) for backing. These worthies agreed to do what they could to help, and sent a message to Sir Francis Walsingham, Secretary of State to Queen Elizabeth, who was the court representative for Scotland at the time. Prefacing their letter with the observation that "good report made to them by sundry of their nation" gave them the confidence to ask the favor, they requested him

> to be good lord to Agnes Cowtie, spouse of George Blak, their neighbour, and to hear her lamentable complaint. She and her spouse being some time wealthy and honourable persons within the burgh of Dundee, are now brought to such extreme wreck and misery by invasion of English pirates, their bairns and servants slain, their especial mariners put to torment, their ship and goods haill taken from them. Beg him to help her in her just suit at the Queen of England's hands, and that she may have some redress of her scaiths to the comfort of her poor husband and bairns.

To his credit, Walsingham did not turn a deaf ear. Clinton Atkinson, celebrating with his wife in a hostelry in Erith on the Thames (where the Gunpowder Plot was devised a few years later, in 1605), escaped arrest only because someone whispered a warning in the nick of time. Francis Hawley, who was the deputy of the Vice-Admiral of Dorset, Sir Christopher Hatton, was brought before the Admiralty judge at the Marshalsea and asked to explain why the Isle of Purbeck in Studland Bay was such a notorious resort of pirates. Hawley did not try to deny the obvious. "In truth," he admitted, "they are my masters." However, he couldn't do anything about the problem, he declared, because he had no means "to encounter their desperate forces"—quite a claim from a man who had once sent word to Clinton Atkinson that he was displeased with him because

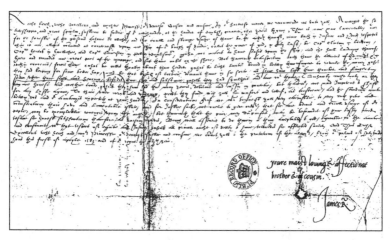

Letter from James VI of Scotland to Queen Elizabeth of England.
Original in the Public Records Office, Kew.

he still hadn't obtained some "arras work he coveted." Then, with characteristically barefaced nerve, Deputy Francis Hawley applied to the Queen for more munitions.

In the meantime, Clinton and Purser looked almost invincible. On December 10, 1582, a Southampton worthy complained to Walsingham that "the archpirate Purser" was selling ships he had seized to local merchants, a Flemish prize profiting him a cool six hundred pounds. Then, the next month, Purser made a "very insolent attack and rebellious attempt" on English and French shipping in Weymouth Road, capturing a sixty-ton bark. He was foiled by the infuriated townspeople, who gathered and attacked, killing seven of his men and wounding others, but there was still a pirate haven in Studland Bay.

However, Agnes Cowtie was still working away at her case. She applied to King James VI of Scotland and went to the Privy Council. The Council submitted a case for "Piracies committed by English men upon divers subjectes of Scotland and the redresse thereof recommended by the Scottish ambassadours." And the King dictated a sincere and impassioned letter to his kinswoman, Queen Elizabeth of England, complaining of the "cruel and strange usage" of the mariners of the *Grace of God* of Dundee.

After relating the circumstances of the capture of the ship and the dreadful torture of the crew, and pointing out that they were so maimed that they "therewith are made impotent to shift for any life again, to their utter wreck and undoing," he requested the Queen "very earnestly to weigh with pity and commiseration their heavy and lamentable estate."

Surely, in the name of justice, she should ensure "that such an odious and cruel usage of our people may be exemplarily revenged upon the authors," and that the "poor men" were indemnified for their losses, receiving "such honest satisfaction therefor as reason craves." Then, after signing the letter, "You're maist lovinge affectionat brother and cousin, James R," he sent it off to his fellow monarch. Evidently, it was a turning point. Two of the Queen's ships descended on Studland Bay, seizing seventeen pirate craft and three of their prizes.

The man in charge of the operation was William Borough, Clerk of the Queen's Ships, who was later to command the *Golden Lion* against the Spanish Armada. According to a popular account of the lives of Clinton and Purser published in 1639, Borough captured these two particular rogues by a trick. Knowing that their ship, *Swallow* was a fast and agile craft, he "provided himselfe of an Hulke, or hoy of slow sayle but great burthen, and stuffed it with able Souldiers." Purser and Clinton fell for it. The moment they sighted the ponderous, heavily laden old ship, they made all sail for her in expectation of a great "purchase"—or prize—"and

Execution Dock at Wapping. Engraving taken from a painting by Robert Dodd, 1723.

the nearer they approached her, the more they were incouraged by reason of her great burthen, and her drone-like sayle." It must have been quite a surprise when they came alongside and threw out grapples, for the "hulke" grappled back, and the *Swallow* was overwhelmed with a rush of hitherto unseen marines.

Both pirate captains were sent off to Marshalsea Prison in Southwark, to be examined by the new, tough judge of the Admiralty Court, Sir Julius Caesar. Inevitably, they were convicted and condemned, to be executed in the traditional fashion. And, on August 30,

1853, the sentence was carried out. Escorted by guards and officers, with a ceremonial silver oar borne before them, the pirates were conducted through the streets of Southwark to Execution Dock on the low-water mark at Wapping.

Purser and Clinton conducted themselves with dignity, it seems, being "as brave in habite, as bold in spirit." As was customary with condemned pirates, they wore their best finery, Clinton Atkinson being dressed in a "velvet doublet with great gold buttons and his velvet Venetian breeches laid with fresh gold lace." As was traditional, too, they took these off before the rope was put around their necks, and distributed them

amongst their private friends who came to sea them dye, that they might remember them after their deaths. Many questions were asked them concerning their Piracies, which they punctually resolved: desiring first, pardon of all men whom they had wronged, and then remission of their sinnes from God, whom they had most heinously offended: when imbracing one the other in their armes, it seemed they no more joyfully lived together than they were willing to dye together: and so being at once turned off from the ladder, it appeared to all the multitude that were then present, that they could not live more irregularly, than they dyed resolutely: and so there they hanged till from that ebbe two Tydes had overwhelmed their bodies, which were after taken downe, and committed to Christian buriall.

And so the bodies of Captains Purser and Clinton swung in chains from the gallows at Wapping until the high tides had covered them twice. Being begged for forgiveness from the scaffold was not enough for Agnes Cowtie, however. The three prizes recaptured by the Queen's force had not included her ship *Grace of God,* so she wrote to a friend in London, Patrick Blair, asking him to try to find out more.

He eventually confirmed her dire suspicions, probably from the evidence of the two pirates' examination by Caesar. The freebooters had indeed sailed the Cowtie craft to Studland Bay, but the Vice-Admiral himself, Sir Christopher Hatton, had disposed of the prize on behalf of the thieves. The *Grace of God,* Blair had learned, was now in Spanish ownership.

So, armed with all these damning details, Agnes wrote to Walsingham herself, and succeeded.

Not only did she get redress for the loss of her ship, but she got compensation for her maimed mariners, too.

Chapter Four

PIRATE QUEENS

Those poor affrighted seamen, not knowing what to do,
They hove their main yard to the mast and let their ship lay to.
These bold and crafty pirates, with broadsword in hand,
They went on board of the merchant ship and slaughtered every man.
—"Bold Manan the Pirate"

It is one of fate's ironies that at the same time that Mistress Agnes Cowtie was seeking redress from the English Admiralty, there was a famous female pirate operating out of Connacht in western Ireland. She was a haughty, dark-featured, gray-eyed Irishwoman, Grania ny Maille—now known as Grace O'Malley, though often called Granuaile ("the bald Grania") because she cut her hair short like a boy's.

Grania was not the only female raider around. Even the Thames at London was plagued with piratical women, some so desperate that they operated on foot, wading out to ships that lay aground in low water and creeping into their holds. One of these wretched creatures operated in cohorts with her husband. "William Patrickson and Elizabetha his wife, in the Thames near the City bridge, did take one hundred pounds English money and various goods," the indictment reads; "and upon Henrico Marten a Doctor of Law, did comit piracy, robbery and murder, between the first and second hours on the 10th day of March 1634." It was a low and grubby crime, but the punishment was horrendous. Elizabeth was confined in "his Maties [Majesty's] Gaole of Newgate, for that she confesseth . . . till she shall speake."

This means she was being tortured. In another indictment her loot was itemized, the list including "one blacke turkey gowne for a woman," various pieces of linen, a dagger, and a "grey clothe doublett," the total value being sixteen pounds. Inevitably, Elizabeth Patrickson was hanged. However, she did not suffer as much as Alice Keeler, who robbed a warehouse near the port. Her punishment was to be publicly and very slowly pressed to death with stones.

Compared with these poor scavengers, Grania was like a magnificent eagle. The O'Malleys had been Gaelic chieftains since about the dawn of time. Indeed, their name derives from *maglios*, the ancient Gaelic word for "chief." Like the Vikings of the not-so-distant Irish past, they were legendary seafarers, locally referred to as Manannans, which means "sea gods of the western ocean." Surprisingly, their coat of arms bears not a sea dragon but a savage red boar aggressively prowling across a field of gold. Nonetheless, it is eloquently indicative of the warrior nature of the tribe.

Born about 1530, Grania was the daughter of Dudara "Black Oak" O'Malley, a mighty chieftain, "strong in galleys and seamen," who owned a great herring fleet. He did a large trade in salt fish with Spain and England, though he was one of the few who never submitted to the English Crown, instead levying a toll on all "foreign" vessels fishing in his waters. Even so illustrious a personage as King Philip II of Spain was not spared, in 1556 being forced to pay a due of one thousand pounds for the right to fish off O'Malley territory for the next twenty-one years. The family had castles at Belclare and on Clare Island, and owned ships which carried cargoes in legitimate trade, as well as craft employed in raids on surrounding territories. An opportunistic man, Dudara also ferried in Scottish mercenary soldiers—the gallowglass—to hire out to warring chieftains. His entire life was in accordance with the O'Malley maxim, *Terra Marique Potens* ("powerful by both land and sea").

In 1546, at about the age of fifteen, Grania was married to Donal-an-Cogahaidh ("Donal of the Battles"), the Tanist, or heir apparent, of the O'Flahertys of Ballinahinch. This was no love match, but a political alliance with another of the most powerful clans of western Ireland. The

Clare Castle. Artist: Ron Druett.

O'Flahertys had such a terrible name that a regular prayer in the churches of Galway ran, "From the ferocious O'Flahertys the Good Lord deliver us." Several children later—including a daughter and her first two sons, Owen and Murrough—Grania found herself a widow, for Donal was killed in battle. According to legend, he was mortally wounded while attacking an island fortress known as Cock's Castle, which had been taken from him by an enemy clan, the Joyces. Grania had been acting in the capacity of clan leader, for Donal was so extravagant and irresponsible that his clansmen had turned to her for help. Thus, she was perfectly capable of wreaking revenge on the men who had killed him. She led the O'Flahertys in a raid of reprisal, regaining the island bastion with a display of such reckless courage that it was promptly renamed Hen's Castle.

Despite this resounding demonstration of leadership abilities, however, Irish law would not allow her to become the chieftain in name, so her husband's cousin was elected to succeed him. Grania recruited the O'Flaherty men who were loyal to her and returned to her father's territory, where she settled her troops on Clare Island in Clew Bay. Then, in the spirit of Princess Alfhild, she took over her father's fleet of galleys and launched herself on a career of piracy.

These galleys were reputed to be highly maneuverable craft, "rowed with thirty oars and sail," each with one hundred good men on board. Obviously, when in the open sea the sails were set, but in the sheltered bays putting out sweeps would give her a tremendous advantage. Within a remarkably short time, Grania had built a reputation as a resolute and reckless admiral. Like Purser and Clinton, she raided the merchant fleets that plied the seas between Scotland, England, and the Continent, robbing them of rich cargoes of salt, wine, silk, and damask. Hunting her down was an exercise in frustration, for Grania's intimate knowledge of the coves and reefs of western Ireland meant that her ships had an uncanny ability to fade invisibly into the seascape.

Naturally, signing up with such a successful raider became considered the path to adventure and fortune. It was also an excellent means of wreaking revenge on the oppressive and rapacious English governors who ruled each county in the name of Queen Elizabeth. For many unfortunate Irish peasants and fisherfolk, survival meant living wild in the forests, eating nettles, berries, and occasionally their comrades' dead bodies, so turning pirate was an attractive option. Thus, Grania's crews came to include ragged and violent men from many tribes, all of whom swore fealty to her, though their clans might be at war with each other. Likewise, her fleet expanded, to include captured and converted ships. Few women have been so powerful at sea. In fact, a female admiral to match the caliber of Grania would not arise for another 250 years, and then it would be a half world away.

This was Cheng I Sao, whose fleets of junks held total sway over the South China Sea in the first decade of the nineteenth century. Her origins were much humbler than Grania's, but equally rooted in maritime tradition. First recorded as a Cantonese prostitute named Shih Yang, Cheng I Sao very possibly plied her trade on one of the many "flower boats"—floating brothels—in the harbor. In 1801 she married Cheng I, the commander of one of the pirate squadrons recruited to fight on the Tay-son side in a Vietnamese rebellion.

In July 1802 the insurrection collapsed, and the Chinese pirates were forced to retreat to southern China, theoretically to resume competing with each other for prizes.

Years of fighting side by side with other pirate captains had taught Cheng I and Cheng I Sao the advantages of collaboration, however, and they set about co-opting their erstwhile associates into a single force. By 1804, their efforts

A Victorian view of Cheng I Sao. Engraving from *History of the Pirates of All Nations.* London, 1837.

resulted in a confederation of four hundred junks and seventy thousand men, under seven banners. They even wrote a constitution, signed in 1805 by the seven major pirate leaders of the area. There was a strict hierarchy within the powerful naval force that resulted, and Cheng I was the chief admiral. Then, on November 16, 1807, Cheng I died, possibly drowned in a gale. And Cheng I Sao, like Grania, took command.

And like Grania, she was able to get away with it because of long-held custom. In Ireland, it was a Celtic tradition that women fought alongside men, and because of that, Grania's participation was never in question. In southern China, women lived with their menfolk on the water, doing an equal share of the work and taking on parallel responsibilities. This happened on pirate vessels, as well as on fishing junks, freighters, passenger boats, and traders. Richard Glasspoole, the young fourth mate of an East Indiaman who was kidnapped by Chinese pirates in 1809, recorded that his captors spent their whole lives on the sea. The captain had the after-

Four views of junks and Chinese riverboats.
Artist: Ron Druett.

part of the ship, and an ordinary seaman was "allowed a small berth about four feet square, where he stows with his wife and family." As in Grania's Ireland, it was common for Chinese pirate women to take part in battle, at times in command of junks. What made Cheng I Sao and Grania different was that they controlled whole fleets instead of just one vessel.

While outright piracy was her avocation, along with the ransoming of prisoners, Cheng I Sao reaped most of her profits from a massive protection racket. Glasspoole was on board during one of the regular expeditions to levy "contributions" from the towns and villages of the Pearl River. He described an intimidating fleet of more than "five hundred sail of different sizes" which plundered and burned uncooperative communities, murdering and enslaving at will. The female villagers were especially vulnerable because their bound feet prevented them from running away like the men. Grania would have levied "contributions" in somewhat the same fashion, for her society was a feudal one, in which paying tribute to the chief was part of the system. This yearly ritual was followed by a great feast in which lots of meat was served—a rare luxury—and much poteen (whiskey) drunk. On the Pearl River delta, Glasspoole recorded celebrations in the shape of opium smoking and gambling.

Marriage of convenience was another feature the two cultures shared. While romantic love had its place in lore and legend, it was often adulterous, and usually ill-fated. In real life, people were more practical. Cheng I Sao regularized her position by becoming the mistress of her dead husband's homosexual lover, Chang Pao, ultimately marrying him even though she had previously adopted him as her son. While she retained overall command of

the confederation, and Chang Pao had formal command of only one of the fleets, he was her mouthpiece. So Chinese historians have focused on Chang Pao instead of the real authority figure, Cheng I Sao. Much the same has happened to Grania, who has been immortalized in Irish folklore but largely ignored by historians. The lives of both pirate queens have been properly researched and described only because of the dedication of two modern scholars, Anne Chambers (Granuaile) and Dian Murray (Cheng I Sao).

In Ireland, Grania strengthened her territory by marrying her younger daughter to a neighboring chief, Richard Gurke of Corraun, whom the English called "the Devil's Hook." Then she followed suit herself, by marrying Richard-an-Iarainn—called "Richard-in-Iron" because he always wore a coat of mail—Burke. The Burkes were originally Franks, descended from Charlemagne, "Burke" being an adaptation of the Frankish name "de Burgos." Richard-in-Iron had the blood of many famous men in his veins, including the legendary Brian Boru, for this was a prolific family. A cousin of his, the second Earl of Clanricard, who died in 1582, was recorded with four wives at once, all legal.

Richard-in-Iron himself was an important Connacht chieftain who owned a fleet of trading vessels. He was described by the English as "a plundering, warlike, unquiet and rebellious man," so he had a great deal in common with his new wife's family—and with her dead husband, too. The Flahertys, O'Malleys, and Burkes had always been known as unquiet people, at

one time specifically forbidden by the Normans who ruled Galway to enter the city. At the same time, there was a horrible enmity between the Burkes and the Flahertys. Thus, that Grania, a Flaherty widow, should marry a Burke seems the essence of romantic drama. According to folklore, however, Grania stipulated that the marriage was only "for a year certain," and after that either party could withdraw if he or she wished. Reputedly, she waited until she had control of his lands, then took over his castle at Carraigahowley, bawling most unromantically from the battlements, "I dismiss you!"

The separation was as unsettled as the marriage, for they remained married in name at least, though it was widely apparent that Grania was the one who wore the breeches. In 1576, Sir Henry Sidney became the first English Crown representative to venture into the west of Ireland, reminiscing in 1583 that when he was in Galway, a most famous feminine Sea Captain called Graine O'Malley" had come to call:

> and she offered her services to me whenever I would command her, with three galleys and 200 fighting men, either in Ireland or in Scotland. She brought with her her husband, for she was, as well by sea as by land, more than master's mate to him. He was of the Nether Burkes . . . called by nickname Richard in Iron. This was a notorious woman in all the coasts of Ireland.

Despite this forthright opinion Sidney made Richard a knight, so that Grania was entitled to be called Lady Burke. It is on record, too, that for once she put on female clothes for the investiture. However, it is difficult to tell exactly why she risked arrest by confronting the Queen's representative. For some years the merchants of Galway had been protesting furiously to Governor Sir Edward Fitton about her piratical activities. Just two years before this meeting with Sidney, Captain William Martin had led a convoy into Clew Bay to lay siege to Rockfleet Castle, but Grania and her forces had driven him off in humiliating defeat, so it seems strange that she put her head in a noose, as it were. She might have taken the risk of being arrested to make certain of Richard's claim to the chieftainship of the MacWilliam clan of Mayo. Basic instinct prevailed, however. Grania invited Sidney on board one of her galleys for a tour of the

Carraigahowley, now known as Rockfleet—a direct translation of its name, which means "stormy rock."
From a 1713 engraving.

Bay of Galway, and when they got back she handed him a bill. Yet still she returned home unhindered.

Richard-in-Iron gave her another son, her favorite, named Tibbott-ne-Long ("Toby of the ships") because he was born at sea. The day after Grania gave birth, a Turkish corsair attacked her ship, and her men were doing so badly that they sent down for her help. Clambering out of bed, she fumed in Irish, "May you be seven times worse in one year, seeing you can't manage for even one day without me." Then, throwing a blanket about her shoulders, she grabbed a couple of blunderbusses and barged up to deck. The Turkish leaders crowded to the taffrail of their ship to gape at this apparition, and she fired both weapons in their faces, hollering, "Take this from an infidel hand!" The Turkish pirate was duly seized, and she hanged the crew at Carraigahowley.

In 1577, Grania raided the territory of the Great Earl of Desmond, at the mouth of the Shannon, and came to regret it, for she was captured by the Earl himself, who promptly threw her into his dungeon. From there she was sent to Governor William Drury, who imprisoned her in Dublin Castle, describing her as "Grany O'Mayle, a woman that hath impudently passed the part of womanhood and been a great spoiler, and chief Commander and director of thieves and murderers at sea." Eighteen months later she was released on condition that she would curb her husband, who was implicated in the rebellion in Munster. When an English official, the hapless Captain William Martin, called to check, however, his way was barred by Sir Richard-in-Iron and "Grany O Mallye with all their force and did swear they would have my life for coming so far into their country, and specially his wife who would fight with me before she was a half mile near me."

Richard-in-Iron died in 1583, but fifty-three-year-old Grania continued her career from her command center at Carraigahowley. In 1584, however, she met another setback, for Richard Bingham succeeded Sir Edward Fitton as Governor of Connacht. It was part of the crackdown on piracy that had been triggered at least in part by Mistress Agnes Cowtie's campaign. Bingham's main mission was to subdue the Irish chieftains, but Grania was a particular target. In 1586 he finally captured her, celebrating by erecting a fresh set of gallows. In the nick of time, however, her son-in-law, Devil's Hook, arrived, and offered himself as pledge and hostage.

Bingham set her free, but felt no scruples about descending to treachery. His brother John rode with his troops to Clare Island, and asked Grania's son Owen for shelter. Owen, a trusting fellow, arranged for them all to be ferried across, but as soon as they were all landed they turned on their host and tied him up with his men, while they rounded up the O'Malley herds of cattle and horses. That night, eighteen of the men were hanged without trial, and the night after that Owen was viciously slaughtered, stabbed no less than twelve times.

Little wonder, then, that Grania set to masterminding rebellion, ferrying in Scots mercenaries the way her father had done. These gallowglass were terrifying figures in iron helmets and long chain armor, their favorite weapon a massive battle-ax with a six-foot handle. Fighting as her forebears had, Grania specialized in ambush, lying in wait, attacking hard, and then dashing away from her stunned and battered targets. Battles were of short duration by necessity, for there were no organized lines of supply, but as a fighting technique it was extremely successful. Indeed, it would have been recognized that Grania's major strength was speed and agility in both attack and retreat—and her ability to disappear like magic. As an Irish bard could well have intoned:

> "Have you seen her
> The Connacht queen in the field?"
> "All that we saw
> Was the shadow under her shield."*

Belief in alchemy was intrinsic to Irish culture. Grania's people used a calendar based on the lunar month, with the twelve extra days of the year being set aside as "the twelve days of Christmas." Samhain, or Halloween, marked the beginning of the year, and February 1, the first day of spring, Saint Brigid's Day. Saint Brigid was a real person, named after the pagan goddess Brigid—in Sanskrit *Brhati,* "the exalted one"—the patron of womanhood and the seasonal renewal of life, which is the reason for the timing of her saint's day. It was a harking back to goddess worship and warrior-queens like Tomyris and Artemisia—and reminiscent of Cheng I Sao's culture, too. In Chinese folklore, mystic powers were attributed to certain women, the most dangerous of whom might materialize as "fox fairies." Glasspoole described joss, or idol worship, the god being propitiated with gifts of roasted pigs that were levied from the villagers. During the collection of levies, one town was spared because "Joss had not promised them success." During a pitched battle, when Glasspoole had

---

*Adaptation of lines from an anonymous Irish poet, quoted in Constantine FitzGibbon, *The Irish in Ireland,* p. 47.

been coerced into manning one of the pirate cannon, he recorded the "chief's wife"—perhaps Cheng I Sao herself—sprinkling him constantly with "garlic water, which they considered an effectual charm against shot."

This engagement came about because Cheng I Sao, like Grania, was fighting government forces. In January 1808, before Glasspoole's spell of captivity, there had been a great pitched battle in which a government fleet, led by General Li Ch'ang-keng, attacked the pirates in Kwangtung waters. The pirates enjoyed a rousing victory in which Li's throat was torn out by a bullet. Many government junks were destroyed, and others were captured. By the end of the year several similar engagements had ended in the same result, and the authorities had lost sixty-three ships. Attempts at blockading Cheng I Sao's squadrons proved farcical, for the pirates simply looted coastal villages, wreaking terrible punishments on anyone who tried to defy them. The pirate squadrons won the battle that Glasspoole described as well. To all appearances, the huge fleet was invincible. Their joss, indubitably, was on their side, but for how long?

In 1592, Grania's run of luck came to an end. Bingham raided her pirate haven at Clare Island and seized her fleet that was anchored in Clew Bay. Grania fled to Ulster, seeking refuge with the O'Neills and the O'Donnells. These were clans with their own grudge against Bingham, for the O'Donnell Tanist, Red Hugh, had only just escaped from a three-year imprisonment in Dublin Castle. After managing to break out, Red Hugh and two O'Neill boys had trekked across the snowy Wicklow Mountains to Ulster, an ordeal that only Red Hugh and one of the O'Neills survived. Once Grania was safely ensconced, Red Hugh and his forces set to devastating all of Connacht as part of their war with the English.

Grania, more coolly, sat down and penned a personal petition to Queen Elizabeth. Like Agnes Cowtie, she was prepared to go right to the top. In a document dated July 1593, she politely requested that her two surviving sons might hold their lands by right of English law. Furthermore, she "most humbly" beseeched Her Majesty "to grant her some reasonable maintenance for the little time she has to live." In return, Grania promised "to invade with sword and fire all your Highness enemies"— quite an undertaking for a lady in her sixties who had just applied for an old age pension. Intrigued, the Queen sent a questionnaire containing eighteen "Articles of Interrogatory," which Grania filled in with eloquent but diplomatic replies. Then she went to Greenwich Palace to meet the Queen herself.

A royal arrival at Greenwich Palace. From *Girl's Own Paper.* August 1885.

It must have been quite an encounter—two valkyria, much the same age, who had led lives of power and manipulation, but on different sides. Grania herself described it as a meeting of equals, though the Queen addressed her as Lady Burke. Instead of being insulted or even amused, Elizabeth, it seems, was impressed. She granted the pension, directing Sir Richard Bingham to organize "some maintenance for the rest of her living of her old years," much to that gentleman's outrage. Additionally, she ordered that Tibbott-ne-Long—who meantime had been arrested on Bingham's orders—should be set free, and that his half brother, Murrough, should be favored.

This, too, has a parallel with Cheng I Sao's story. Tired of losing ships and men in the war with the pirates, in February 1810 the Chinese government offered amnesty. The first conference was inconclusive, so on April 18, Cheng I Sao, taking along a company of pirate women and children, arrived unarmed at the governor general's headquarters in Canton. It was an impressive gesture, which led to a bout of very shrewd negotiations. Instead of being punished, the pirates were rewarded, especially husband Chang Pao, for he was given military rank and allowed to keep a private twenty-junk fleet, along with a large sum of money. In return, Cheng I Sao went into retirement, which meant the end of the huge federation of pirates. The operation had been kept together by this one woman's charisma. Once she had gone, the cohesive element was lost. Their joss, in effect, had been Cheng I Sao herself.

In the same situation, Grania was somewhat more reluctant to retire, because by agreeing to the request to "pursue, during her life, all Her Majesty's enemies by land and sea," Elizabeth had given her nothing less than a very tempting privateering license. That was Bingham's conclusion anyway, for he protested that Grania could not be trusted, being a notorious "traitoress, and nurse to all rebellions in the Province for 40 years." In an attempt to fend off the consequences of his monarch's rashness, Bingham quartered soldiers on Grania's land and ordered that she should carry a guard on every voyage, but in 1595 he was recalled in disgrace. And so, at the age of sixty-six, Grania was back to roving.

Before long, she and officialdom were at loggerheads again. In 1601 she was in action with the English sloop of war *Tramontane,* the leader of the small squadron of Queen's ships in Ireland, which managed to capture one of her galleys. When an Ulster chieftain passed over Tibbott and created another man the Mac William, however, Grania finally remembered her commitment to her "fellow princess." She put Tibbott-ne-Long in charge of her remaining ships, with orders that he was to sail in Her Majesty's service.

This was the end of her pirate operation, for, like Cheng I Sao's federation, it had been kept in focus by her charisma. Tibbott fought on the English side at the Battle of Kinsale, while Red Hugh O'Donnell, whose family had sheltered Grania less than ten years before, was one of the defeated Irish forces. Red Hugh fled to Spain, where he died mysteriously, probably poisoned by a spy. Tibbott-ne-Long, by contrast, was knighted Sir Theobald Burke in 1603—the same year that two valkyria died, one his mother, Grania, and the other his monarch, Elizabeth.

And Cheng I Sao, who had spent her last days peacefully running a gambling house of ill repute in Canton, died in 1844, aged sixty.

Chapter Five

CAPTURED BY CORSAIRS

"O hail her! O hail her!" our gallant captain cried,
Blow high, blow low, and so sailed we;
"Are you a man of war or a privateer," said he,
"Cruising down along the coast of the High Barbaree!"

"O, I am not a man of war nor privateer," said he,
Blow high, blow low, and so sailed we;
"But I'm a salt-sea pirate a-looking for my fee,
Cruising down along the coast of the High Barbaree."
                                                    —Sea chantey

One dark night in 1638, the distraught father of a dishonored girl piloted seven boatloads of Barbary corsairs into a secluded cove near his home village of Nicotera, in the far south of Italy. His name was Giovanni Andrea Capria, and his daughter had been seduced by the feudal lord. Smarting for revenge, Capria had offered himself to the Tunisian pirates as their guide. In the course of the raid that followed their landing, Capria found and killed the girl with his own hands. Before he could make his escape he was seized and hanged from the bow of a galley that had been captured from the pirates, but in the meantime his terrible vengeance had been wreaked.

This operalike scenario is typical of the many harrowing tales of the pirates of the Barbary Coast—the Mediterranean shores of the seventeenth-century North African regencies of Tunis, Tripoli, and Algiers, together with the empire of Morocco. Since the early eighth century the Moors and Turks had built up a fearsome tradition of freebooting, but because of their fragile galleys, they had been constrained to the Mediterranean Sea. With the change in the official attitude to piracy back home, however, a number of English rovers turned to operating out of North Africa. For a

Corsair galley. From *Historie van Barbaryen* Amsterdam, 1634.

while their sturdy, square-rigged, well-armed ships gave them a huge advantage. John Ward, for instance, created a sensation when he captured several Venetian argosies, including the *Reniera e Soderina* with a freight of indigo and other goods valued at one hundred thousand pounds. The "Turks," however, quickly learned about European-style ships and ship-handling from the Elizabethan rovers' example.

The ability to handle "round" ships and heavy cannon gave the Barbary corsairs the capability to invade the Atlantic and hunt grounds as far from home as Iceland and Nova Scotia. Soon, none but the most heavily armed merchantmen were immune. A Christian renegade, John Nutt, was in command of a whole fleet—twenty-eight ships—off the Irish coast in May 1623, when he stopped a bark at the entrance to Dungarvan Harbour and found about a dozen women on board. They were all "ravished by the pyrates' company," the wife of a Cork saddler being favored by the captain himself. Nutt carried her into his cabin "and there had her a week." This, however, was unusual, for if the "pyrates' company" managed to keep their hands off captured women, they got a lot more money for them when they were put up for sale in the North African slave markets.

And the market in slaves was a huge one. For example, the mayor of Plymouth claimed that the Moslems had taken a thousand men of that port in 1625 alone. It was dangerous even for fishermen to ply their trade, for the humblest of craft were raided for slaves, eighty men from the Cornish fishing village of East Looe being captured over a period of just ten days in

1626. By 1636, the shipowners of Exeter, Plymouth, Dartmouth, and other West Country ports were sending frantic petitions to the Lords of the Council begging support, for the swarms of freebooters in the English Channel made it almost impossible to send ships to sea.

Whole towns were raided. Like their Mediterranean forebears, the corsairs descended at night, carrying off complete populations including women and children, all headed for sale on the Barbary Coast. Italy, being in such close range, was one of the earliest targets. In 1534, Aruj Barbarossa—"Redbeard"—led a savage attack on the Italian town of Fondi with the aim of capturing its regent, the spectacularly beautiful, pious, and cultured Contessa Giulia Gonzaga, who was destined to adorn the harem of the Grand Signior—the Ottoman Sultan. Luckily, the Countess was roused in the nick of time to make her escape in her nightdress, but the town was ravaged and many of its inhabitants killed or enslaved. In 1631 a similar attack on the Irish port of Baltimore was led by the Dutch renegade Murat Reis (Jan Jansz of Haarlem), yielding 109 men, women, and children to be sold in the slave market in Algiers.

The alternative to slavery was ransom—if the captive or the captive's family could afford it, though sometimes the government provided the money, such as in the case of Eliza Bradley. Eliza, wife of Captain James Bradley, was thirty-four years old when their ship *Sally* sailed from Liverpool on May 12, 1818, bound for Tenerife. Five weeks out, they were overtaken by a tremendous storm, during which the ship ran ashore on the Barbary Coast. Eliza, her husband, and the thirty members of the crew struggled to the beach and set up camp at the fringe of the desert, subsist-

"Horrid abuse of the helpless women in the cabin." Ellms, *Pirates Own Book.* Boston, 1837.

ing for the next five days on a barrel of flour and a keg of salt pork, brought on shore from the wreck. When that ran out, they set off along the beach, surviving somehow on mussels and the half-rotted corpse of a seal. Their only reward for this feat of endurance was to be captured by Arabs, who stripped them all nearly naked and divided up the party as spoil. To Eliza's horror, she and her husband were separated. His "master" took him one way, and hers another, informing her he intended to sell her in Morocco.

The subsequent trek was even more terrible than the one along the coast. Eliza, though allowed to ride on camelback, was wearing nothing but "my petticoat and shimmy" because her bonnet, gown, and shoes had been confiscated. The men in her party, who were forced to march, had only trousers, so suffered terribly from sunburn as well as hunger due to a diet of little else but insects. Eliza's "master" was a terrible and intimidating figure, being

> about six feet in height, of a tawny complexion. His hair was stout and bushy, and stuck up in every direction like bristles on the back of a hog; his eyes were small, but were red and fiery, resembling those of a serpent when irritated; and to add to his horrid appearance his beard (which was of a jet black, and curly) was of more than a foot in length!

Eliza was allowed a tent of her own, but this did not help her to sleep any more easily, for she was told that she was given this luxury only because the English Consul at Mogador (modern Essaouira) would pay twice the ransom for a female captive in good condition as he would for a man. She had lots of visitors, for the women of the village used to come to watch her cry. Five months later, the nightmare came to an end, when Mr. Willshire, the British Consul resident at Mogador, ransomed her, having already redeemed her husband.

This ransoming business could add up to a large public expense, with the result that at one time a proposal was presented in England to try exchanging useful male captives for "idle and lascivious" women. However, this met with no success, the corsairs being so insistent on hard cash. After a petition to Parliament in 1640 claimed that more than three thousand English men, women, and children were languishing in captivity on the Barbary Coast, representing about £150,000 in ransom demands, in 1646 a British envoy, Edmund Casson, was sent to Algiers with a purse of just under £40,000 to redeem as many as he could.

He ransomed 244 of them. The basic price for one Englishman was £38, but—as we have seen from Eliza Bradley's tale—women were reckoned to be worth at least twice as much. As it was, Casson paid out £200 for Elizabeth Mancor of Dundee, £800 for Sarah Riply of London, £1,000 for Mary Riply and her two children, £1,100 for Alice Hayes of Edinburgh, and £1,392 for Mary Bruster of Youghal, Ireland, who must have been unusually beautiful or else known to have rich connections.

Their towns of origin being major shipping ports, these women were probably seized from ships and could well have been captains' or merchants' wives, which would also account for their unusual value. While large numbers of women and children were captured at the same time as their menfolk during raids on towns, the proportion of women taken from ships or shipwrecks was, of course, much smaller. English consular records for the 1680s show that of a sampling of two hundred English captives taken to Algiers from seized ships, only ten—or five percent— were women.

However, this does not diminish the terror the women must have felt as their vessels, either becalmed or tricked by false flags into hauling aback, were brought to by European-style vessels bristling with cannon, or overtaken by slim, agile corsair galleys. Corsair craft had smooth hulls that were greased to slip as easily as arrows through the water, while all the time the Moslem crews ululated their distinctive, bloodcurdling battle cries. Even more ominously, the teams of naked, heavily chained, half-starved slaves who thrust and hauled the fifteen-foot oars were all too often the women's own countrymen.

Paying ransom was their best option, as the only alternative to slavery. The variable was how much money was demanded. As we can see by the vastly differing amounts paid by Casson, some people were considered a lot more valuable than others. Thus, sophisticated captains' wives and female passengers would strip off jewels and finery to keep their captors' estimate of their ransom value as low as possible. The corsairs were up to such tricks, however. A close inspection sorted out the soft skin of the privileged from the calluses of the lowly, and a powerful emetic produced any coins or jewels that might have been swallowed.

After the galleys arrived at their home port, to the accompaniment of a delirious salute of guns, female captives were sent to the house where the captain (raïs) of the corsair craft lived. There, they were confined in shadowy seclusion. Miss Tully, a relative of the British Consul in Tripoli, described apartments where the "windows have no glass, but are furnished with jalousies of wood curiously cut: these windows produce a gloomy light, being admitted through spaces a quarter of an inch wide, and crossed with heavy bars of iron; and as they look into an inward court-yard, they are well calculated to calm the perturbed mind of the jealous Moor."

There, the women were subjected to an intimate scrutiny. As observed by Joseph Pitts, an English slave in Cairo, the professional auctioneers had the liberty

> to view their faces, and to put their fingers into their mouths to feel their teeth; and also to feel their breasts. And further, as I have been informed, they are sometimes permitted by the sellers . . . to [physically examine] whether they are Virgins or no.

Women who were worth a ransom were set aside and closely guarded until payment and release had been arranged, though in 1747 one woman, along with her two small children, did manage to escape for a brief and ghastly hour. This was Mrs. Jones, the wife of one of the officers belonging to the Hibernian Regiment. She had been captured with her husband and brought to Algiers, where she somehow got out into the street.

There she wandered, dazed, through dirty, unfamiliar alleys where sand drifted down the central gutters and cobbles were heaped with animal droppings. She would have been buffeted by whining, buzzing flies and clouds of fine, clinging dust, lost in a maze of walls and iron screens and tall, barred gates. People would have pressed close, most in rags, some men in magnificent gold-embroidered robes, their women muffled to the eyes in layers of cloth like walking tents. The noise would have been deafening, vendors' cries mingling with shrill screams and the grim shouting of sudden brawls. Depending on the time of day, the ghostly calling of the muezzin would have set flights of birds to wheeling in the sky.

Inevitably, Mrs. Jones became an object of curiosity. Assaulted by one of the Pasha's soldiers, she fled into a loft. In her panic, she left the two children behind. The soldier grabbed one of them and threatened to hurt the child unless she came down. When Mrs. Jones refused, the janissary cut off the child's hand and hurled it at her. Sick with disgust, she grabbed a piece of a broken millstone and threw it down on him with such force that it broke his leg. At that, he killed the child.

Screaming with shock and loathing, she heaved the rest of the stone over the edge of the loft, knocking him senseless. Mrs. Jones jumped down, took his scimitar, and cut off his head. Then, sobbing, gathering the corpse of her child into her arms, she gave herself up.

*   *   *

Women who were not ransomed were taken to the Bedestan—slave market—where they joined the men who were also waiting to be sold. This might be the last chance of seeing a husband, brother, or father. Over three successive mornings the captives were stripped and prodded by raucous auctioneers. Saint Vincent de Paul, then a young professor at the University of Toulouse, recorded that after being captured in the Gulf of Lyons in 1605, he and his companions were loaded down with chains and "paraded through the streets of Tunis" to the marketplace, there to be inspected by merchants who behaved "just like people come to the sale of a horse or an ox, making us open our mouths to see our teeth," and testing the captives' strength by set-

ting them to lifting heavy weights, fighting with each other, and so forth.

The fate of men was hard enough. Miss Tully recorded in 1783 that they were set to "the lowest and hardest kind of work, while in the country[side] they are sometimes obliged to draw the plough instead of horses." Seamen were assigned to the galleys, while others labored endlessly on construction sites. Saint Vincent de Paul was sold to an alchemist whose wife took pity on him and persuaded her husband to help him escape, but few captives had that kind of luck.

The Bedestan. From *Historie van Barbaryen.* Amsterdam, 1634.

Pretty girls, particularly if they were virginal, were headed for a harem—a place impossible to flee. "The wall surrounding it is thirty feet high," wrote Miss Tully after visiting the Bashaw's seraglio in Tripoli. Within, the only men who were allowed to come within sight of the women were the master and his eunuchs. Any other man discovered, even in the gardens, was beheaded instantly. Miss Tully described passages so long and dark that she had to be ushered by attendants with flaring torches, despite the broad daylight outside. "Could the subterranean ways and hidden corners of this castle tell the secret plots and strange events that happen daily within its walls," she mused, "they would be most extraordinary to hear."

Strange, indeed. The story of one unfortunate girl is told by Francis Brooks, a man from Bristol who managed to escape from Moroccan slavery in 1692, and published a harrowing account of his experiences to stir up public sentiment on behalf of the miserable Barbary slaves.

Seven years previously Veneziano Raïs, who was a particularly audacious Italian renegade operating out of Morocco, seized a ship bound for Barbados from London. Much to his delight, he found four women on board, two of them a mother and her young daughter. Noticing the tender age of the daughter, the corsair asked "who the young Woman was, and whether she was ever married?"

Christian slaves in Algiers. Engraving by Flameng, 1869.

The answer was no— which meant that she was a virgin, a reason for special treatment, virgins having a high market value. "Account being given him concerning her, he ordered her to be put in the Cabin, lest any of his own barbarous Crew should offer to lie with her"—thus drastically reducing her price—and forthwith steered speedily to the port of Sallee. From there the four women were transported to Meknes, and "brought before the Emperor's Eunuchs, and an account given to the Chief of them by the Moors Captain, that one of them was a Virgin, and she was immediately sent to the Emperor's Women : and the Eunuch sent to the Vice-Roy, acquainting him how he had disposed of the Virgin, who ordered the other Women to be brought to his House."

It is easy to imagine the panic, particularly that of the girl, who must have been terrified at being so abruptly separated from her mother. Even if she did not have any clear idea of what lay ahead, the older women must have been able to guess. As it was, the Chief Eunuch lost no time in sending "word to the Emperor, that he had a Christian Virgin amongst the rest of his Women."

This was the Emperor of Morocco, Mulai Ismail, a most unappealing character who was notorious for taking a personal delight in the act of killing. He once sawed a living man in half *vertically,* and he kept a menagerie of wild beasts he occasionally fed with screaming slaves.

Thomas Phelps, another Englishman enslaved by the Moroccans, testified in 1685 that in the space of one day he saw the Emperor "Lance Seven and twenty *Negroes* one after another," and then went on to observe, "yea his Women are not able by all their Charms to avoid his Fury, but are more the objects of his implacable rage than any other passion."

"The swarthy Infidel," as Phelps dubbed him, had a huge harem—he sired at least five hundred sons by the time he died in 1727—but the prospect of possessing an English virgin was nonetheless enormously tempting. So, according to Brooks, Mulai Ismail sent for the girl to be brought to his camp, "with a parcel of his Eunuchs to guard her thither" and make certain that she remained untouched until the moment she received the honor of being deflowered by the Emperor himself.

There was a problem, however. A good Moslem would not lie with a Christian, so first the girl had to be forced into changing her religion. Accordingly, when she arrived at the camp "the Emperor urged her, tempting her with Promises of great Rewards if she would turn Moor [Moslem], and lie with him." The girl flatly refused, an act that must have taken courage. Not only was Mulai Ismail a fearsome figure in exotic, flowing robes and turban, but he was also notorious for going black in the face when enraged—and he flew into a rage very readily.

"When he could not prevail so, he fell to threat'ning her," Brooks related,

> and caused her to be stript, and whipt by his Eunuchs with small Cords, so long till she lay for dead; and he caused her to be carried away out of his Presence that time, and charged his Women none of them should help her till he sent for her, which was not till two days after, and in the meantime to have no Sustenance but that black rotten Bread: at which time he sought again to prevail with Promises and Threats, which she still withstood . . . then he prick'd her with such things, as commonly his Women use instead of Pins. Thus this beastly and inhuman Wretch by all ways he could invent, sought to force her to yield, which she resisted so long, till Tortures, and the hazards of her Life forced her to yield, or resign her Body to him.

And so eventually the girl gave in, eschewing her own religion and taking on his by whispering the fateful words, "There is no God but God, and Mohammed is his prophet."

Triumphantly, Mulai Ismail "had her wash'd, and clothed her in their fashion of Apparel." To the bewildered girl, it must have felt as if nightmare had been succeeded by hallucination, for all European observers found Moorish costume so overwhelmingly exotic. Miss Tully described chemises of transparent gauze, some in the "finest crimson," with "rich silk stripes of the same colour," topped with waistcoats of silver, gold, or elaborate embroidery. According to Brooks, the women of the Moroccan tyrant's harem covered their heads with "a piece of Silk of Red or Yellow Colour," and their bodies with loose fine smocks that were girdled with silk at the waist and worn over diaphanous drawers, which were "open or slit in the middle."

The toilet was equally strange. Miss Tully recorded that large quantities of powdered cloves were brushed into the hair, which was then packed out with many strands of silk that were "prepared with strong perfumes," so that it plaited up into two massive braids. Every hair of the eyebrows was painted individually with kohl, unwanted hairs tweaked without mercy. With equal care, the face was painted red and white, and the palms of the hands and soles of the feet dyed with henna. About "the Wrists of their Hands they wear on each a Silver Shackle, and likewise upon the Small of their Legs; and on their Feet red Slippers," wrote Brooks. The shackles, as it happens, were not a mark of slavery, instead symbolizing the subservience of women, even queens wearing gold or silver fetters. However, it is very likely that the girl found them a terrifying confirmation that she was, indeed, in bondage.

Having had her thus prepared for his pleasure, Mulai Ismail "lay with her." Deflowering accomplished, he promptly lost any further interest. Having "his desire fulfilled, he inhumanly, in great haste, forced her away out of his presence; and she being with child, he sent her by his eunuchs to Meknes to the Chief Eunuch, after that she was delivered of two children." What happened to the girl after the birth of the twins is unknown.

While the tribulations of the Barbary captives were terrible almost beyond belief, there was also much misery in their homes. When, in 1626, the mayor of Plymouth complained that the "Turks" had taken a thousand seamen of that port, he emphasized the "pitiful lamentations that are made by wives and children"—something that must have deeply troubled many of the captive seamen themselves. As a mariner from Dover confided in his memoirs, throughout his slavery he was haunted by the knowledge that "I had not the wherewithal to release myself, so that I knew not but that I might a ended my days a slave under the hands of merciless men; [and]

then the consideration of my poor wife at home . . . now big with the second child."

This "poor wife" was Mary Highway, who was born in Dover in 1632. In 1655 she married Edward Coxere, a remarkable man who has left an eloquent record of what it was like to be a seaman at the time. Seven weeks after the wedding, Edward (called "Ned") sailed off as gunner in the *Diligence* of London, at the rate of forty-eight shillings a month, taking all the spare household cash with him to invest in a "venture" (a small stockpile of trade goods with which he hoped to make a profit)—though, as he admitted in his memoirs, it "left my wife very bare of money." Somehow, Mary was expected to cope. It is unlikely that she expected anything different, her father, Richard, and her brother, Thomas, being seamen just like her new husband. And, as we shall see, she proved quite resourceful.

Meantime, Ned's voyage turned out to be an interesting one. His captain was a crackpot who ordered a boat lowered every time he felt the urge, so that he could be rowed to the nearest beach, "where he tucked down his breeches and eased himself." Returning very drunk after being entertained by the Governor of Tangier, he declared that the wind was fair and they must be off, although the air was dead calm. Solemnly, the men all pretended to obey. They "weighed" the anchor, leaving the cable slack, and loosed the limp sails while the captain roared instructions to the helmsman. "And we fast at anchor. A very noticeable whimsy of a commander."

Then, when they did get to sea, they were overtaken by a storm. By the time it was over they were floating, crippled, off the Barbary Coast. Coxere managed to get the ship under jury rig, but "all our labour and hopes was in vain," for the *Diligence* was seized by a Spanish man-of-war. On arrival at Málaga, however, Ned was able to "slily" make his escape in the boat which had brought some whores on board. He talked the skipper of a Fleming ship into taking him into the crew, and thus made his way to Amsterdam and thence to Dover, arriving in May 1656. He had lost everything—his books, his clothes, and his navigational instruments. The only profit from nine months of "troublesome voyage" was a bolt of linen cloth he had bought with his wages in Holland.

And throughout that nine months, Mary had spent most of the time alone. Both her father and her brother had departed on voyage, and so

> coming into our house, I found only my poor wife and a young child of three weeks old in a cradle. She, being surprised, could hardly speak to me, for she knew not before whether I was dead or alive. I laid down my pack, and rested myself, and had my relations come about me with

joy. My wife soon turned the holland [cloth] into money, which we had then occasion for. As I remember, it sold for nine pounds, which was then our stock; for my wife, having good friends, with her own industry kept me out of debt.

Not only had Mary endured pregnancy and birth alone, but "with her own industry," she had kept the little family solvent. It was lucky she could do it, for within weeks Ned was off again. This time he sailed with her brother, Thomas, who had been given command of a small vessel, the *Friendship* of London. It was a short and prosperous voyage, which must have been very heartening for the young couple, but the next, in 1657, proved a disaster. The ship arrived safely in Venice, loaded with wine and currants, but on the way back to England, they were attacked by the *Vice-Admiral* of Tunis and "forced to yield to those unreasonable barbarians, to whom we became their slaves, a heart-breaking sorrow."

Knowing full well that his only hope of release was a ransom, Ned Coxere "desired my brother Hiway that he would not call me brother nor acknowledge me to have been his mate, that thereby they might have the less esteem of me to set the less ransom on me." Brother-in-law Thomas disregarded this plea, telling their captors that Coxere was the mate of the ship, and therefore more valuable than they had thought. "I was not pleased," wrote Ned, understandably, particularly as his brother-in-law, being a relatively wealthy man, was able to buy his own freedom two months later, for the sum of eight hundred pieces of eight (about £150).

Left behind, Ned worked in chains and existed on bread, horsebeans, olives, and water, greatly troubled with "thoughts of my wife at home, knowing that this news must needs be a heart-breaking to her, having lost all and liberty too, and not [the] wherewithal to be released out of this miserable life of slavery." He would have had the chance to better himself if he had consented to give up his Christian faith. After he was put into the ship *Rear Admiral* as boatswain, he was told "if I would turn Turk I might be captain of the ship. I told him 'no': I had a wife and children at home." His guards told him "that was nothing; I might have a wife there." What was unsaid, but understood, was that Ned would have become a corsair as well.

It was common enough for renegade Christians to marry local women. In the early sixteenth century a Portuguese writer, Fernão Mendes Pinto, told a story about being on board a ship that attacked and seized an Arab vessel in the Indian Ocean. When the Portuguese captain found out that the master of the captured ship was a renegade, having renounced his Christian faith in order to marry a Greek Moslem girl, he offered him the chance to return to his old religion. The renegade refused, so he was bound hand and foot, a great stone was tied to his neck, and he was tossed overboard.

However, this did not necessarily mean that apostates neglected their family responsibilities at home. Mary Coxere might have been much better off if Ned had accepted the double-edged offer. The wives of some of the renegade corsairs settled in the Low Countries to be nearer their husbands, and saw them relatively often. Furthermore, the pirates commonly sent money home by English ships that were encountered at sea. John Ward and Anthony Johnson entrusted the master of the *Husband* with two hundred pounds in Barbary gold to deliver to their wives, which he did. It was not the safest system in the world, though, for the temptation for the courier to sail off with the cash was a strong one. On one occasion the marshal of the Admiralty Court was accosted by a group of irate pirate wives who had not received some promised gold. Ward went on record as wreaking revenge on a Captain Fisher of Redriffe, who had been entrusted with one hundred pounds to carry to his wife. Finding out that Fisher had abused his trust, Ward hunted him down, had Fisher ducked at the yardarm, and then killed him.

Ned Coxere was a man of strong principles, however, who stuck to his decision despite harsh treatment, and despite living in terror of being put to work in a galley, where the guard was a notorious Moor who had once "cut off a slave's arm and beat the rest of the slaves with it to make them row the more." However, he was fortunate. After he had been captive five months, a fleet of English frigates arrived in Tunis and ransomed seventy-five English slaves, including Ned and two women. "Some had been there under this bondage five years, some ten; one old man had been there thirty-two years." After that, Ned became a gunner on a man-of-war, fighting against the Spanish. He had the good luck to plunder a bag of gold ducats from one of their prizes, but this was stolen by a so-called English consort (comrade). Thus the months dragged by, with Ned existing on his wits and his skill as a linguister (translator) until at last he arrived back in Dover

> [with] only my clothes to my back to my poor wife, but poor and penniless yet glad to see each other in health again after these troubles. My son Robert died whilst I was a slave, and Elizabeth was born. I was pitied by many, [and] counted unfortunate. At this time my wife did

begin to keep shop, there being a necessity for something to be done for a livelihood. Here ended this troublesome voyage.

After such a long tale of profitless woe, it would seem logical that Coxere should swallow the anchor and settle down to help his wife keep the store. Instead, however, Ned borrowed fifteen pounds "to fit myself with books, instruments, clothes, and a venture." Then, he hied himself to sea again, shipping as chief mate on a ship commanded by Mary's brother, Thomas—the same man who had let him down so badly in the Tunisian jail—on a voyage to Newfoundland for a cargo of "poor jack" (salt cod).

Oddly, Mary could have been with Ned all this time. Since medieval times the captains of small merchant ships had taken their wives along, particularly in the Mediterranean trade. If a valued member of the crew had accommodations that were roomy enough to carry his wife, it was common for him to take her, too. Indeed, it was to everyone's advantage, for the women on board would be expected to help with the work of the ship. Shipowner John Tilly was surprised that Ned did not take Mary on voyage, or settle her in Amsterdam, where he would have seen her more often. However, "it did not suit with me to carry my wife from her relations," and Mary Coxere spent her life in Dover, keeping the family financially secure by whatever means she could contrive.

If she had sailed, though, Mary would have been enslaved by the Barbary corsairs. Ned's decision proved to be the right one.

Chapter Six

THE WIDOWS

Then she got a shore tailor
To rig her young sailor
In fine nankeen trousers and blue long-tail coat;
And he looked like a squire
For her to admire
With a dimity han'kercher tied round his throat.

—Sea chantey

In the 1660s, when Ned Coxere was sailing to the shores of North America after cargoes of "poor jack," the only Europeans he encountered were the men who caught the cod and then, helped by their women, processed the fish at the flaking tables. These wretched laborers lived in such appalling conditions that pirates regularly sailed to Newfoundland when they needed volunteers to fill out their crew lists. It took religious discrimination and an error in navigation (for the Pilgrim Fathers believed they were heading for Virginia) to make the northernmost part of the American continent respectable. And so, by 1674, when a tall, muscular second-generation pioneer married the widow of a "well-bred" Boston merchant, Massachusetts had been populated by English men and women for just fifty-three years.

Twenty-three-year-old William Phips hailed from what his biographer, Cotton Mather, described as "a despicable plantation" on the Kennebec River in Maine. Raised along with many siblings by his mother after the early death of his father, William was barely literate. He seems to have caught the widow's attention simply because he was an attractively sunburned giant with the gift of the gab. His new wife, Mary, taught him to read and write, and helped him rise to the stature of ship carpenter. She probably kept him on the right side of the law as well, for instead of turning to buccaneering to make his fortune, which was a course many similar men took at the time, Phips made up his mind to hunt for treasure.

On voyages to the West Indies, he heard about the treasure galleon *Nuestra Señora de la Concepción,* which had sunk off Hispaniola (now the Dominican Republic) in 1641. The story caught his imagination, and he became obsessed with the notion that he was the one who was fated by the gods to uncover this rich trove. It is a testimony to William's eloquence that Mary agreed to fund a voyage to England to talk the King into backing an expedition, and that, even more amazingly, the strange mission succeeded. Sir John Narborough, a man who had been fascinated by stories of the wreck for a number of years, was swept up by William's compelling personality, and Charles II succumbed, too. Phips was given a ship that had been captured from the Algerine corsairs, and permission to go off and hunt for treasure.

That first voyage was a strange one. The King had put a couple of "spies" on board—John Knepp and Charles Salmon—to look after the royal interests, and Knepp in particular objected to just about everything, starting off by grumbling that the only bed he was assigned was the lid of a chest. Then the crew, a scruffy bunch who were paying their own way in return for a share of the treasure, went ashore in Ireland to provision the ship by shooting sheep. Even more infuriatingly, they raided the spies' store of liquor, and when Knepp complained about that they talked thoughtfully and openly about marooning him.

When the ship arrived at Boston, Phips hung about the harbor showing

Boston harbor, 1723. Contemporary print.

off, the honor of commanding "an actual mann of warr" having given him ideas above his station. Despite Knepp's scandalized arguments, he was determined to force all other ships to strike their colors in deference to his "royal" flag, firing across the bows of any captain who failed to do so. Then, to add insult to injury, he sent over a boat with a bill for six shillings and eightpence for the cost of the shot. His men got into drunken brawls on shore, but when Phips was summoned by the Governor's constables to do something about it he merely informed them "he did not care a turd for the Governor," and invited the policemen to kiss his arse. No doubt, he was getting his own back for various snubs the Boston gentry had handed out to him in the past. Somewhat naturally, Mary was alarmed by these shenanigans, realizing that Knepp's report was going to do her husband a lot of harm once it arrived in England. Consequently, she was insistent that William make certain that Knepp was on board when they set sail for the Caribbean. Salmon got to hear of this, and when he told Knepp, the spy jumped to the conclusion that if he did sail, he was unlikely to return, and accordingly he made sure he missed the ship when Phips finally departed.

Shipboard life was no quieter without Knepp. Phips was forced to put down two attempts at mutiny, for his men decided they would rather turn pirate than hunt for treasure. The first time, William waded in with boots and fists, and the second time he aimed the ship's cannon at the troublemakers, hollering, "Stand off, ye wretches, at your peril." Then, Mary's fears were proved well founded, for he was summoned back to London to explain away Knepp's report. While he was in England, in 1685, Charles II died, to be succeeded by James II, who had no interest in treasure whatsoever. Phips had to go about finding backers again.

He did not have much luck at first, but then the Duke of Albemarle, encouraged by his madcap wife, the former Lady Elizabeth Cavendish, agreed to put up a quarter of the capital. At that, Sir John Narborough's interest was revived, and he agreed to put up an eighth. He could certainly afford it. His second wife (another Elizabeth) had brought him a huge dowry, to add to the fortune in prize money he had reaped from three successful expeditions against the Barbary corsairs. The partners bought a ship, diplomatically named her *James & Mary,* sold the other shares to five more investors, and off Phips sailed, for a second attempt. As Daniel Defoe later described it, " 'twas a mere Project, a Lottery of a Hundred Thousand to One odds." And yet it proved to be the greatest commercial success of the seventeenth century

For in February 1687, Phips's divers found a coral-encrusted wreck.

Over six more weeks of intoxicated "fishing," he oversaw
the retrieval of thirty-four tons
of treasure, including a chest
of rubies, emeralds, and diamonds, more than 63,000
pounds of silver, and 347
pounds of plate. In one fell
swoop, he had taken more
treasure than Henry Morgan
had seized throughout his lifetime, without the loss of a

Drift whale. Engraving by Van der Gouwen, 1598.

man. The expedition reached London in June, and Samuel Pepys, Secretary of the Admiralty, placed it under guard while the treasure was
counted and the Duke of Albemarle and the other investors celebrated
with Phips and the crew.

The King's tax on the haul came to £20,872, and Phips's portion was
£11,000. There was some talk of a yard-long chain of gold that he had
failed to declare, but everyone was too happy to cast aspersions on the
hero. Indeed, James II was so delighted he created Phips a knight, so that
the farm boy from Maine was now Sir William. All kinds of fine positions
were offered in England, but Phips was anxious to return home to Mary,
and so they made him Provost-Marshal of New England, just one rank
away from the governorship, which he eventually achieved. It was a marvelous triumph for a rowdy ship's carpenter who had been taught to read
and write by his wife, and had been snubbed by half of Boston.

And Mary, who had backed him all the way, was sent a cup of gold
worth £1,000 by the Duke and Duchess of Albemarle—and gained the
"fair brick house" in Green Lane, Boston, that her husband had promised
her, thirteen tempestuous years before.

All this time on Long Island, New York, other men, and women, too,
were reaping riches from the sea. However, this was in much less flamboyant fashion, for they were the pioneers of American whaling.

The Reverend Thomas James of Southampton was one of the earliest
speculators in the whaling trade. In 1658 he negotiated with the Montauk
Indians for half of all drift whales cast up on the beach. The market was
such a good one that in the 1660s several "whale Companeys of East

Hampton and Southampton" were organized, for the good reason that there were not enough whale corpses drifting onto shore to meet the demand. The answer was a "whale designe," which was an arrangement for going out to hunt the whales in the sea. The pioneers did not do it themselves, but employed Indians instead, supplying them with cedar boats, iron harpoons, and lances. Then, when the whales were towed up onto the beach, everyone helped cut off the blubber and boil the oil in pots set up on the strand.

While the system worked, it resulted in some nasty dissension, simply because there were not enough Indians to go around. In 1678, Minister James entered "a Solemne Protest" in the Town Books "against any person or persons who have or shall Contrary to all Law of God or man, Justice or equity goe about to violate or infringe contracts or agreements with ye Indians made by me and my Copartners for the Whale designe." To put it baldly, someone was stealing his Indians. And one of these "persons" could easily have been Martha Tunstall Smith, wife of the man who was known throughout New York as Tangier.

Colonel William "Tangier" Smith got his nickname because he had been the English Governor of Tangier, a town in Morocco. Sometime before 1684, when the city fell into the hands of the Barbary pirates, Tangier sailed to New York, probably because he and Thomas Dongan, a fellow soldier who had been appointed Governor of the colony in 1682, were such close friends. It was a good move, for Dongan's influence helped turn Smith into one of the landowning aristocracy. Starting with a generous land grant and extending this with purchases from the Indians, Tangier established an enormous estate on Long Island called St. George's Manor, which stretched clear across from shore to shore, from Little Neck Bay to the present site of John F. Kennedy International Airport, from where he ran his "whaling designe."

Tangier's wife, Martha, was known about the island as "Col. Smith's lady," and had her own seat at the table in the meetinghouse, a rare privilege for a woman. She appears to have been respected as some kind of "cunning-woman," too, her "receipt" for deafness reading, "Take hare and fleece him & roast him & let the party put some of the fatt in his ear and he shall recover his hearing in a short time." Between them, she and her husband administered a virtual kingdom, for Martha and Tangier— like other manor holders such as John Gardiner of Gardiners Island and Robert Livingston of the Hudson River Valley—held almost unlimited power within their territory. Being so close to Governor Dongan, Tangier would have been an important voice in colonial affairs as well.

With the accession of James II to the throne of England, there was a change in policy, however. Tangier's friend Thomas Dongan was replaced by Sir Edmund Andros, who governed from Boston, leaving New York in charge of the extremely unpopular Lieutenant Governor Francis Nicholson. When James was forced to turn over the throne

Natives hunting whales. Engraving by De Bry, 1602.

to his daughter Mary and her husband, William, Prince of Orange, the people of Boston celebrated by throwing Andros into prison. New York followed suit on May 31, 1689, seizing Fort James and appointing Captain Jacob Leisler to lead a people's rebellion against the local aristocracy of manor holders and merchants.

Somewhat naturally, Lieutenant Governor Nicholson appealed to that local aristocracy for help, but Smith was among those who declined to assist in putting down the rebellion, his hasty excuse being that he was afraid of personal vengeance. Nicholson "retired aboard a vessel" and sailed home to England. Tangier was probably very wise to keep his head down, for controversy reigned, culminating in March 1691, when Henry Sloughter was appointed Governor, and Leisler was duly executed. Whether Tangier was around to congratulate himself on his wisdom is debatable, however, for around this time he died.

Martha, like many a widow, developed into a commercial force, taking over all her late husband's affairs, not excluding his "whaling designe." Just like Minister James and his "Copartners," she recruited Indian crews and sent them out in boats with whaling craft and gear, while her men and her sons waited on the beach to flense the catch. She did very well, averaging twenty whales a season. Her account book for 1707 reads, in part:

Jan. 16, 1707—My company killed a yearling whale, made 27 barrels.

Feb. 4—Indian Harry with his boat, struck a stunt whale [an adolescent male] and could not kill it—called for my boat to help him. I had but a third, which was 4 barrels.

Feb. 22—My two boats, and my son's, and Floyd's boats, killed a yearling whale, of which I had half—made 36. My share is 18 barrels.

Feb. 24—My Company killed a school whale, which made 35 barrels.

March 1—My company killed a small yearling, made 30 barrels.
March 17—My company killed two yearlings in one day; one made 27,
the other 14 barrels

In all, her take for the 1707 season was worth £315, less duties, her tax
receipt reading, "New York, this 5th June, 1707, received of Nathan Simon, ye sume of fifteen pounds, fifteen shillings, for acc't of Madam
Martha Smith, it being ye 20th part of eyle, by virtue of a warrant from
my Lord Cornbury, dated 25th of March last past, 1707. Per me, Elias
Boudinot."

This twenty percent tax was a bone of contention with the Long Island
whalers, who did their utmost to avoid it by shipping their oil to Boston or
New London, rather than through New York, as was legally required.

New York, about 1700. Engraving by de Ram.

The merchants of New York
had their own good reasons,
too, for evading the law.
While trade with the West Indies had flourished, with large
quantities of whale oil, tallow,
and beef—much of it from St.
George's Manor—sent there
in exchange for wine, rum,
sugar, cocoa, and Spanish gold
coins, the English Parliament
prohibited any direct trade
with Europe or India. Every-
thing had to come through England, which meant that levies were ex-
acted on imports and exports alike.

Little wonder, then, that smuggling had flourished since the early days
of settlement. The merchants of New York, however, had a highly original method for beating the system, which reached its peak when Benjamin Fletcher became Governor of the colony in 1692. They simply
evaded the tax by dealing with pirates. Ships were loaded with small
arms, gunpowder, food, and liquor, crewed with adventurous young
New Yorkers, and sent off to a pirate hideout to do some bartering.

This was usually St. Mary's Island on the northeast coast of Madagascar, in the Indian Ocean. Here, pirates had a kingdom of their own, often
called Libertalia, where they lived in lush luxury with multiple wives,
armed bodyguards, slaves, and harems, no doubt having got a lot of their
ideas from the Barbary Coast. They did not lose their sense of family re-

sponsibility entirely, however. It was so common for pirates to write wills to make sure that their loot went to their families that women regularly sent legal documents to Madagascar laying claim to the estate when they heard that the husband or father was dead. In the 1690s the *compradore* here was Adam Baldridge, a former buccaneer with New York connections. His was a very lucrative business, the exchange of arms and foodstuffs the New York ships had carried, for looted gold, silver, silks, spices, dyes, and slaves.

This merchant-pirate trade was so blatant that pirate captains traveled freely to New York, and were entertained by the highest echelons of society while their black-hulled craft were being refitted. Intriguingly, as late as 1811 it was reported in the *Philadelphia Press* that one of these flamboyant and glamorous characters was a woman, the commander of "a French privateer" who had been seen visiting a New York bank to deposit "a large quantity of doubloons and other specie for safety." Though "of masculine appearance, tall, robust," she was definitely a "lady," and "superbly dressed," to boot.

Back in the 1690s, lower Manhattan was like a reincarnation of Studland Bay, and Governor Fletcher was like another Vice-Admiral of Dorset. He did not just protect pirates from the law, but fitted out their ships in New York and Rhode Island as well, receiving nice gifts in return—once even a whole vessel, probably a prize, which he sold for eighty-eight pounds—along with "rich presents for his wife and daughter." During his time, doing business with pirates was the most profitable commerce of New York, all without a cent going to the tax gatherers, so it is little wonder that the English Parliament decided that it was high time for it to be brought to a stop.

Richard Coote, Earl of Bellomont, was the man who was chosen for the job. He arrived in New York in 1695 and found the situation even worse than expected. Long Island, he reported, was "a receptacle for pirates and the people generally a lawless and unruly set," and in New York, "the pirates are so cherished by the people that not a man of them is taken up." Accordingly, he listened with interest to a proposition for a privateering voyage to hunt down "Pirates, Freebooters, and Sea Rovers," as the commission later phrased it. Backers were found in England, including King William, four English peers, and a director of the East India Company. Two New Yorkers contributed six thousand pounds, one of them the manor holder Robert Livingston. And the other was a woman, Sarah Bradley Cox Oort Kidd, though it was invested under the name of her third husband. With the money they formed a company and fitted out the ship *Adventure Galley*—and put her under the command of Sarah's current husband, the "trusty and well-beloved" Captain William Kidd.

Kidd's past was murky. The son of a Scottish Presbyterian minister, he was first recorded in 1689 as a buccaneer in the Caribbean. In 1688, he had been one of the pirates recruited by William of Orange to help fight the war against France. Having diplomatically renamed his ship *Blessed William,* Kidd sailed along with the Royal Navy, acquitting himself well in a battle off the island of St. Martin. Unfortunately, his crew seized the *Blessed William* while William Kidd was on shore and sailed off without him, to become proper pirates again. However, the authorities in the Caribbean exhibited a very decent understanding, presenting Kidd with a captured vessel, which he renamed *Antigua* and sailed to New York.

There he met Sarah Bradley Cox Oort. John Oort, a shipping magnate, was her second husband. She was very comfortably off, having married well both times. No doubt she was impressed when she met William Kidd, a large and "very lusty" man with a dashing reputation. John Oort died, and just days later, on May 16, 1691, Sarah and William were married. She brought him a sizable dowry, including two substantial houses, one on Wall Street and the other on Pearl Street, both conveniently close to the wharves. They shifted into the Pearl Street one, and Kidd should have settled down to a life of respectability, domesticity, and ease.

Instead, he became involved in the privateering-after-pirates idea. To Sarah, it must have seemed a very good investment, simply because of the good prospect of much loot—or, as the commission phrased it, the "Goods, Merchandizes, Treasure and other Things which shall be taken from the said Pirates." One fourth of this was to go to the crew, and of the rest Livingston and Kidd would share one fifth. Additionally, if prize goods to the value of one hundred thousand pounds or more were delivered to Bellomont in Boston, Kidd could keep the *Adventure Galley.*

Sarah must have waved goodbye quite optimistically on the morning of September 6, 1696, when William sailed away from New York with a crew of 152 "desperate" men. Ominously, however, after a year of little or no news, strange tales drifted back to New York—that Captain Kidd, who had gone to sea to fight the corsairs, was flying the pirate flag himself.

He had been attacking friendly Moorish ships, and innocent trading vessels, too, and the East India Company had declared him a pirate. No doubt Sarah was extremely embarrassed, for Lord Bellomont and the other backers most certainly were. They rapidly dissolved the company, washing their hands of any connection with Kidd, while King William made up for his disastrous decision to back the enterprise by offering an amnesty for all pirates who would give themselves up—except for Henry "Long Ben" Avery and Captain William Kidd.

Meanwhile, Kidd had abandoned the outworn *Adventure Galley* and shifted his headquarters to a ship that had been a rich prize, the *Quedagh Merchant.* Selling off the contents of her hold as he went, he steered for the Caribbean. The first Sarah saw of him was when he materialized in Long Island Sound on board a sloop named *San Antonio.*

Early in June 1699, John Gardiner, Lord of the Manor of Gardiners Island, "noticed a mysterious six-gun sloop riding at anchor off the island." There was little movement to be seen, and no attempt at communication with the shore, so after a couple of days Gardiner rowed out to pay a visit. According to his account, Kidd received him very courteously. He asked him to look after three slaves while he paid a call on Lord Bellomont in Boston. A tribute of six sheep and a barrel of cider was demanded, and given cheerfully enough, it seems, for Kidd gave Gardiner two pieces of Bengal muslin for his wife and four pieces of gold to his men for loading the tribute onto the sloop. And then they parted, the sloop firing a salute of four guns and steering for Block Island. And this is where the legends start, for no one knows how much of the *Quedagh Merchant* treasure Kidd was carrying.

As the sloop dawdled off Gardiner's Island, Kidd received visitors, including his wife, Sarah, his daughters, Sarah and Elizabeth, and his New York lawyer, Joseph Emmot. After some lengthy consultation Emmot was sent to Boston with a present of a fancy box containing jewels for Lady Bellomont, to bargain with the Governor. According to Bellomont's deposition, Emmot told him that Kidd had sixty pounds' weight of gold, a hundredweight of silver, and a few bales of East India goods on the sloop, and had left a great ship loaded with treasure on the coast of Hispaniola, presumably the *Quedagh Merchant.* In return for a pardon, Kidd would bring the sloop to Boston and then fetch the ship. He also sent Bellomont two French passes that had been taken from on board two Moorish ships he had captured—vital evidence that he was a privateer, not a pirate, for he had the King's permission to seize French prizes.

While Emmot was doing his utmost to convince the Governor of Kidd's innocence, Kidd and Sarah were conferring. He gave her a part of the fortune—probably all of the bills of exchange he was carrying, and certainly a six-pound bag of pieces of eight—and John Gardiner was asked to look after a part of the trove. According to Gardiner, Kidd came back to his island three days after departure and asked him "to take and keep for him a chest and a box of gold, a bundle of quilts, and four bales of goods, saying that the box of gold was intended for Lord Bellomont." Also, according to a list that Gardiner made later, there was a bag of gold dust and pieces of eight, another bag of rubies great and small, silk, silver and gold coins, a piece of crystal, a bag of unpolished stones and broken silver, coral necklaces, lamps, and silver buttons, all undoubtedly seized from passengers on the ships that had been despoiled.

Gardiner agreed to look after the loot, and the chests were buried in the swamp at Cherry Harbor, near the manor house. Momentarily, Kidd's mood became ferocious, and he threatened Gardiner that "he would take his head, or his son's" if the treasure was missing. Then, just as abruptly, he was convivial again, requesting Mrs. Gardiner to roast a pig for him, "and was so pleased with the result that he gave her a piece of cloth of gold." Then Kidd, tricked by a long, reassuring letter from Bellomont, took on a pilot and sailed to Boston, where he, Sarah, and their two little girls found lodgings at the house of the postmaster, Duncan Campbell, a fellow Scot. Kidd spent the next few days writing an account of his voyage and frequenting the Blue Anchor Tavern while he waited for a private interview with Bellomont. Then, abruptly, he and Sarah were arrested.

Both Kidd and Sarah were clapped into jail, and all the property she had brought to Boston was seized, including her clothing and personal plate. The room where they lodged was searched, and a bag of gold worth about a thousand pounds was confiscated, along with a bag of silver. Lacking any real reason for holding her, Bellomont had to let Sarah go, but William was less fortunate. In February 1700 a man-of-war arrived in Boston to carry him to London for imprisonment at Newgate.

He was not brought to trial for over a year—a year in which the two lifesaving French passes mysteriously disappeared. Then, he was

A French pass of the kind that would have saved Kidd's life. Public Record Office, Kew.

given just a fortnight to find them. "I beg your lordship's patience till I can procure my papers," Kidd repeatedly pleaded. "I had a couple of French passes, which I must make use of in order to my justification." His petition, however, fell on obstinately deaf ears. Whether guilty or not, he was doomed, for Bellomont needed a scapegoat.

He was not even tried for piracy at first, but for the murder of his gunner, William Moore, it being charged that he did "violently, feloniously, voluntarily, and of malice aforethought, beat and strike" Moore over the head with a bucket, the blow causing a "mortal bruise." Kidd argued that the gunner was inciting mutiny at the time, but the jury found him guilty nonetheless. His fate being sealed, a per-

"Captain Kidd hanging in chains."
From Ellms, *Pirates Own Book.* Boston, 1837.

functory trial for piracy followed. On May 23, 1701, William Kidd was hanged at Execution Dock in Wapping.

He was, in fact, hanged twice, for the first time the rope broke, and the hangman had to go through the procedure again. Then his body was bound in chains to keep its human shape as it rotted, and gibbeted near Tilbury on the lower reaches of the Thames River, to be a "terror to all that saw it." Instead, this man who was little more than a violent and unlucky blunderer became the stuff of myth and legend, for the name of Captain William Kidd is still the one that springs to mind whenever pirates are mentioned.

Back in New York, Sarah was an object of great attention, too, for a while. People constantly intruded on her privacy in the hope of picking up vital clues to where the fabled loot might be hidden. However, she was meantime quietly regaining her property, even managing to pick up part of her husband's plunder, probably including the bills of exchange. Then at last, unlike her husband, Sarah was forgotten. In 1703 she married Christopher Rousby and resumed a quiet domestic life. Sarah Bradley Cox Oort Kidd Rousby finally passed away in 1744, a woman in her seventies who had successfully outlived four husbands and a scandal.

Chapter Seven

BONNY & READ

*I had my fill of fine gentlemen in the sugar planta-
tions. . . . They can't ask a girl for what they want
without simpering and playacting. And then along
came Calico Jack like a great roaring stallion.*
—Anne Bonny,
in the 1934 play *Mary Read,*
by James Bridie

On a balmy tropic evening in November 1720, a privateer commanded by Captain Jonathan Barnet raised a black-hulled sloop lying
dark and silent at Negril Point. This was buccaneer territory, off the extreme western end of the island of Jamaica, and Barnet—like Kidd
twenty-five years previously—had a commission to hunt down pirates.
The privateer coasted along slowly, studying this enigmatic stranger. Silence, save for the ripple of silky water along the run of the hull—and
then, the sudden sound of a gun. Barnet ordered a change of course to investigate. At the sight of his craft, the black ship hurriedly began to put on
sail, looking more furtive than ever, so Barnet gave the order to make
chase.

It is easy to recapture the stream of commands, from a stirring near-
contemporary description. "Out with all your sails, a steady man at the
helm, sit close to keep her steady . . . Ho, we gather on him." At ten, the
stranger is in hailing distance. "Is all ready? Yea, yea. Every man to his
charge. Dowse your sail, salute him for the sea. Hail him! Whence your
ship?"

And the bold reply echoed back, "John Rackham, from Cuba!"

This enlivened Captain Barnet more than somewhat, "Calico Jack" Rackham being very high up on the pirates-wanted list. Not only had Rackham broken the terms of the amnesty he had accepted the previous year, but the twelve-ton sloop *William* he was sailing had been stolen from the harbor of Nassau in an act of barefaced insolence less than three months before. Barnet bawled out a demand to surrender, but the only reply was the firing of a swivel gun, along with a few shouts of defiance, some of them remarkably shrill.

Despite the darkness Captain Barnet immediately launched an attack. It lasted no more than a few moments, for the first broadside carried away the pirates' boom, effectively disabling the *William*. Then, when Barnet and his men boarded Rackham's sloop, the hand-to-hand combat was even briefer. While it would not have surprised Captain Barnet to find two women in the pirate crew—Governor Woodes Rogers's pirates-wanted list including "Ann[e] Fulford alias Bonny, & Mary Read"—it must have amazed him that the girls were the only ones who offered resistance. Anne and Mary were armed to the teeth with cutlasses and pistols, and their language, to say the very least, was unladylike, but they failed to rouse their shipmates, who were cowering cravenly down in the hold. According to legend, Mary was so furious at this that she fired her pistol down among her erstwhile comrades, wounding a few and killing one, but the fact of the matter is that the outcome of the battle was never in doubt.

Bonny and Read. Artist: Ron Druett.

While Bonny and Read certainly existed, their stories are even more murky than William Kidd's, simply because of all the speculation and embroidering ever since. Some of the earliest retelling of their yarns was included in a book that first came out in London in 1724, *A General History of the Robberies and Murders of the Most Notorious Pyrates* by Captain Charles Johnson, believed by many to be Daniel Defoe, the writer who took the real adventures of the self-marooned pirate Alexander Selkirk and turned them into the classic story of Robinson Crusoe. If it was Defoe who produced this early record of the two pirate girls, the details should be reliable, for he was famous for his painstaking research, but as it is, the stories are a little hard to credit.

As the writer himself admits, "some may be tempted to think the whole Story no better than a Novel or Romance."

Anne Bonny's, in particular, reads like one of the more racy of Chaucer's *Canterbury Tales*. Anne was born in Ireland, in a town near Cork. While a certain lawyer was her real father, his wife was not her mother. The lawyer's wife, in fact, was not even at home at the time Anne was conceived, being at her mother-in-law's house. In the lawyer's house, instead, was "a handsome young Woman," a serving maid named Mary. Maid Mary had another swain, a young tanner who was fatally light-fingered, "whipping three Silver Spoons into his Pocket" one day when Mary's back was turned. When the maid noticed that the spoons were missing, she knew exactly whom to blame. The tanner denied it, but she threatened to go to a Justice of the Peace, so he surreptitiously returned the spoons, hiding them in the maid's own bed, imagining that she would discover them that night. But, strange to say, she did not.

Next, the Mistress came to hear of it. She returned home, and Mary reported the theft. The young tanner, keen to clear his name, went to the lawyer's wife privately to inform her that he had returned the spoons, telling her exactly where he had put them. Naturally, the "Mistress could scarce believe it." But, when she went to the maid's room and turned down the covers, there indeed lay the missing silverware. The deduction was obvious, but she decided to make certain. So, in a series of compli-cated maneuvers worthy of a modern French farce, she arranged it so that she slept in the maid's bed that night and the maid slept somewhere else.

After she had been in the maid's bed some time, "she heard some Body enter the Room." As the stealthy footsteps approached the bed she silently agitated about thieves, but "when she heard these Words, Mary, *are you awake?* She knew it to be her Husband's Voice." The Mistress said noth-ing, pretending to be asleep, and lo, her "Husband came to Bed, and that Night play'd the vigorous Lover." The knowledge that he thought she was someone else was more than a little mortifying, but she lay still "and bore it like a Christian."

As soon as the lawyer was sleeping deeply from his exertions, she stole out and told her mother-in-law about it. Then, to wreak revenge on the maid, she "sent for a Constable, and charged her with stealing the spoons." Mary was arrested and thrown into prison, and the lawyer flew into a rage. At that, his wife promptly left him, to take up residence with her mother-in-law again. In due course, both the maid and the Mistress were found to be pregnant (this last greatly surprising the lawyer, who was not aware that he had slept with his wife), Mary was released and delivered of a daughter whom she named Anne, and the wife was delivered of twins.

This string of events meant that the lawyer was very short of money, for he was dependent on his wife for an income. His wife, however, relented and made him an allowance—until she found out that he had taken in his illegitimate daughter and was bringing the child up to be a lawyer's clerk, dressing her as a boy. So, she stopped the allowance. Driven onto his beam-ends, the lawyer sold up his business and embarked for Carolina with Maid Mary and little Anne.

Captain Calico Jack Rackham.
From *A General History of the Pyrates.*
London, 1724.

All went happily there for a while, but first Mary died, and then Anne exhibited an extremely bad temper. There was gossip that she had killed a servant-maid with a "Case-Knife" (which Johnson declares to be untrue), and she half-killed a young man who tried to seduce her. Then, she infuriated her father by marrying a penniless seaman, James Bonny. Forthwith, he threw her out of the house.

Bonny, who had married Anne for her father's money, was naturally very disappointed. Making the best of a bad job, he took her to the Isle of New Providence, hoping to find employment there by informing on pirates, as an alternative to turning to piracy himself. It was contrary-natured Anne who became the buccaneer, after being seduced by the dashing Jack Rackham.

Donning men's clothes, she went to sea, but "beginning to grow big, *Rackam* landed her on the Island of *Cuba*," and there she had his child. According to some accounts, the infant died, but Johnson does not mention the child's fate. Whatever, as soon as she was up and about again,

Anne rejoined Calico Jack on his ship. The amnesty interrupted their pirating career for a while, but as we have seen, they both fell back into their old piratical ways. And it is at this part of the drama that Mary Read arrives on the stage.

Mary Read's mother was a solo parent, a young woman who had borne a baby boy some months after her husband, a seaman, had gone off on a voyage. Though she was living with his family, she "met with an Accident" and found herself pregnant again, so she beat a strategic retreat into the countryside, taking the infant boy with her. The boy died, Mary was born, and about three or four years later the young mother ran out of money, though not out of ideas. The obvious ploy was to dress Mary in boy's clothes and pass her off to her mother-in-law as the deceased son, and that is exactly what Mary's mother did. There was a bit of a hitch when the old lady took a fancy to the "son" and wanted to keep him, "but the Mother pretended it would break her Heart to part with it; so it was agreed betwixt them, that the Child should live with the Mother, and the supposed Grandmother should allow a Crown a Week for its Maintenance."

Thus, Mary Read was raised as a boy and that so thoroughly that she became set in masculine ways. In her teens, she shipped on a man-of-war. Being of a restless temperament, she soon got tired of the sea, so joined the army in Flanders "and carry'd Arms in a Regiment of Foot, as a *Cadet.*" As she was unable to purchase a commission, she tired of this, too, and joined the cavalry, at which point nature intruded, for she fell obsessively in love with a fellow soldier, a Fleming. It altered her whole character, for she followed him about like a lovesick pup. For a while the whole regiment thought she was mad, but then when she and the object of her passion were sharing a tent "she found a Way of letting him discover her Sex, without appearing that it was done with Design."

Naturally, he was surprised. Even more understandably, he was delighted, as it was highly unusual for a humble soldier to have a mistress all to himself. However, when he embarked on "gratifying his Passions," he found her disappointingly uncooperative, for Mary had something very different in mind. To cut the story short, as soon as the campaign was over they were publicly married, much to everyone's amazement.

Some of the officers were so amused and intrigued that they clubbed to set the couple up. Mary and her swain took their discharge and went into the "Eating-House" business, their establishment being "the Sign of the

Three Horse-Shoes, near the Castle of *Breda,* where they soon run into a good Trade, a great many Officers eating with them constantly." Obviously, notoriety was good for business. Unhappily, however, Mary's husband died just as "the Peace of Ryswick[,] being concluded" put an end to both battle and trade. This seems a mistake, for the Peace of Ryswick was concluded on September 20, 1697, which means that Mary was a woman in her mid-forties when she was captured. It is more likely that the Peace of Utrecht, co-signed with France on April 11, 1713, was what the narrator really had in mind, for it puts Mary into a much more plausible age group.

Preferring not to starve, Mary shifted back into men's attire and shipped on a voyage to the West Indies. It was an action that determined the course of the rest of her days, for the ship was seized by pirates, and the pirate captain invited her to join his crew. This was common enough, for pirate ships needed large numbers of men and in fact gained most of their recruits in this way. According to Johnson, Mary vowed upon cross-examination that she had been coerced, "that the Life of a Pyrate was what she always abhor'd, and went into it only upon Compulsion," but if

Rackham's hoist. Artist: Ron Druett.

she did say this, she was telling a lie to save her life. All the evidence points the other way. For instance, she accepted the same amnesty that Anne Bonny and Calico Jack Rackham did, but within months she returned to her old piratical ways, entirely of her own volition. Two Frenchmen who had been captive on Rackham's craft deposed that she, like Anne Bonny, was there of her "own Free-Will and Consent."

It is Mary's motive for joining the pirate crew in the first place that inspires curiosity. When the pirates offered her a berth on their ship, they did it under the misapprehension that she was a British seaman. Mary, on the other hand, knew perfectly well that the danger of being uncovered as a woman was constant. This was in contrast to Anne Bonny who, apart from that brief time in her childhood when her father dressed her as a boy to mislead his wife, never pretended she was not female. To put it baldly, Anne Bonny was a camp follower, while Mary Read, a much more complicated person, was a transvestite seaman-soldier.

Pirates were a great deal more familiar with camp followers than they

One result of this was that every now and then the artists of the expedition painted the same scene twice, one work being true to life, and the other *sans* Madame. This subterfuge was necessary for the official record, *Voyage autour du Monde . . . exécuté sur les corvettes de S. M. L'Uranie et La Physicienne,* which was prepared by de Freycinet and published between 1827 and 1839. Madame herself was embarrassed that her presence was so informal. She was not comfortable in men's clothing. The only time she was glad of it was when the corvette was pursued by an Algerian corsair. The prospect of being enslaved was bad enough, but "the thought of a seraglio evoked even more unpleasant images in my mind, and I hoped to escape that fate thanks to my male disguise." Luckily, the corsair veered off after counting the corvette's cannon, and the possibility of the disguise being penetrated was averted. Then, after a disastrous meeting with the Governor of Gibraltar, it was decided that she should abandon male dress altogether, to her vast relief.

Catherine Fryer and Mary Haydon.

It is easy to make guesses about the reason Mary Broad was in Plymouth instead of back in her home in the coastal village of Fowey, Cornwall. Nineteen years old, dark-haired and gray-eyed, Mary was a seaman's daughter. Her father, William Broad, was away at sea at the time, and Mary could well have been

Dockside scene. From an engraving by
Thomas Rowlandson, 1811.

sent to Plymouth to meet his ship or to see him off because the family was in such desperate need of the money he was earning. Or she may have been one of the many girls who moved to the port to live off the sailors. As the "Gosport girls" sang in 1780:

> *Don't you see the ships a-coming?*
> *Don't you see them in full sail?*
> *Don't you see the ships a-coming*
> *With the prizes at their tail?*
> *Oh! My little rolling sailor*
> *Oh! My little rolling he;*
> *I do love a jolly sailor,*
> *Blithe and merry might he be.*
>
> *Sailors, they get all the money,*
> *Soldiers, they get none but brass;*
> *I do love a jolly sailor,*
> *Soldiers they may kiss my arse*
> *Oh! My little rolling sailor,*
> *Oh! My little rolling he;*
> *I do love a jolly sailor,*
> *Soldiers may be damned for me.*

For a teenaged girl living in hard times, consorting with seamen could have seemed enticing. There was a certain gaiety and glamour about it. The mariners on liberty—or leave—gathered up these girls in their bois-terous wake as they swaggered from one tavern to another, spending

Seamen carousing in port. Caricature by George Cruikshank.

freely until their money ran out. Henry Mayhew, in his portrait of the port of London in the 1840s, described streets that were "alive with sailors, and bonnetless and capless women. The Jews' shops and public-houses were all open"—despite the Sabbath—"and parties of 'jolly tars' reeled past us, singing and bawling on their way." The boys would have been dressed up in their best shore rig, colored tape along the seams of their white duck trouser legs, silver buckles on their shoes, embroidered ribbons in their hats. Little wonder that their sprees were the subject for many a chantey, no matter how sordid the transactions—and sordid they definitely were. As Mayhew also pointed out, the women's "bare heads told their mode of life."

Mary Broad and her two friends may even have been on board the vessels in port. During the seventeenth and eighteenth centuries it was common for women to be ferried out to the Navy ships because on many men-of-war the seamen were not allowed liberty on shore. Because they could not go out to find female company themselves, the women had to be carried out to them. This transport of women from shore to ship was a grubby business, described by a man who served in the Navy from 1805 to 1811, and whose memoirs were published under a pseudonym, Jack Nastyface, his real name probably being William Robinson.

"On the arrival of any man-of-war in port," he wrote, "these girls flock down to the shore, where boats are always ready; and here may be witnessed a scene, somewhat similar to the trafficking of slaves in the West

Indies." According to him, the boatman would inspect them all, choosing only "the best looking and the most dashingly dressed; and in making up his complement for a load, it often happens that he refuses to take some of them observing (very politely) and usually with some vulgar oath, to one that she is *too old;* to another that she is too ugly; and that he shall not be able *to sell them;* and he'll be damned if he has any notion of having his trouble for nothing."

Apparently, the boatman carried the women as a venture, for if they were "sold," he got three shillings for each one. The officer in command of the gangway had his own selection process, however, and was apt to send some away, saying "that he should not bring such a cargo of damned ugly ducks on board, and that he would not allow any of the men to have them." Thus, the rejected cargo would have to be returned on shore with no pay to the boatman, much to his disgust. "A boat usually carries about ten

Women being carried out to the fleet.
Caricature by W. Elmes.

of these poor creatures at a time, and will often bring off three cargoes of these ladies in a day; so that if he is fortunate in his *sales,* as he calls them, he will make nearly five pounds by his three trips. Thus these poor unfortunates are taken to market like cattle," Jack concluded, "and whilst this system is observed, it cannot with truth be said that the slave-trade is abolished in England."

As it happens, a good number of the women were decent wives and daughters who simply wished to be reunited with their menfolk, which makes the selection process all the more mortifying. The procedure, in fact, had respectable beginnings. The ships spent much of their lives lying outside ports—often a surprising number of miles outside—being re-provisioned and refitted for sea, so it seemed only humane for the married men to be allowed to have their wives and families on board during those lengthy intervals. This meant that the ship resembled a village more than it did a vessel of war, with bustling streets instead of decks. Women sat in groups and gossiped, and children ran around everywhere, while opportunistic traders displayed their wares. "There were also shops and stalls of every kind of goods," wrote an observer in the late eighteenth century, "and people crying their different commodities about the ship." It was an age of folk musicians, and in the evenings the planks vibrated with hearty jigs and reels.

But it must be remembered that the winter of 1786 was a quiet time for the British Navy. Whatever the reason, Mary Broad did not have enough money to go home to Fowey—or perhaps she was too ashamed. Instead, she and her two friends were reduced to the level of "forest-dwellers," living in the rough and preying on those who were unwise enough to travel by.

And so Agnes Lakeman was robbed of her silk bonnet and the value of eleven guineas while journeying on the road that led into Plymouth, but she screamed so loud that her three assailants were caught. And thus Mary Broad was hauled up before the judges at the Exeter Lenten Assizes, which opened on March 20, 1786. Her trial was an academic exercise. She and her comrades had been caught red-handed, and Agnes Lakeman had been injured during the attack. This was an era when punishments were even more out of proportion to the nature of the crime than they had been in Elizabethan days. The sentence of death was inevitable.

Four days later, however, it was commuted to transportation, this being a popular remedy for what was perceived as a crime wave. Few people seemed to think that removing the causes of crime—poverty, lack of education, the great gap between the rich (many of them newly and ostentatiously rich) and the very poor—would help. Instead, it was popularly believed that the best way to eliminate felony was to remove the felons, originally by sending them to the other side of the Atlantic. In 1786, however, there was nowhere suitable to send them, the colonists of America having most inconsiderately won their independence.

And so, while the authorities were making up their minds about her future destination, Mary and her comrades were herded with thousands of other condemned men and women into stinking hulks that were beached along the Thames River. The name of her particular prison was *Dunkirk,* and she and her companions endured appalling conditions within its rotting, overcrowded confines for many months while the matter was debated at leisure.

For a while it seemed that no one would come to a decision, but then the hulks deteriorated so horrifyingly into verminous pits of infection that the matter became urgent. That August the resolution was made to send a test party of 750 convicts to Botany Bay, New South Wales, to see if the foundations of a penal settlement could be established there. On October

12, Captain Arthur Phillip of the Royal Navy was chosen to be Governor of the operation, and on May 13, 1787, the First Convict Fleet set sail.

The eleven ships carried 191 female convicts and 568 male prisoners, including a Cornish fisherman and smuggler by the name of William Bryant. Thirteen convicts' children went along, too, condemned to the penal settlement because of their parentage. To guard the complement were 211 marines and officers, along with their wives and children, these totaling forty-six. Governor Phillip and his staff of nine completed the list.

Governor Phillip, who established the penal colony at Port Jackson.
Artist: Ron Druett.

Both Mary Broad and William Bryant were assigned to the transport *Charlotte,* Captain Thomas Gilbert, embarking at Plymouth on 7 January. "Barque-built" in a Thames shipyard in 1784, the ship was relatively new when chartered by the Navy. However, she was certainly not luxurious. Rated at just a little over 335 tons, the *Charlotte* was 105 feet long, yet 108 convicts were packed into her holds, twenty of them female. As on all eleven ships, the two sexes were separated by stout bulkheads below and a spike-topped fence on deck. While the authorities managed to keep the male and female convicts apart, though, they did not experience nearly the same success in keeping the female convicts away from the seamen and soldiers.

It must be acknowledged that some of the females were very tough customers. Two of the women on the *Friendship,* Elizabeth Barber and Elizabeth Dudgeon, had been transported once already, in 1782. They were sent off to Nova Scotia on the *Mercury,* and had taken a leading part in a mutiny before the ship had even left English waters. Bad weather had forced the captain to head for Tor Bay, on the south coast of Devon, and during the night the convicts released each other and overpowered the crew. Then they escaped to shore in the ship's boats, but many—including the two Elizabeths—had been recaptured. They were lucky not to have been hanged. As it was, they caused such trouble throughout the voyage that both were put in irons for brawling and insolence, and Elizabeth Dudgeon was flogged.

The major source of the problem, it seems, was drunkenness—quite a comment on the state of matters on board the ships, for it was common for a marine or a crew member to be able to buy a woman's services with a tot of rum from his daily ration. According to Surgeon John White of the *Charlotte,* the women were by no means unwilling participants in this shoddy business. On the *Prince of Wales* a woman received six lashes. Other women were punished with thumbscrews, while others had their heads shaved, but the bad behavior continued. Neither shame "nor the fear of punishment could deter them from making their way through the bulkheads to the apartments assigned to the seamen."

Mary Broad was unlikely to have been one of them. She was already pregnant when she embarked, giving birth to a girl on September 8, 1787. The identity of the father of the child—who was named "Charlotte," after the ship—is unknown. She also seems to have been one of the well-behaved ones, for when she and William Bryant applied to be married after arrival at their destination, Governor Phillip was pleased to agree. Otherwise, however, the treatment and behavior of the female convicts of the First Fleet set the pattern for a very dark page of maritime history.

The *Lady Juliana,* which was the earliest transport to sail after the First Fleet had departed, carried all female convicts. Within days of departure, the ship was nothing more than a floating brothel. "When we were fairly out to sea, every man on board took a wife from among the convicts," wrote the steward, John Nicol. Whenever the ship touched land for provisions, seamen from the other ships in port swarmed on board to take part in the free-for-all. This did have the advantage that the death toll on all-female transports was much lower than on other ships because of the abundant fresh air and leisurely spells in port—and was preferable to the deliberate starving of convicts that was common on the all-male or mixed-sex transports—but was evidence of the disgracefully lax conduct of the officers.

Some of the fellows who should have been setting a good example for their crews were slyly opportunistic as well. While this scurrilous trade was being conducted, Captain Aitken of the *Lady Juliana* was blithely taking advantage of the penned-up labor on board. Having brought a good supply of linen, he set the women to sewing shirts, which he sold at great advantage when they finally arrived at the penal settlement. Severe punishment was the rule, not the exception. On the "hell-ship" *Britannia,* which sailed from Cork on December 10, 1796, the master, Thomas Dennott, was a sadist who took pleasure in personally whipping the women. One girl, Jenny Blake, was shaved and then brutally beaten over the face, back, and shoulders for the sin of trying to commit suicide. Other women were locked into neck yokes and put on public display for no apparent reason at all.

Yet, with decent treatment, the hardest of convicts could have demonstrated a good-hearted willingness. Much later, in 1815, the *Francis and Eliza,* commanded by Captain William Harrison, with a full complement of Irish convicts under the hatches, was seized by an American privateer in Long Island Sound even though the Treaty of Paris, which signaled the end of Anglo-American hostilities, had been signed. Worse still, during the confusion Harrison's crew broke into the spirit room and started a riot, and so many members of his crew deserted to the American craft that it was impossible to work the ship. In the middle of the incident, the convicts all broke free. Instead of taking over the vessel, however, the men and women divided themselves into watches, and sailed and navigated the ship under Harrison's command.

Hellish as the voyage of the First Fleet might have been, no one on board the eleven ships could have had any concept of the nightmare that awaited. The fleet dropped anchor in Botany Bay on January 18, 1788, to find a hot, sere, utterly inhospitable landscape. Governor Phillip was forced to send out parties in search of a more promising place. On January 26 the fleet weighed anchor and made sail for Port Jackson, the site of the future city of Sydney. Eleven days later, on February 6, the female convicts disembarked from the ships and headed for the small hamlet of tents that had been prepared for them by the men.

It was a moment of celebration, for which most, pathetically, had tried to dress up, arraying themselves in the fragments of finery a few had managed to preserve. Ominously, however, thunderheads were gathering overhead, so darkness descended prematurely. As they were trudging up the beach, the first loud clap of thunder sounded, just like some strange signal. The women turned uncertainly and the male convicts rushed in on them, closely followed by drunken seamen. Throughout a night of unmitigated horror most of the 188 girls and women were clawed down into the mud and repeatedly raped by a mass of more than five hundred men.

Whether Mary Broad was one of the victims is not determined. As we have seen, she had agreed to marry the Cornish fisherman and smuggler William Bryant. Toward the end of the voyage Governor Phillip, urged by his chaplain, the Reverend Richard Johnson, had offered to take down the names of willing couples, and Mary Broad and William Bryant had been two of those to step forward. It was certainly not a love match—for they scarcely knew each other—but a marriage of convenience. For William, it meant he had sole sexual and domestic rights to a woman, and for Mary, it meant that she and her infant had a protector. Whether he was able to protect her on that dreadful night of February 6, however, is unknown.

More privations lay directly ahead, for never had a set of pioneers been so badly equipped. Officialdom back in London had imagined rich, virgin Australian soil, which would produce a bounteous harvest within a year of arrival, but that proved an impossible goal. The company had no draft animals, no plows, and very few useful skills. Most of the convicts were the products of city slums and had no idea how to work the land, yet they were expected to found an outpost of Britain on the far side of the world with little more than their hands.

Near-starvation was inevitable. William Bryant was the only fisherman, and at times the result of his labors was all that kept the colony alive. Appreciating this, Governor Phillip put him in charge of the cutter, which was the only good-sized sailing craft in the settlement. And, as a mark of his importance, William and Mary had their own hut, where they could live apart from the rest with her two children—Bryant's son, Emanuel, being added to the family in April 1790. Greed or hunger got the better of Bryant, however. He was caught selling some of the fish on the side, and was punished with a bloody flogging—one hundred lashes of the cat-o'-nine-tails on his bare back, the scars of which he would carry for the rest of his life. He and Mary made up their minds to escape.

Other convicts had tried to run off overland, but none had succeeded. The desert, starvation, and conflict with the wandering aborigines had spelled an end for every single one. So Mary plotted escape by sea. It was no small proposition, involving an open boat voyage from Sydney to Timor, covering more than three thousand miles through the treacherous shoals and reefs of the Coral Sea and Torres Strait. However, it is very unlikely that the thought of staying behind with her children even crossed her mind, for the same reasons that had impelled her to marry William Bryant. It was a matter of self-preservation.

Finding a boat was easy, for the Governor's cutter could be stolen. The notion that by filching the boat they were taking away the settlement's major source of protein food does not seem to have crossed her mind. Instead, Mary concentrated on the problem of charts and navigational instruments. Obviously, it would be suicidal to set off without them. Then, in October 1790, she had a piece of luck.

A Dutch East Indies trader, the snow *Waaksamheyd,* dropped anchor in the harbor, having come from Batavia (now Jakarta, Java) with stores to sell to the desperate colony. Her master, Captain Detmer Smit, was a shrewd businessman who drove a hard bargain. While he and officialdom were dickering, Mary Bryant approached him, offering to do his laundry, carry messages, and so forth. These favors were eventually rewarded with gifts of a compass, a quadrant, muskets, and a chart of the waters between Sydney and Timor. These were hidden in the floor of the hut. Then the Bryants bided their time until there were no ships in the harbor to pursue them when they left.

Finally, on the night of March 28, 1791, the Bryant family, along with seven other convicts who had been stealthily recruited, boarded the six-oar cutter, rowed out of the harbor, set sail, and turned north. It was an act of calculated desperation. Almost exactly two years previously, Captain William Bligh had astounded the world with his remarkable open boat journey to Timor, after having been set adrift by the mutineers of the *Bounty.* Now, this small, underequipped, and inexperienced party, which included a woman and two very small children—one of them a baby still at the breast—was attempting almost exactly the same feat.

At first, the voyage went relatively smoothly, as they were able to catch mullet in a net, and go ashore for fresh water and the hearts of cabbage palms, which they boiled and ate. Then they had problems with the native people, who actively opposed their attempts to land. The boat began to leak and they were forced to caulk the seams with soap. An adverse wind drove them out to sea, and they were not able to replenish supplies for three weeks. "I will leave you to Consider what distress we must be in," wrote James Martin, one of the party; "the Woman and the two little Babies was in a bad condition, everything being so Wet that we Cou'd by no means light a Fire, we had nothing to Eat except a little raw rice."

The men were on the verge of giving up, but Mary rallied their courage. According to the *Annual Register of Events,* published the following year:

> The resolution displayed by the woman [was] hardly to be paralleled. At one time their anchor broke, and the surf was so great that the men laid down their oars in a state of despair, and gave themselves up as lost; but this Amazon, taking one of their hats, cried out "Never fear!" and immediately began to exert herself in clearing the boat of water. Her example was followed by her companions and by great labour the boat was prevented from sinking until they got into smoother sea.

And that particular ordeal did have an end, for they were blown onto one of the atolls of the Great Barrier Reef, where they were able to catch and kill a turtle, which, according to Martin, furnished "a Noble Meal this Night." Butchering more turtles, they dried the meat into jerky and continued on their way. They reached the island of Timor on June 5, 1791, having sailed 3,254 miles in sixty-nine days without the loss of a single life. Considering their condition, it was easy for them to convince the Dutch governor that they were survivors of a shipwreck.

And, at that, they could sit back and breathe a sigh of relief. All they needed to do was keep their counsel and recruit their health while they waited for a ship to carry them to England. Inexplicably however, perhaps because he had a fight with his wife, William Bryant got drunk, went to the Governor, and babbled the truth.

The party was imprisoned immediately. Then, in September, Captain Edward Edwards arrived. A brave but most unattractive officer, he had been in command of HMS *Pandora,* his mission to hunt down and capture the *Bounty* mutineers. He had taken some in Tahiti, confining them in a "Pandora's Box," a hutch built on the quarterdeck. Then his ship was wrecked on a reef south of New Guinea, with the loss of thirty-one crew and four prisoners, who were trapped in the hutch as the ship went down. Then, Edwards and the ninety-eight other survivors had sailed the thousand-mile journey to Timor in the four ship's boats.

Edwards immediately took charge of the Bryant party, clapping them into irons and shipping them onto a Dutch East Indiaman that was headed for Batavia. Tragedy closely pursued disaster. By confessing, William Bryant had signed a death warrant for both himself and his son, for he and Emanuel died of fever before Christmas.

The next passage was to the Cape of Good Hope. Three more convicts died on the way. At Cape Town, Mary Bryant, her daughter, and the four remaining convict men were put on board HMS *Gorgon* for London—and this is where another Mary enters the story—Mary Ann Parker, wife of the captain of the *Gorgon.* If she was aware of Mary Bryant's amazing accomplishment, Mary Ann certainly did not confide it to her journal, or describe it in the book she published after soliciting subscriptions, in 1795. "[A] Dutch Indiaman arrived from Batavia," she wrote, "and shortly after we were gratified with the company of Captain Edwards, of his Majesty's ship the *Pandora,* who a few days after landing embarked, and afterwards pursued his voyage in our ship: the convicts also who had escaped from Port Jackson were taken up at sea by the *Pandora,* and returned to England in the *Gorgon.*"

Seventeenth-century Batavia. Contemporary print.

Mrs. Parker's only other reference to Mary Bryant is an oblique one and, as with the other, tacked onto the end of "more interesting" news. On April 23, she wrote, "we anchored in 15 fathom, at Ascension Road. At this uninhabited island we found the *Betsy,* an American schooner, with the master, his wife, and four or five men on board, without a grain of tea or scarcely any provisions. . . . The sea continued tranquil and the ship still, which made our short stay very agreeable. After leaving the body of a child on shore for interment, we again set sail on the 25ᵗʰ."

And so little Charlotte died, and Mary was entirely alone when she was committed to Newgate Prison as an escaped felon However, she soon became the focus of much public attention, as word of her amazing voyage got about to a much more interested audience than Mary Ann Parker. Even Bligh became intrigued, badgering the governor of Timor for William Bryant's journal, which he partially copied before it was lost.

In particular, Mary Bryant gained the attention of the kindhearted writer and political lobbyist James Boswell, who adopted her cause with gusto, tirelessly petitioning the authorities for her release. Finally, in May 1793, she received an unconditional pardon. Boswell settled an annuity of ten pounds on her (which his heirs promptly rescinded when he died in 1795), and at last Mary had the wherewithal to return to her home in Fowey, Cornwall. Whether she rejoined her family or married again is unknown, for she was never heard of again.

Chapter Eleven

FATAL IMPACT

Slaves to the Devil & their own lusts.
—The Reverend Dwight Baldwin of Lahaina

In view of the publicity given to Mary Bryant's open boat voyage, it would be surprising if other female transportees did not try to emulate her. A pair who succeeded, though with very mixed results, were Catherine Hagerty and Charlotte Badger.

Charlotte, a very fat woman, "with a full face, thick lips, and light hair," was a London pickpocket who had been sentenced to transportation for life. At the time of the escape, she had an infant. It is a pity we don't know what Catherine Hagerty was sent down for, as she is the more intriguing of the two. Blonde, nubile, and husky-voiced, "fresh complexion, much inclined to smile," Catherine was definitely in the Anne Bonny mold. Catherine and Charlotte must have behaved themselves reasonably well at Port Jackson, for the month of April 1806 found them on the forty-five-ton brig *Venus,* on the way to the new penal settlement at Hobart Town, Tasmania, to work as convict servants. There were two male convicts as well, one of them an ex–gunner's mate named Richard Thomas Evans, who had been sentenced to fourteen years in the penal colony for desertion from the Royal Navy, and the other an emaciated little fellow by the name of John William Lancashire, who had been a painter. Richard Thompson, a private in the New South Wales Corps, was there in the capacity of guard.

The American captain of the brig, Samuel Rodman Chace, had been hired to freight grain, flour, and salt pork to the settlements, and after that he intended to join a sealing gang at Macquarie Island, far to the sub-Antarctic south. In the meantime, Chace was not happy, for the ready smile of Catherine Hagerty had seduced his first officer. This man, a fellow American by the name of Benjamin Barnet Kelly, does not sound particularly handsome, being "about 5 feet 7 inches, pock-marked, thin visage, brown hair, auburn whiskers," but Catherine was not worried about that, for her sights were set on the ship.

By June 16, when the *Venus* dropped anchor at the mouth of the River Tamar, on the northern coast of Tasmania, there were open ructions. Chace had publicly accused Kelly of breaking into the hold to broach a cask of spirits, and Catherine had thrown a box of ship's papers overboard, evidently to muddy the trail once the brig was seized. The captain spent the night on board another ship after conducting business at Port Dalrymple. Next morning, as he pulled back toward the brig, to his amazement and horror he saw the *Venus* make sail and stand briskly out to sea.

Incited by Catherine, three of the men—Kelly, Evans, and Private Thompson—had knocked down the second mate, Richard Edwards, and locked him up. When he came to, he did not appear to hold any umbrage, for he opted to join their gang. The young Malay cook, Thomas Ford,

Bay of Islands.

and his teenaged assistant, William Evans, came over to their side as well, apparently for the hell of it. Then they had tackled the six seamen. One of these, a mulatto by the name of Joseph Redmonds, also volunteered to join them, but the five others had been forced off the brig at gunpoint.

And so the ten pirates—Charlotte, Catherine, first mate Kelly, second mate Edwards, soldier Thompson, convicts Evans and Lancashire, two young boys, and the seaman Redmonds—made away with the ship. A proclamation, complete with detailed descriptions, was promptly posted in Sydney, but meantime the *Venus* got clean away to the Bay of Islands, New Zealand. There, Catherine, Kelly, Charlotte, and Lancashire decided to disembark. The *Venus,* now under the command of Redmonds, sailed off, and the two couples set to building a hut.

Maori chief. Engraving by Edward Finden from a drawing by R. Read. London, 1823.

From that point onward the voyage of the *Venus* became a litany of sexual greed, stupidity, and callousness. While the two women were on board a veneer of civilization prevailed, but once they had gone it collapsed. Redmonds had told them he planned to return to Sydney. However, he did not know how to navigate, so he did not dare sail out of sight of the coast. Accordingly, he cruised to Cape Brett in the north, then turned south to sail along the east coast of the North Island of New Zealand, picking up Maori women on the way.

These were not humble maidens, but close relatives of eminent chiefs, who were not at all happy about their sisters, daughters, and nieces being forcibly incorporated into the traveling harem of a bunch of mutineers and pirates. Then fury was fanned to bloodlust when the chiefs found out that as the mutineers tired of the women, they were sold to rival chieftains—a fate that meant slavery for all the princesses, and being killed and ceremoniously eaten for most.

This brutal, forced prostitution was a direct result of a cultural misinterpretation that had prevailed ever since the Europeans had penetrated the South Pacific. The first mariners to arrive at such island groups as the Marquesas had been bewildered by what seemed to them to be a scene of hysterical excitement. Native men whistled, strutted about, pranced aggressively one moment, and beckoned with obvious friendliness the next, while the gestures of hospitality from the women were unmistakable. Andreas Sparrmann, a rather priggish young Swede who was a botanist on Cook's second voyage, described a typical arrival at a tropical island in remarkably coy terms—

> In the harbour our ships were frequently surrounded by swimming natives of both sexes. We often amused ourselves by putting their skill as divers to the test by throwing them glass beads or nails. Some of the older divers and the younger girls rested astride the anchor-cable and were besmirched by the fresh tar with which it had been coated. The men were obliged to go back to their swimming without anybody to help them clean themselves, but I understood that, when it was a question of the fair sex, the boatswain would give them soap and help them to wash.

Some intellectual and pompous types tried to find some explanation for the strangely free behavior. In Tahiti, the scientist Joseph Banks remarked on the singular fact that making love was "the chief occupation, the favourite, nay almost the sole luxury of the inhabitants," and postulated that it might be because "the bodies and souls of the women are modelled into the utmost perfection for that soft science." Furthermore, the soil and climate of the tropical isles inevitably led to a life of ease, indolence, and far too much spare time, he mused, a great deal of which was "given up to love"—out of boredom, perhaps.

Other men were too charmed to pose questions. As Charles Murphy, the poetic third mate of the whaleship *Dauphin* put it, in 1822:

> *The graceful damsels from the shore*
> *As soon as we were moored*
> *Came paddling off in their canoes*
> *While others swam on board.*
>
> *And now our decks with girls are filled*
> *Of every sort and kind*
> *And every man picked out a wife*
> *The best that he could find.*

'Twas here the girls, including all
(To speak it rather dryly)
The sailors' amorous wants supplied
And think they are hon'red highly.

The natural result was a great deal of sexual congress, along with the tropical Pacific's swiftly spreading reputation as some kind of paradise, where the airs were balmy and the houris eagerly available. This tempted a great many young men who might not have otherwise sailed to sign onto voyages, particularly on whalers and sandalwood traders. It was certainly a deciding factor in the mutiny on the *Bounty*. However, many women did not wish to take part in what rapidly declined into mass prostitution. William Wilson of the Connecticut whaling bark *Cavalier* noted at Ponape, in February 1850, that the girls came on board very unwillingly, "have to if brother tells them to—if they cry they are beat." In the 1830s, Captain Rhodes of the ship *Australian* made active attempts to procure girls for his mutinous crew—for he did not dare allow them on shore to find their own, knowing they would promptly run away—but was turned down more often than not. In Tonga, he was informed that the girls were only available to shipmasters who called often, "and they are considered as wives and kept taboo'd." And close relatives of important New Zealand Maori chiefs were not likely to consider even that option.

Naturally, once the sensational details of the seizure of the *Venus* and the sordid aftermath filtered back to Port Jackson, the whole settlement was agog for the rest of the yarn. They had to wait six months, but then the South Seas whaler *Commerce* arrived into port. The master, Captain Eckstein, had much news. Kelly had been captured in the Bay of Islands, and Captain Hussey of the whaleship *Britannia* had taken him in irons to London. Captain Brothers of the *Russell* had done the same to Lancashire, so the two men were off to their just reward.

Later, the colonial schooner *Mercury* came in with an even more stirring report. The Maoris had caught up with the brig *Venus* on the Coromandel Peninsula and seized her. The vessel had been hauled up on the beach and burned for the iron in her hull—and the crew? Most appropriately, they had been killed and eaten in a cannibal feast. However, they left a legacy of tribal feud, as chiefs also sought vengeance on the rival chiefs who had bought, enslaved, and killed their women, resulting in over a thousand deaths and enslavement for many more.

But what about Catherine Hagerty, whose constant and beguiling smile had triggered the whole sorry saga? The same day the *Commerce* came into port, the whaler *Elizabeth* arrived, too, and Captain Bunker was able to satisfy part of the public curiosity on that score as well. Husky-voiced Catherine Hagerty was dead, probably of disease. So the only convict still at large was Charlotte Badger, living with her child in the hut at the Bay of Islands.

It is only possible to guess what happened to the fat woman who played such a minor part in the tale, yet who is now known as "Australia's first female pirate." Fourteen years later news reached Sydney that a white woman was living with a minor chieftain at the Bay of Islands, and this may have been our Charlotte.

There is another tale, however, of an American whaling captain who found a white woman and her half-caste son on the island of Vavau in the Tonga group, and who carried her off on his ship. She told him she was Charlotte Badger, and—who knows? She might have been telling the truth.

Samuel Rodman Chace, the captain who had watched with furious incredulity as the brig *Venus* sailed away with Catherine Hagerty and her co-conspirators in charge, was involved in yet another sensational incident. He arrived at Port Jackson on March 12, 1810, in command of the whaler *King George,* with grisly tidings. The transport *Boyd* had been seized by Maoris in New Zealand, and ransacked and burned. There were just four survivors from the general massacre of passengers and crew, three of them female.

The *Boyd,* a Thames-built three-decker of 392 tons, had arrived in Port Jackson on August 14, 1809, with a complement of convicts from Cork. As soon as the "immigrants" were discharged, the ship was chartered by one of Sydney's most prominent merchants, Simeon Lord, who loaded her with a cargo of timber, coal, seal-skins, and sperm oil for the Cape of Good Hope. On November 8 she sailed for New Zealand, it being the intention of her master, Captain John Thompson, to top up her lading with spars from the forests about Whangaroa, in the far north. There were between sixty and seventy people on board. It is difficult to be exact about how many of these were passengers; there were fourteen in the passenger list, but other names came to light later. Three women were named—Ann Morley, Ann Glossop, and Catherine Bourke—but there was also a Mrs. Broughton, whose husband was an official with the Victualing Commission. She had her little daughter, Betsy, with her.

Ann Morley also had a child, a baby girl. Ann's past is obscure, but it seems likely that she was a convict who had worked out her sentence and moved on to commercial enterprise. She and her husband had operated an inn—probably a combination of tavern, accommodation house, and brothel—in Sydney, which had been much frequented by Maori seamen. Then, becoming estranged from her husband, Ann had made up her mind to ship out of Sydney, taking passage on the *Boyd*. It was a fateful resolve.

Among the crew were four or five New Zealand Maoris who had left whaling vessels in Port Jackson and were working their passage back home. One of these, Tara George (probably Te Ara), may have been Ann's lover. He must have been an attractive character, for when he fell ill during the passage the second mate and the steerage boy, Thomas Davis, took care of him. Captain Thompson was not so humane. Instead, he flogged Tara for laziness. This was another fatal move, for Tara was the son of a chief.

At the time, however, no threats were made. The *Boyd* dropped anchor in the beautiful harbor of Whangaroa early in December, and was immediately surrounded by native canoes. A Maori party came on board, including Tara's brother, Te Puhi. The scars of the flogging must have been obvious—and Tara may even have been flogged again before being sent ashore—but still nothing was said. Thompson bargained for spars, and three days later three ship's boats were lowered with most of the ship's company, to be escorted by canoes up the river and into the forest. Thompson went with them. None of the Europeans returned. Deep in the trees, there had been a swift massacre.

After that, the vengeful Maoris turned their attention to the ship. Dressing up in the dead mariners' clothes and carrying their muskets, they set sail in the *Boyd*'s boats down the river to the harbor. They arrived by night. The officer on watch hailed them, and they told him that the captain had decided to stop on shore, to get an early start on cutting wood in the morning. Then they began to clamber on board. When the officer objected, they killed him.

The seamen on board were surprised and killed one by one, except for four or five who clambered into the rigging and clung there, trembling, while the Maoris plundered the cabins and holds. One woman passenger who came to the companionway to investigate the noises was killed halfway up, and the sounds of her fall alerted the others. Running about in a panic, they were quickly slaughtered.

Meanwhile, a friendly chief, Te Pahi, arrived alongside in his canoe, originally intent on an innocent fishing expedition. When the men in the rigging cried out to him for help, he told them that if they jumped down and swam to his canoe, he would carry them to land. At about the same moment that the seamen were escaping, Ann Morley was discovered, cowering in a corner with her baby. Instead of killing her immediately, her assailants hauled her out onto the deck. According to some of the stories, she wept so bitterly that some of the Maoris took pity on her and suggested that she should be ransomed instead of killed. It is also possible that Tara was one of those who argued that she should be spared.

Whoever interceded for her life did so successfully. Te Puhi, distracted because he had just glimpsed the rescued seamen running out onto the beach, agreed. And so Ann was carried safely to shore, as Te Puhi assembled a party and went in hot pursuit of the boys Te Pahi had done his best to save. Te Pahi, struggling to get free, was forcibly held while the seamen were caught and killed. Afterwards, it was reported that Ann saw the dead bodies laid out on the beach.

This pursuit, ironically, saved Te Puhi's life, for back on the *Boyd* a warrior found a powder keg, knocked it open, and poured powder into the pan of a musket, the way he had seen Europeans do it. Then he struck the flint. There was a deafening flash, followed by a huge, nightmarish explosion in which pieces of butchered flesh flew all about, and fourteen Maoris were killed. Crazily, Tara's father repeated the blunder, opening another keg and pouring powder into another musket. This second explosion killed him and most of the Maoris on deck, tore the ship from her chains, and sparked a fire that burned her down to the waterline.

A few days later, a Maori arrived in the Bay of Islands and asked for a private interview with the master of the *City of Edinburgh,* which was lying there loading spars. He told the captain, Simon Pattison, and the supercargo, Alexander Berry, that a ship had been captured in Whangaroa, and warned them that a warrior party, armed with stolen weapons, was on the way. It took awhile for him to make himself believed, but finally, on the thirty-first, Berry took three armed boats up the coast.

Berry, a medical man and free settler who prospered greatly in Australia, was no lover of the Maori people. He may have held a particular grudge against Te Pahi, who had visited Sydney and been received with great civility by the Governor of New South Wales. In fact, Berry had been publicly derisive of Te Pahi's attempt to dress correctly in European clothes for formal occasions, once likening the chief's outfit to "the garb of a clown." However, he was greeted in surprisingly friendly fashion by Te Puhi and his fellow chieftains.

Those who had been involved in the massacre approached, and when Berry asked if there had been any survivors, they replied, yes. "Give us axes, and you shall have the prisoners."

After dickering over the ransom they came to an agreement, and Berry and a party went up to the *pa*. There, chillingly, they found that a number of the women were dressed in European female garments. However, as Berry recorded, in due course the natives, "according to promise, brought to our quarters a young woman with her suckling child, and a boy belonging to the vessel, about fifteen years old." The boy, Thomas Davis, had saved himself by hiding in the hold until he saw a chance to slip over the side. Captain Pattison declared later that the Maoris had spared the boy because he had a club foot, but it is more likely that Tara remembered his kindness on the passage to New Zealand.

When Berry asked Ann Morley if there were any other survivors, she said yes. According to the deposition Berry sent to Sydney with Captain Samuel Chace, the second mate had been kept alive for two weeks so that

Maori village, or pa. Engraving by Polack, 1838.

he could show the tribe how to make fishhooks out of iron hoops, but he had made such a bad job of it that they killed and ate him. How true this is, is uncertain. However, there was another person alive—"the infant daughter of Mr. Commissary Broughton." Berry forthwith demanded the child, but such a long time elapsed that he feared she, too, was dead.

However, it turned out that they were trying to make the little girl presentable. "It was tolerably clean, with its hair dressed and ornamented with white feathers in the fashion of New Zealanders," he wrote. The toddler's only garment, however, was Captain Thompson's shirt. "The poor child was greatly emaciated," having refused to eat. In later years, she declared that she vividly remembered watching her mother being slaughtered.

The four survivors sailed away on Pattison's ship. Ann Morley never arrived home, for she died while the ship was at Lima—"as a consequence of her own irregularities," as Berry phrased it. Some kindhearted whaling wife took over the baby and little Betsy Broughton, and they were carried to Australia. The Morley girl grew up to be a schoolteacher. Betsy was raised by her father, and eventually married a prominent Sydney citizen, giving birth in future years to seventeen children. Thomas Davis was sent to England, but returned to Australia, where he worked on one of Berry's properties until he was drowned in 1822.

And the reprisal mission of two hundred men from five British whaleships, which was led by Captain Parker of the New Zealander and motivated by Berry's undoubtedly biased report, made a terrible mistake. Instead of attacking and killing the vengeful Te Puhi, they murdered the people and razed the village of Te Pahi, the chief who had tried so hard to save the seamen who had taken refuge in the rigging.

Chapter Twelve

THE DECEIT OF DRESS

The apparel oft proclaims the man.
—Shakespeare

On February 22, 1797, in a scenario fit for a Gilbert and Sullivan comedy, four French ships landed an invasion force of twelve hundred troops on the beach two miles west of the little Welsh village of Fishguard. Why the French naval authorities had made the strange decision to invade the remotenesses of Pembrokeshire is uncertain, but they might have been misled by intelligence reports that there was a peasant revolt in the area. One of the officers asked the first man he met if he had landed in Ireland, and was very confused to be told that it was Wales. All of them, in fact, must have been somewhat bewildered, for they made such a very bad job of it.

As it was, there were only about six hundred genuine soldiers in the force, the rest being a mixture of convicts and Irishmen. Their leader was Colonel William Tate, an Irish-American who had fled to Paris when American officialdom found out that he was doing his utmost to sell Florida to the French. No great military genius to start with, he had a bit of bad luck when his men happened across a Portuguese wreck on the shore and looted it for its cargo of wine. Drunkenly, they ambled across the countryside, plundering a couple of farms on the way, while the militia fired blanks at them from the cannon of Fishguard fort, lacking any powder or shot.

Meanwhile, a messenger on a horse had been sent hotfoot to the gentry, who were obliviously partying at the mansion of a wealthy landowner, Lord Cawdor. His lordship immediately mobilized a force of six hundred yeomanry, mostly armed with scythes and other farming tools. "There never was shewn greater loyalty," wrote George Devereux, Viscount Hereford, proudly claiming that every able-bodied man in the area had responded to the summons.

However, the extempore army was not needed. The invading force had been stopped in their tracks—by the women of the village, led by the commanding figure of Jemima Nicholas, the local cobbler. In fact, the French soldiers were in a highly demoralized state, very eager indeed to trade in their muskets for cheese and bread and seek surrender terms, which were forthwith signed in the Royal Oak pub.

Jemima, a formidable female armed only with a pitchfork, had captured twelve French soldiers all by herself and locked them up in a

Welsh women in national dress.
Girl's Own Paper, November 1884.

church. After she died, in 1832, it was recorded in the burial register that "she marched against the French and could overcome most men in a fight." The real reason the French force caved in so easily, however, was that the Welsh women were wearing their traditional dress of tall black hats and red cloaks. From a distance, to drunken, poorly led invaders, they looked just like a regiment of British redcoats.

Obviously, then, dress was very significant. While the women of Fishguard were not pretending to be anything other than themselves, they were mistaken for soldiers, and that was what counted. In times when men and women wore very different kinds of garb, one could persuade others that he or she belonged to the other sex simply by changing his or

ALMIRA PAUL,

A YOUNG WOMAN, who, garbed as a Male, for
of the last preceding years, actually served as a com
Sailor, on board of English and American armed ve as

Frontispiece of The Surprising Adventures
of Almira Paul. Boston, 1816.

her outfit. Thus Jeanne Baré, who became the first woman to circumnavigate the world by disguising herself as the valet of her lover, Commerson, to sail with him on the French discovery ship *Boudeuse* in 1765, got away with it until they arrived at Tahiti in April 1768. The native men realized at once that she was a woman, for they were used to recognizing a person's sex by posture and shape, not dress. They could not understand why she would not grant them the same sexual favors that their women were granting the French seamen and complained about it, so Jeanne's secret became common knowledge.

This use of dress to fool the audience is the basis of the longstanding folklore of women dressing as men to go to sea. There are dozens of ballads and chanteys on this theme. Very popular, for instance, was the song of the lovelorn Susan who

> *Put on a jolly sailor's dress,*
> *And daubed her hands with tar*
> *To cross the raging sea*
> *On board a man of war*

in order to be near her William, who, of course, did not recognize her until the dénouement of the story. This is not particularly plausible, for it would have been easy enough for Susan to get on board William's man-of-war in port without bothering with a disguise, and with any luck at all she could go to sea as well, still without putting on trousers.

The same grain of salt should be taken with a 1771 report in the *Annual Register* that a transvestite by the name of Charles Waddall had been uncovered on the man-of-war *Oxford,* which was lying at Chatham. According to the account, Ms. Waddall's true sex had been revealed when she was condemned to a flogging for desertion and then stripped to the waist for the stipulated two dozen lashes. She played for sympathy, pleading

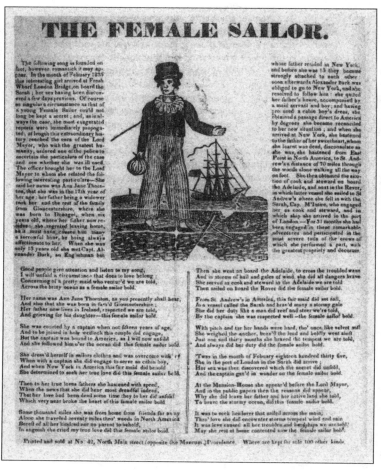

Broadsheet, "The Female Sailor," the ballad of Ann Jane Thornton.
Note the use of the same woodcut.

that she had joined the ship under the misapprehension that her lover was on board, but finding he had run away, a week later she had decided to run away, too.

Her ploy was outstandingly successful, for Admiral Dennis, touched to the heart, gave her a present of some money, as did the Commissioner of the Chatham Dockyard and many of the officers. On reflection, however, those kind gentlemen must have realized that her excuse was unlikely to be the truth. Not only could she have come on board openly, as her lover's girlfriend, but the lapse of a week before taking off after him needed a lot of explaining. It is highly probable that she made up the romance to get out of her scrape.

As it happens, though, teenaged girls being traditionally romantic, some of the sentimental charades really did happen, though not usually on men-of-war. One such was Ann Jane Thornton, who conformed to the legend so neatly that she was memorialized in a ballad of her own.

"Good people give attention and listen to my song," the troubadour begins,

I will unfold a circumstance that does to love belong
Concerning of a pretty maid who ventur'd we are told
Across the briny ocean as a female sailor bold.

In February 1835, sixteen-year-old Ann Jane Thornton was summoned by the Lord Mayor of London to appear before him at Mansion House, because he had read about her in the papers and thought she might have been ill treated by the captain and crew of the ship where she worked. The shipmaster, Captain McIntire of the *Sarah,* was summoned, too, to give evidence on his own behalf. He had met Ann at St. Andrews in North America, he said. She had been dressed as a sailor, and he had engaged her in all innocence, giving her the job of cook and steward for the fair wage of nine dollars a month. The crew had been suspicious of her right from the start, he said, because she would not drink grog like a regular seaman. Then, they found her out for sure when they saw her washing herself in her berth, and reported to the captain that the cook was a girl.

Her sex was then discovered which the secret did unfold
And the captain gaz'd with wonder on the female sailor bold.

This posed quite a problem for McIntire, for the ship was in the middle of the Atlantic, the weather was rugged, and he needed every hand. So he told her to carry on as before. Ann agreed that McIntire had treated her as humanely as possible under the circumstances, for he had told her to go to him with any complaints about the crew. Some of the sailors had struck her, she admitted, for not working hard enough—presumably meaning not as hard as a man—but she had kept her own counsel instead of running to the captain. For his part, McIntire had no complaints, testifying that she had performed the duties of a seaman to admiration. She would run up to hand the topgallant sail in any kind of weather, he said.

She'd had a hard time, for the passage had been a very rough one, but through it all she had borne it excellently, and in his opinion she was a capital seaman.

With pitch and tar her hands were hard, tho' once like velvet soft
She weighed the anchor, heav'd the lead and boldly went aloft
Just one and thirty months she braved the tempest we are told
And always did her duty, did the female sailor bold.

The Lord Mayor was being well rewarded for his benign interest in the case. Here was a girl worthy of an excellent recommendation, being not just clean and sober, but a brave and willing sailor as well. So he asked her why she had set out on this strange career.

Her widowed father had moved the family from Gloucestershire to Donegal when she was six, she said, and when she was thirteen she had fallen in love with a visiting shipmaster, Captain Alexander Burk of New York. When he left, she dressed as a cabin boy and worked her passage to join him, only to find that he had died just a few days before she arrived.

Then to her true love's father's she hastened with speed
When the news that she did hear most dreadful indeed
That her love had been dead some time they to her did unfold
Which very near broke the heart, of this female sailor bold.

To keep body and soul together while she looked for a ship that would take her back home, Ann signed onto a craft called *Adelaide* as cook and steward, and then onto the Belfast-bound ship *Rover*. But then the *Rover* was redirected to the West Indies, so she shipped with McIntire instead.

And here she was, in Mansion House, still not home after years of trying to get there. Profoundly touched, the Lord Mayor gave her enough money to get to Donegal, and that is the last that we hear of her.

It was to seek her lover that she sailed across the main
Thro' love she did encounter storms tempest wind and rain
It was love caused all her troubles and hardships we are told
May she rest at home contented now, the female sailor bold.

The crux of the matter, however, is that she hadn't been *paid*—for that is the reason Ann was still hanging around in London instead of heading for home. Because she was female, she did not warrant a seaman's proper wage. It was for this that the Lord Mayor had hauled her up before the bench, and not because he wanted to be entertained by a yarn. This discrimination in the matter of pay is even more eloquently demonstrated by the case of Elizabeth Stephens, who did not bother with cross-dressing at all. Elizabeth went to court in December 1821 to file a suit against the ship *Jane and Matilda* and her master, Captain Chandler, for monies due for three voyages between England and Spain.

Like Ann Jane, Elizabeth had shipped as cook and steward, and had carried out the duties of a seaman, too. Elizabeth "stood watches, took her turn at the helm and hauled ropes on deck"—just as Ann Jane did a decade and a half later—even though she had shipped as a woman, not a man. The difference was that she did not have to go aloft to work on the sails. Otherwise, her case was the same: Captain Chandler had refused to pay her. His excuse was that she was not eligible for the wages that would have been due to a man.

It took a long time for the case to get due attention (perhaps because it was not as sensational as a cross-dresser's would have been), but it was finally heard on July 12, 1823, with Lord Stowell at the bench. A staunch conservative, he heard out the evidence with much distaste, weightily deploring "a woman doing man's work on board ship," his reasoning being that "it could lead to moral disorder." Lord Stowell wondered much about the propriety of the business altogether. Indeed, he wondered if the full facts of the case had been laid before him. Had "the captain engaged the services of this woman in more capacities than those described?" Had Elizabeth Stephens acted "in character of his wife, or in a less honourable connection?" Was she, in fact, the captain's doxy, just pretending to be a seaman so that she could accompany him on voyage?

Everyone emphatically denied this nasty assertion. All Elizabeth wanted, she said, was her rightful wage, which had not been forthcoming. And finally Lord Stowell conceded her case, awarding her ninety-one pounds and two shillings, pronouncing, "sex alone does not create a legal or total disqualification."

And so it seems that a major reason for a woman's passing herself as male was to get money for her seaman's work. Even if she managed the feat of signing up as a female, as Elizabeth Stephens did, her employer was likely to weasel out of handing over her rightful wages. If dressing in man's clothes meant a basic wage, then pretending to be male was logical.

In 1807 the London papers reported that an old woman named Tom Bowling was brought before the magistrates, charged with some trivial offense. She told the magistrate that she had served as boatswain's mate on board a man-of-war for upwards of twenty years, and had a pension from the Chatham Chest. She had always dressed as a man, she replied stoutly, when asked. Apparently, no one asked her why—perhaps because her motive was so obvious. Not only had she received a seaman's pay "for upwards of twenty years," but as long as she could pass herself off as a man, she received a pension as well.

This was a very good motive for keeping up the cross-dressing after retirement. The *Annual Register* for 1761 reported that a transvestite who had served five years as a marine was picked up by a press gang in Plymouth. She was forced to reveal her true sex when they

Deception was not particularly difficult, especially in the lower ranks. Sketch of a cabin boy by Thomas Rowlandson, c. 1780.

shoved her into a prison cell, but went on record as saying she "would not have disclosed herself if she had been allowed her liberty." She did not give her reasons, but money would have been a good one.

As far back as 1692, an unnamed "gentlewoman" petitioned the queen for a pension on the grounds that she had "served in man's clothes on board the *St. Andrew,* which was engaged in the fight with the French." There is no record of whether she got any money, but the fact that she had to go all the way to the top to plead her case is an indication that her sex was against her. At the other end of the social scale was the story of the poor girl whose family forced her to do men's work, commented upon by the *Naval Chronicle* in 1808. Her "father-in-law" had apprenticed her to a collier in Whitby, and she had served for four years without her sex being discovered. Finally rebelling against this unnatural existence, she had run away and was found in the streets of London in a destitute condition by parties who sent her to the Lord Mayor.

The mercenary side of the transvestitism is also amply demonstrated by the case of one of the most famous cross-dressers. It was first described by the *Annual Register* in October 1807, in an article reporting on the court-martial of William Berry, first lieutenant of HMS *Hazard*. Twenty-two-year-old Berry was on trial for "the unnatural and detestable sin of sodomy with Thomas Gibbs, a boy of the second class belonging to the said sloop [*Hazard*], punishable by the Twenty-ninth Article of War"—this last being an edict which ran, "If any person of the fleet shall commit the unnatural and detestable sin of sodomy with man or beast, he shall be punished with death by the sentence of a court martial."

Obviously, the affair was sensational enough in itself. The really riveting passage ran thus, however:

> One of the witnesses in this awful and horrible trial was a little female tar, Elizabeth Bowden, who has been on board the *Hazard* these eight months. She appeared in court in a long jacket and blue trousers.

Back in February, Elizabeth, a fourteen-year-old orphan from Truro, Cornwall, had walked to Plymouth, put on boy's clothes, and joined the Navy under the name of John, being both destitute and starving. As the newspaper put it, "she was obliged through want to disguise herself and volunteer into His Majesty's service." This was an excellent motive for pretending to be a man, but also a good reason for the court to trust not a word that she said. However, despite this demonstration of opportunism, her extreme youth, her sex, and her lack of naval experience, the evidence she gave was considered permissible.

Prompted by the prosecutor, Elizabeth testified that she had spied on Berry through the keyhole of his stateroom door, with the result, she said, of seeing "Thomas Gibbs playing with the prisoner's privates." Such sneaky surveillance is not attractive, particularly when the reader learns

Sketch by Rowlandson of a seaman, c. 1780.

that Bowden fetched the gunroom steward and told him to have a look, too, which he refused to do, advising her to go up on deck and mind her own business. There is a definite hint of mischief-making about both her evidence and her actions. The spying happened on a sunny Sunday afternoon as the *Hazard* was cruising back to Plymouth, and there is an unavoidable impression that Bowden, being off duty, was bored and looking for trouble.

Even the prosecutor seemed uncertain of the credibility of this strange young witness, questioning whether the boy Gibbs had ever complained or even talked about "what passed between him and the prisoner in the past."

"Gibbs has never told me anything that has happened," Elizabeth replied.

So what, in the name of all providence (though not in so many words), "induced you to look through the keyhole?"

"He [Gibbs] was called in several times," replied Elizabeth frankly, "and I thought I would see what he was about."

"Are you sure that it was the prisoner's private parts that you saw Thomas Gibbs have hold of?"

"Yes."

There was one candle lit in the cabin, Elizabeth was sure of what she had seen, and so the outcome was determined, despite Berry's emphatic denial that anything of the sort had happened. Berry said Thomas Gibbs had made it up, because he had threatened to thrash the boy for stealing. The gunroom steward supported this, testifying that Gibbs was a notorious thief and liar. There must have been some public sympathy for young Lieutenant Berry, for when the testimony was published a woman came alongside the ship and offered to save his life by marrying him. She had been informed that a reprieve could be obtained by these means—erroneously so, for Berry was hanged at the starboard foreyardarm of the *Hazard* on 19 October. What happened to the boy Gibbs—who must have been under fourteen, for he was never charged—is just as unknown as the fate of the interfering Miss Bowden.

Chapter Thirteen

DECENTLY SKIRTED

*MALE ATTIRE—Dr. Mary Walker, and her unique
costume do not now excite quite so much of the
public attention as they did some time ago. The
style adopted by her has none of the hideousness of
deformity about it, whatever may be its faults as a
becoming and womanly dress.*
—New Bedford newspaper,
August 1869

One thought-provoking aspect of the trial of the unfortunate Lieutenant Berry is that the clothes Ms. Bowden wore in court were as interesting to the public as her presence on the ship, if not even more so. Young Elizabeth was wearing male clothing as a gesture, it seems, for everyone was perfectly well aware that she was not a boy, but a girl. The captain and officers of the *Hazard*, in fact, had known it for more than six months, for, according to the *Annual Register,* she had been able to maintain her deception for only six weeks. It seems very odd that she was not dismissed and sent ashore the instant the ship had arrived in port; indeed, it could have saved a lot of grief for the lieutenant and notoriety for the ship if she had disappeared before the case was heard. Instead, "the captain and officers have paid every attention to her; they gave her an apartment to sleep in, and she still remains on board the *Hazard* as an attendant on the officers to the ship."

This raises a very interesting question, quite apart from the obvious one of whether anyone thought to check whether Thomas Gibbs was himself a boy, and not just another cross-dresser. Just how prejudicial was it to a woman's character when it was found she had been dressing as a man?

Deuteronomy 22:5 says, "A woman shall not wear that which pertaineth to a man, neither shall a man put on a woman's garment; for whosoever doeth such things is an abomination unto Jehovah thy God." But how strongly was this dictum held?

It depended on the society and the era. When Anne Chamberlyne cross-dressed to join her brother's ship in 1690, to take an active part in a battle against the French off Beachy Head, her contemporaries were most uncritical. After she died, a memorial was placed on the wall of Chelsea Old Church on Cheyne Walk, London, certifying in Latin that on June 30, 1690, at the age of twenty-three, "aspiring to great

Bloomer dress. Artist: Ron Druett.

achievements unusual to her sex and age," she went on board in men's clothing and "fought valiantly six hours against the French, under the command of her brother." Ironically, Anne survived unhurt, to die in childbirth exactly sixteen months later. "This monument, for a consort most virtuous and dearly loved, was erected by her husband," John Spragg, Esquire.

Mary Stuart, Queen of Scots, loved to cross-dress, reputedly because she had such perfect legs. At a banquet staged for the French ambassador, she and her ladies-in-waiting—her "Maries"—all appeared as men. She cross-dressed for more serious reasons, too, riding at the head of her troops in male garb in 1565. Despite the declamations of such men as the Scottish Protestant reformer John Knox, who dismissed the whole of womankind as "weak, frail, impatient feeble and foolish creatures," the philosophy of separate spheres for separate sexes had not gripped the popular imagination at the time. Mary Stuart's court jesters, for instance, were female, a particular favorite being Nichola "La Folle," who accompanied Mary from France to Scotland, and was sent back after her mistress lost her head.

Reportedly, Admiral Horatio Nelson's mistress, Emma Hamilton, used to squeeze her abundant and voluptuous form into a midshipman's uniform to accompany her lover to the waterfront taverns of Palermo. This is more plausible than it may at first appear, for after Nelson and the Hamiltons were back in London, the Goat Tavern on Stratford Street was a favorite trysting place. Emma was not in male dress then, possibly because she was carrying Nelson's child, but if she were, it would not have been as scandalous as the actual meeting of the two lovers—and in a tavern, at that. In the higher echelons of society, in fact, cross-dressing was considered to be socially acceptable fun.

"We were gone to bed," wrote an eleven-year-old girl in her diary, on September 11, 1789,

> when all of a sudden there was a musketry discharge, and shouts of joy in the court-yard which startled us, and made us leap out of our beds. We found the whole house in the drawing room, [both] servants and masters. Then followed the loveliest and maddest of balls, mascarades, changing of sex, tumbling of women and men on the floor—in short, we stayed up, all of us, still dancing, until after midnight.

Young Betsey Wynne and her four sisters belonged to the spectacular milieu of the wealthy and privileged in Europe who whiled away the hours gambling, play-acting, attending the opera, and entertaining each other in castles and mansions. Their whole reason for life was to have a good time. Betsey's father was the rich, well-connected Riccardo Gulielmo Casparo Melchior Balthazaro Wynne, half Venetian, half Welsh; her mother was French. Back in 1786, Richard Wynne had sold his extensive holdings in Falkingham, Lincolnshire, and removed his family, along with a large retinue of cooks, maids, grooms, dancing master, tutor, secretary, horses, and dogs, to the Continent. There he had adopted a roving, epicurean lifestyle, settling down in various European resorts whenever the fancy took him.

Betsey's early journals testify to plenty of socially acceptable cross-dressing. On September 14, 1789, for example, Richard Wynne hosted an entertainment where the girls' nurse, Mary, was dressed as a man, while Richard himself and the older girls' tutor, M'sieu Jaegle, were dressed as women, and a groom named Charles "dressed up as a girl." The kitchen maid "dressed up as a man," and so did the cook. The cook, it seems, took every opportunity of getting into breeches and stockings. "She has very fine legs." Not only did it give her a chance to show off these splendid limbs, but this was an era when men's fashions were often more elaborate and beautiful than women's.

Such flamboyant behavior was certainly not confined to the privacy of the home. Betsey recorded that her aunt's lover, Benincasa, "dressed up as a woman" when he called on the family on an afternoon in August 1789, while Tante Justiniana was dressed as a man. "I came downstairs without recognising them. But at last Mons. Benincasa made such an absurd curt-sey that I knew him and my aunt also from her voice." Richard Wynne not only "supped in his travesti," but wore women's clothes while promenading in St. Mark's Square, Venice, to see how many of their friends he could fool. Nor was "changing of sex" a family eccentricity. In February 1791, "The monks of St. Justina made a great mascarade 24 of them drest in womens cloaths."

Masculine attire was much more dashing than female gowns. Captain Woodes Rogers accosting Spanish ladies. Detail of William Hogarth engraving.

As late as 1848 a seaman visiting California, William Ryan, recorded attending a ball in the port of Monterey where he "found a motley crowd of persons assembled, amongst whom were several well-dressed females and young men, both Yankee and Californian." Two of the young men attracted his particular attention because of their agility and beauty, and he was not particularly surprised to find that they were young women. "This practice of the women disguising themselves in male attire is not by any means confined to females of easy character," he remarked. "On several occasions, I detected married Spanish women of unblemished reputation dressed in male costume at these fandangoes, and was amused to observe the jealous watchfulness with which they regarded their husbands."

On board ship, dress was a matter of practicality. While a woman in skirts might stand watches, take her trick at the helm, or haul ropes with the men—as Elizabeth Stephens did—it was dangerous to climb tall masts and grapple with heavy sails in women's garb, which is why going aloft was not part of Ms. Stephens's job description. It was only common sense for women who climbed the rigging, like Ann Jane Thornton, to wear the same gear as the men. The trousers were not part of a charade anymore, but a sensible convenience.

Similarly, a cross-dressed seaman by the name of William Brown was able to rejoin her ship after everyone had found out that she was female. According to a newspaper report in September 1815, Mrs. Brown had served in the 110-gun ship of the line *Queen Charlotte* for about eleven years, "highly to the satisfaction of the officers." She was a real regular seaman, "rather handsome for a black," who exhibited "all the traits of a British tar and takes her grog with her late messmates with the greatest gaiety." Apparently, she had gone to sea to escape her husband, who had since found out that a lot of prize money was due to her, and had claimed it as his legal due. Whether Mrs. Brown managed to hang on to her rightful loot is unknown, but she rejoined her ship with no comment from the captain or officers, still in the guise of a seaman.

By contrast, after Jeanne Baré—the young lady who cross-dressed to sail on the French discovery ship *Boudeuse* with her lover—was recognized as a woman by the Tahitians, the commander of the expedition, Bougainville, complained that "it was difficult to prevent the sailors from alarming her modesty." This could have been because those seamen also knew the reason for her cross-dressing, and had promptly sized her up as a woman of easy virtue. On the whole, though, it took thinkers like the Reverend John Knox to attach importance to the gender of dress, a narrow-mindedness that meant, among other things, that a captain's knee-jerk reaction when a transvestite was discovered on his ship was to rush about getting the girl dressed "decently"—that is, in a skirt.

On October 18, 1693, Captain Thomas Phillips of the slaver *Hannibal* found to his consternation that one of the soldiers he was carrying to the Guinea coast "was a woman, who had enter'd herself into their service under the name of John Brown, without the least suspicion, and had been three months on board without any mistrust, lying always amongst the other passengers, and being as handy and ready to do any work as any of them." Ms. Brown would have got away with it even longer, but was unlucky enough to fall sick. The surgeon prescribed an enema, and when his mate went to administer it, he got quite a surprise. Naturally, he went to the captain, "whereupon, in charity, as well as in respect to her sex, I order'd her a private lodging apart from the men, and gave the taylor some ordinary stuffs to make her woman's cloaths." The young woman, who was "about twenty years old, and a likely black girl," did not just reassume female clothing, but took on her traditionally female role as well. Phillips found her "very useful in washing my linen." It never occurred to him that her reason for dressing as a man might have been to avoid that kind of fate.

Falling ill or getting wounded in an intimate place was a fast route to exposure. According to the seaman-soldier Hannah Snell, after she was badly wounded in the upper thighs she avoided detection by taking a serving woman into her confidence. The servant stole some lint and ointment from the surgeon's medical chest, and between them they extracted all the musket balls, using only their fingers, and then dressed the wounds.

Not everyone had this kind of grit, and many were too feverish to think of it. One of these was Ann Johnson, who in 1848 shipped as a seaman named George Johnson on the Nantucket whaler *Christopher Mitchell.* According to a boatsteerer on the *Charles W. Morgan,* Nelson Haley, who was one of the first outsiders to hear about the impersonation, "George" was a brave and popular young fellow, remarkable only because he was a much better hand at doing his laundry than the rest, and had a tendency to blush when the language about decks became ungentlemanly. At the beginning of July 1849, however, George had the misfortune to be put off duty, being sick and feverish. And on the fifth one of the hands, who had gone into the forecastle to light his pipe, came hurtling up to deck, hollering, "That young fellow who is sick is a woman!"

Naturally, the officer on watch wanted to have a look for himself before bothering the captain, but "sure enough there lay before his astonished gaze a beautifully formed woman." Apparently Ann, who had kept her bosom flattened with a special canvas corset, had shrugged this off in her fever, and thus "disclosed what she had kept an inviolate secret." She was roused up and hauled before Captain Thomas Sullivan, who promptly conformed to convention by giving her "some of the calico and white cotton we had on board for trading

> and she made herself quite an outfit, and when dressed in her proper attire she was a pretty girl, even if her face was rough and sunburnt. Of course her hands were rough, but they still were a pretty shape.

According to convention, too, Haley related that she had cross-dressed for a romantic reason. After falling in love with a young man, Ann had left home with him, but the rotten cad had run off. Learning that he had joined the crew of a whaler, Ann made up her mind to do the same and track him down somehow in the five hundred–plus fleet of American whaling ships that were plowing the Pacific at the time. And what would she do if she found him? "I would kill him like a venomous snake!" she declared with flashing eyes. Here was the essence of Victorian melodrama, and a story which surely helped the sale of Nelson Haley's book, after he'd got back home and written it. However, the truth, as it was gradually revealed, was somewhat less elevated.

Having organized Ann into proper dress, Sullivan changed course for Paita, Peru, where he dropped her off into the care of the United States consul, whose name is a bit of a mystery. Captain Sullivan called him Bathurst, and it was indeed a Mr. Bathurst who sent a report to Nantucket, published in the *Nantucket Inquirer* of August 16, 1849. First, he quoted a statement written out by First Officer Wood of the whaler, which related that Ann was the daughter of George Johnson, a Rochester, New York, shoemaker. She claimed to have left home in July 1848, and then, having "cast off the petticoats," set out to see the world, initially Nantucket, where she signed onto the *Christopher Mitchell.* And here is the first contradiction of Haley's romantic version: "She is 19 years old," Bathurst reported; "and gives as a reason for coming to sea, that she was told she would get some money in the business."

The consul did not appear to be disappointed that sentimental motives had suddenly changed to mercenary ones, perhaps because he was such an opportunistic character himself. He concluded by writing, "Miss J. is now a guest in my family. She is a very fine young girl, extremely well bred, and has not yet acquired any of the conversation so frequently practiced by sailors. I have promised her my paternal care, for which she appears very grateful." What he did not mention was that he had handed Captain Sullivan a grossly inflated reckoning for said "paternal care."

At this stage of the saga the consul's name changed to Ruden, for the bill he presented ran like this:

Woman's clothing—$84.00
Room and board in Payta—$19.00
Passage to the United States—$100.00
Traveling expenses—$20.00
Postage—$2.00
Commission to A. Ruden—$11.25

Not only was he charging an outrageous sum for his "paternal care," but the consul was raking in a commission as well! Understandably, Sullivan was furious. Being a respectable Quaker, he could not keep Ann on board because of the risk of scandal, so he had no choice but to pay up. He promised the consul that the ship's owners would be taking the matter further, and then, still extremely disgruntled, took his ship back to sea.

A little later, another Nantucket whaleship called into the port, the *Nantucket,* whose master, Captain Benjamin C. Gardner, was most probably carrying his wife. Another passenger was not mentioned, yet he was able with propriety to take Ann Johnson to the States. It would not have done his pocket any harm, either, though it is doubtful that Gardner was paid the whole of that extortionate hundred dollars.

According to the *Nantucket Inquirer,* the *Nantucket* arrived at Woods Hole, Massachusetts, on January 7, 1850. And here Ann Johnson left the ship, with $52.75 in her pocket. According to the ship's accounts, this was what was left of her whaleman's lay—or share of the oil—at the time of her discharge, once the advance she was paid when she signed Ship's Articles had been subtracted. It was quite a large sum by her standards (if not by Mr. Ruden's), and she hied herself off to New York to enjoy it.

And enjoy it, she did. On January 17 the *Nantucket Inquirer* printed a report that had appeared in the *New York Herald* the previous day, under the headline "A FEMALE SAILOR":

> Constable Joseph arrested yesterday, on suspicion, a young woman, called "Shorty," whom the officers found on the Five Points, flush of money, and spending the same very freely. He brought her before the magistrate, where on being questioned, she said that about thirteen months ago, she came off Blackwell's Island, having served out a sentence of three months as a common prostitute; and not wishing to engage again in the same pursuits in life . . . she assumed male attire by procuring a suit of sailor's clothing, and determined to go on a sea voyage. Consequently, to fulfill her designs, she proceeded to Nantucket . . . and then took passage in a whaling ship for a three years' cruise.

So it seems that Ann had yet another motive—or perhaps she figured that the magistrate would lend a more sympathetic ear to a plea that the cross-dressing was an eccentric attempt to reform her wicked ways than he would have to a bold statement that she had heard whaling was a good way to make money.

As it was, it was the money that had got her hauled up before the bench. According to the report, she had arrived in New York about a week before, "and having over $60, which she had made by her trip, she was spending it at various groggeries." That is, until she had been arrested, on the suspicion that the money was stolen. She was innocent of this crime, of course, but nonetheless it was startling behavior from the "extremely well-bred" girl the consul had pictured in his letter to Nantucket. The New York reporter gave a very different description of young "Shorty," though he did allow that she was "very good looking." Broad-built in figure, her hair cut short, Ann "both chewed and smoked tobacco, and talked sailor lingo very fluently," with the result that she seemed more like "a young man dressed up in female clothing" than a regular girl.

And so it would appear that Ann Johnson had a lot more in common with Mary Read than she did with Anne Bonny. Whatever the truth, she was certainly not the conventional heroine drawn in Nelson Haley's romantic version. As it was, it was proved that she had come honestly by the cash—for it seems that the officers of the whaler had sent the hat around to collect extra money before she left the ship in Paita—and Ann was discharged from custody. And that is the last we hear of her, though that is not quite the end of the matter. The owners of the *Christopher Mitchell* took their outrage over the consular bill all the way to the U.S. Secretary of State, but it does not seem as if they were ever reimbursed. And Captain Thomas Sullivan made confounded certain that he carried his wife on every voyage after that.

It is a lot easier to romanticize the story of another whaling cross-dresser, George Weldon. This young woman, whose real name was Georgiana Leonard, signed Articles on the whaling bark *America,* Captain John Luce, in the fall of 1862. No one asked any questions, for this was the height of the Civil War, and whaling hands were very hard to find. She looked likely enough, being tall, strong, and sturdy, though only about twenty years old. George claimed that she had served in the Confederate cavalry, and explained a newly healed cut on her cheek as a wound sustained during hand-to-hand combat. She had been taken prisoner and sent to a Union hospital, then released.

Once at sea, George proved a capable and well-liked member of the crew. She danced the best jig, and had a good fund of ballads, sung in a fine tenor voice. It was her temper that got her into trouble. First, she got into a ruckus with the "big black cook," and won the fight. "If he wasn't such a mean hard cuss I'd say he was a woman," Jethro Cottle, the third mate, observed at the time. All he got, according to his recollection, was a general laugh, but then, on Friday, January 9, 1863, everyone abruptly remembered what he had said.

The boats had been off a-whaling, but had returned to the ship because George had done her utmost to kill Robert G. Smith, the second officer. After several hours of rowing she had decided it was time for a rest, and when Smith decided to persuade her otherwise by punching some sense into her head with a paddle, she pulled a knife on him. The rest of the boat's crew had subdued her after a lively struggle, and then returned to the bark, so Smith could report her mutiny to the captain. Luce ordered a flogging, which involved stripping to the waist. Sullenly, George forestalled what would have been a riveting sight for the assembled crew, by letting on that she was female.

The laconic log entry for that day, apart from the usual seamanlike notations of weather and whales, reads, "This day found out George Weldon to be a woman, the first I ever suspected of such a thing." The chatter did not stop, however, neither then nor later. Harriet Allen, seafaring wife of whaling master Captain David E. Allen, of the bark *Merlin,* noted on August 25, 1869, that Captain John Adams Luce had come on board "to pay me a visit, and entertained me with a story about a woman who once went to *sea* with him, in men's clothing."

George was not put on shore for another six months. Luce had a lot more in common with Captain McIntire than with Captain Thomas Sullivan, for instead of worrying his head about getting Georgiana into skirts, he merely ordered her to trade jobs with the cabin boy. He didn't care about the proprieties, and as it proved, it didn't signify, anyway. As Jethro Cottle frankly admitted, "We couldn't think of her as a woman at all:

> She still wore her sailor togs, and besides, when you have come to look on a chap as a tough fellow, smoking tobacco and dancing jigs, and fighting with the cook, it's hard to change your mind and regard her as a woman.

The crew treated her well, however, no doubt regarding it as a capital joke, and were quite sorry when the *America* sailed into Port Louis on the island of Mauritius, and Georgiana left the ship. At long last she adopted woman's dress, Luce having organized a job for her as stewardess on a homebound clipper ship that was also in port. John Luce was displaying his practical streak yet again, for this meant she worked her passage home, so he avoided being stuck with the kind of bill that had so embarrassed Captain Thomas Sullivan.

For some reason, the episode was the making of young Georgiana. By sheer coincidence, both the clipper and the whaling bark were back in Port Louis on June 14, 1864, exactly one year later, and Georgiana was still serving as stewardess. She had done her job so well that the captain of the clipper had signed her on for another voyage. She came on board and visited all her old shipmates, and confided that she had fallen in love with the second officer of the clipper, and that they intended to marry. The crew of the *America* were all highly approving, finding her a "neat, prosperous looking woman."

The *America* got home on May 4, 1865, to the accompaniment of a great deal of public interest. The men were pestered for reminiscences of their erstwhile shipmate, and a New Bedford pub, The Sailor Boy, was dedicated to Georgiana. She herself did not drop entirely out of sight. Years later, after John Luce had retired to a Martha's Vineyard farm, she and her husband paid a call on him, which went so well that they repeated the visit several times in the following years.

Georgiana, without a doubt, had reformed, but this did not put a halt to her story being retold many, many times, usually in highly exaggerated form, and often to Captain Luce's great discredit. In a newspaper piece written in 1903 by a certain Ellis L. Howland, the dramatic revelation of Georgiana's true sex presented an unsurpassed chance for histrionics:

> "Yer will mutiny, will yer?" shouted the captain, plying the lash again. "Just peel his back, boys, and let's see how this cat feels on his cussed hide." The prisoner at bay gave one fearful yell. "Stand back, you cowards," he hissed. "Don't disgrace your manhood by striking me. You don't know what you're doing. Call me vile names if you will, but I'll kill the first man who tries to touch me. I am no man. I'm a woman."

"The writer," Howland blandly confessed, "feels inadequate to the portrayal of the scene of consternation which ensued"—which is even harder to believe than his version of the yarn. He had plenty of competition, though, as other authors transferred the story to other ships and other voyages, each producing his own melodramatic description.

One was a fictional account of the 1848 voyage of the *Lalla Rookh*, which was published in a racy little pamphlet called *History of Nantucket*

The Flogging. "The snow-white bosom of the maiden suddenly burst upon their view, in all its voluptuous beauty." As the satirist George Cruikshank might have seen it.
Adaptation by Ron Druett.

4 Year's Whaling Voyage. In this, the steerage boy, though popular and much admired for having saved the life of a fellow seaman, gets into trouble with the mate by collapsing with exhaustion in the boat. "You young rascal!" roars the officer, for they have lost the whale—a hideous crime in a whaler—and promises to teach him a lesson.

Seizing a rope, he braces for a hearty blow, but the boy interrupts him by crying weakly, "Please don't."

> "I will!" cried the thoroughly excited officer.
> The boy struggled to his knees, and, clasping his hands, said: "Do not dare to strike me, for I am—Oh, my God! I am a woman!" and fell forward in a swoon.

This kind of stirring situation was even more easily transferred to fiction, a good example being an 1848 novel, *Orlando Melville,* which was written by Herman Melville's old shipmate Ephraim Curtiss Hine, and evidently based on the Charles Waddall case. Hine's cross-dressed heroine is Kate Loraine, who disguises herself as a man so she can find her beloved, Orlando, who has been pressed into the British Navy. Falsely accused of attacking the ship's steward, she is sentenced to a flogging:

"Strip yourself, sir!"

"Never!" replied Kate, firmly, feeling that the crisis of her fate had now indeed arrived.

"Then I'll soon find a way to strip you—you insubordinate rascal! Quarter masters, strip that boy, and seize him up at the gangway. I'll learn him to refuse to obey my orders." . . .

In less than two minutes her jacket was unbuttoned, and literally torn off her by brutal force!

It is unnecessary to portray the astonishment—the amazement which took possession of everyone present, when the garment having been stripped from her shoulders, the snow white bosom of the maiden suddenly burst upon their view, in all its voluptuous beauty.

Unnecessary, indeed. The captain, muttering, "Whew! Here's a go," and "By George, we shall never hear the last of this affair," orders her instant release.

Chapter Fourteen

WAR BRIDE

*Dined at Nelsons and his dolly—called on old Ud-
ney, went to the opera with him. He introduced me
to a very handsome Greek woman.*
                    —Captain Thomas Fremantle,
                    Royal Navy, December 3, 1794

In May 1796, when Betsey Wynne was just eighteen, she noted that Napoleon had celebrated his brilliant victory against the Austrians by leading his triumphant forces into the city of Milan. The Wynne family was living in Florence at the time, uncomfortably close to this scene of action, and despite the usual social round of parties, masked balls, operas, and concerts, her father, Richard, was beginning to feel concerned. Then, in June, Napoleon signed one armistice with the kingdom of Naples and another with Pope Pius VI. Taking fright, Wynne gathered his family and fled to the Tuscan port of Leghorn (now Livorno), and begged the protection of the British fleet.

Betsey did not want to leave Florence at all. "Everybody laughs at his being so great a coward," she wrote. They "arrived at Leghorn at eleven in the morning," to find "a most terrible bustle and noise—All packing up and getting on board the ships. We hardly had time to get a little break-fast, they hurried us so terribly to quit the place and Captain Fremantle took us on board his Frigate the *Inconstant* a most beautiful ship."

Despite having earlier expressed "not the least wish of going a sea voyage," Betsey was instantly reconciled. "I found the *Inconstant* so fine so clean so comfortable so many civil persons that I was quite delighted and regretted no more that the french had obliged us to run away." Not only was the ship beautiful, and the officers amazingly sociable, but the captain, Thomas Fremantle, was entrancing. "He pleases me more than any man I have yet seen."

Though not handsome, there was something about "his fiery black eyes" that she found quite captivating—and he was kind and gallant as well, for he immediately hosted a little party, complete with harpsichord sent on board. Then, when it became apparent that there was nowhere to

Betsey Wynne. Artist: Ron Druett.

lay their heads because of the crush of refugees like themselves in the port, he was "so obliging as to propose us staying on board his ship—he did the honor's so well, that we all got a good Bed or Cot and he had *none*." In short, he had won Betsey's heart from that first fiery, dark-eyed glance.

At the time of this strange and hectic meeting, Thomas Fremantle was thirty years old. He was a thorough seaman, having been in the Navy for eighteen years, and was a longtime friend of Horatio Nelson, though the two men were outwardly very different.

Nelson was a small, restless man, seven years Fremantle's senior, while Thomas Fremantle was large, prone to indolence, and a dedicated bachelor. Nelson, on the other hand, was a respectably married man with a stepson, having wed Frances Herbert Nisbet in March 1787.

According to the stories, Nelson had fallen in love with the demure, pretty, very proper twenty-seven-year-old widow the moment he had first laid eyes on her. For him, the match was a good one, for Fanny was somewhat out of his class. Her connections were excellent—and Nelson, who was extremely ambitious, needed good connections to rise as he wanted in the Navy. Her father, William Woolward, had been a senior judge. When they met, Fanny was hostess of Montpelier, the mansion that belonged to her wealthy uncle, President John Herbert of Nevis. One of Nelson's earliest admirers, Prince William, third son of George III (and future King William IV), approved of the match so highly that he attended the wedding.

However, Nelson had probably mistaken his own feelings, for when he decided he was in love with Fanny Nisbet, it was on the rebound from an infatuation with a much more sophisticated woman, Mary Moutray. He took Fanny from the balmy shores of the island of Nevis to the cold fogs of England, which did not suit her health. While she and his widowed father, the Reverend Edmund, immediately hit it off, he found she was absentminded in domestic affairs. Though she worked hard at cultivating the right contacts, she did not share his craving for social rank and acclaim. Why should she, when she loved him the way he was? Probably worst of all, she did not give him the child of his own that he craved.

More pertinently, Fanny Nelson was not sensual. In reticent England, Nelson probably wouldn't have wanted a lascivious wife anyway, for he himself put it on record that he would not allow her to take erotic liberties with his body.

Captain Thomas Fremantle.
Artist: Ron Druett, after Edmond Bristow.

Here in the Mediterranean, however, Nelson was just as susceptible to the flashing-eyed, full-breasted Italians as his friend Fremantle. Indeed, they were both connoisseurs of the dollies, as courtesans were called then, Thomas Fremantle everlastingly confiding to his diary that he was in love with this, that, or the other dolly.

This sort of behavior was not at all unusual, Navy captains being a goatish set, on the whole. Some even took their dollies to sea. Captain Richard Bennett of the *Fame* had a "Miss Jen——gs on board as his mistress," who had come with him all the way from England. "She was a lovely-looking woman," one of his men reminisced, "and modest in a great degree, compared with the majority who ploughed the seas on the same footing." Alas, the demure Miss Jennings was sent home from Minorca and replaced with a voluptuous brunette.

Much of this feminine company was found in Leghorn, the same port where Fremantle took the Wynnes on board his ship in June 1796. Both he and Nelson consorted a good deal with the British Consul there, Mr. Udney, who seemed to think that one of his most important duties was introducing lonely naval officers to attractive and available women. Through Udney, Nelson met Adelaide Correglia, an opera singer who pleasured the hours of many a naval officer, and may have been a British spy as well. She became his kept mistress, for he sent her money through an Admiralty contractor. In the summer of 1795, he had La Correglia aboard his ship, Fremantle expressing the private opinion that his friend "makes himself ridiculous with that woman."

To make the social situation even more interesting, Fanny's son (and Nelson's stepson), Josiah, was on board as well. By the time of Fremantle's first meeting with Betsey, however, Nelson had dropped the opera singer, and Fremantle had taken her up himself. In fact, the night he so gallantly organized beds on the frigate for the Wynne contingent, he found his own comfort in Adelaide's arms.

On board the well-named *Inconstant,* however, Betsey was both unsuspecting and very happy. Next morning, she "got up much earlier than I thought I should, but there was such a noise in the ship that there was no means of sleeping." The view from the stern gallery was a bustling one. "There is a vast number of English ships here, they are all going to sail for Corsica except the *Inconstant* which will stay to the Last and then will go to join the fleet off Toulon. We dined with Captain Fremantle who continued to treat us with the greatest kindness—just as if he had known us

Frigate Inconstant. Artist: Ron Druett.

these great many years and we only saw him yesterday for the first time."

And so the convoy with all the refugees sailed for Corsica, where Betsey disconsolately prepared to say farewell to this new idol, the Wynnes being left in the care of Lord Garlies of the frigate *Lively.* To Betsey's delighted surprise, though, Fremantle arrived with the news that he had "asked leave of the Admiral for to convey us on board the

Britannia a hundred gunned ship and he will take us in a few days to the Fleet, there we will remain till we have a safe opportunity of going to England." To the casual reader, taking a family of frivolous civilians on board a man-of-war that was lying under the guns of the hostile port of Toulon might seem the height of foolhardiness, but Betsey merely exulted.

To celebrate, a "very pleasant Ball" was staged on board the *Lively* that night. Two days later, Fremantle reciprocated by staging his own ball— "the deck was most elegantly drest up and looked really like a charming large Ball room all the guns being removed." The party went on so late that the family slept on board, but then, next day, the war suddenly intruded again. "Whilst we were sitting very quietly at dinner Captain Fremantle received a letter from the Vice Roy which obliged him to sail immediately."

The Viceroy of Corsica, Sir Gilbert Elliot (later Lord Minto) was the kind of man a mere captain obeyed at once, without question. The gun deck had been stripped of guns, the frigate's commander was busy entertaining guests, some of the ship's complement were still on shore, but nonetheless all sail was instantly set. "I dare say had we not been on board his ship we could not have went with him, for he was in such a hurry that he could not wait for some of his officers that were on shore and remained behind. I cannot conceive where we are going," Betsey blithely added, but "as long as we stay on board the *Inconstant* with this excellent man I do not care what part of the world we go to."

On July 14 they came up with the fleet. It must have been a magnificent sight, Betsey writing, "Nothing so fine as the sight of this Fleet always under sail and so near Toulon that you may easily see the town and the french shipping." She was subdued, however, for the Wynnes were to be shifted to the *Britannia*, as Fremantle had received orders to sail to Algiers. Betsey couldn't help but be impressed with the grandeur of the bigger vessel, writing, "I was not a little surprised when I first came into this ship as it is one of the largest that ever was made it has 100 guns 260 men, a three decker of course. I find it like a Castle." Captain Thomas Foley, the commander of the *Britannia*, "behaves with the greatest kindness towards us." In fact, he was delighted to have a jolly party on board. "We will have there as good accomodation," wrote Betsey, "as we would have in any house on shore."

Nevertheless, she was desolate. Fremantle had bid her a somewhat equivocal farewell, giving her a ring as a keepsake and promising to correspond (a promise he didn't keep), but also informing her that "an imprudent match at present would be his ruin and make him lose the fruits of eighteen years service and pain. What can be done!" Betsey agitated, and answered, "Wait with patience." For his part, Fremantle admitted, "Serious thoughts about Betsey. If I was not such a poor wretch." Just before the *Inconstant* left the fleet, he penned a quick note, promising to persuade Admiral Sir John Jervis to allow him to take the Wynnes to England when his current mission was over, a prospect which made Betsey feel "exceedingly happy."

Admiral Sir John Jervis. Nicknamed Hanging Jervis for his strict disciplinary nature, he was made Earl of St. Vincent after the Battle of Cape St. Vincent in 1797.
Artist: Ron Druett, after Lemuel Abbot.

Life on board the *Britannia* was as social as it had been on the *Inconstant*. "We lead a very regular life here. Breakfast at 8 dine at half past two sup before 9 and go to bed at ten. Captain Foley keeps an excellent good table his ship is a little Town—you get all your desire in it." Like Fremantle and Lord Garlies, Thomas Foley put on parties for the Wynnes' entertainment, inviting other captains from the fleet to come and dine and dance, though one fellow, Sir Charles Knowles—"an old bachelor who Commands the *Golliath*"—got himself into a scrape by doing so: "he went so near shore that he was within gun shot."

Then, on July 29, the family received a note from the admiral, Sir John Jervis, asking them to dine with him on board the flagship *Victory*. They accepted this summons "with infinite pleasure," even though it had been sent at the peculiar hour of four in the morning. When they arrived, the admiral "was on Deck to receive us with the greatest civility and kindness nothing stiff or formal about him and we were not at all embarrassed as I feared we should be." Jervis, who had been nicknamed "Hanging Jervis" because of his strict disciplinarian nature, and was known as a deeply religious man of high integrity, was about to display a side of his character that most history books do not reveal. "He desired we should pay the tribute that was due to him at our entering his Cabin," Betsey related:

This was to kiss him which the Ladies did very willingly. Lord Garlies came soon after us. The Admiral abused him for not having yet saluted us, the consequence was that we were kissed a second time. . . . Nothing can express how kind, gallant and friendly the Admiral was to us, he is a fine old man, though past seventy, he is as fresh and brisk as if he was only thirty. He said he would wish us to stay with the Fleet all the summer that when we were tired of Captain Foley we should go on board the *Victory*. . . . It was a large party and we were very gay, laughed much and made a monstrous noise at table. . . . We were obliged to sing a duet after dinner. We did not stay late for as Admiral Jervis gets up at two oclock in the morning he goes to bed at half past eight.

Sir John dubbed the Wynnes "the Amiables," and often invited them on board the *Victory*—"a much finer ship than the *Britannia*." The "Amiables" were easy on the eye, and useful, too, Betsey and her sister Eugenia being summoned to interpret when some Germans were being cross-examined. Their reward was more kisses—"The old Gentleman is very partial to kisses."

And so life in the fleet went on, while the lines of ships sailed back and forth, back and forth. It was not all plain sailing. A couple of times the weather cheated them of a promised ball, and another time Betsey got a bad pain in her side, which she attributed to lack of exercise, but she managed to "dance it off" successfully. Suitable gowns had to be fashioned and furbished, Sir John himself taking much interest in this, noting in a letter to Nelson that it was fashionable to wear fine velvet gowns, which fell open to reveal petticoats "of white crape or gauze which the ladies embroider or ornament for themselves."

There were some frights. On August 9, "Sir John Jervis got us all in a terrible scrape." The fleet suddenly lost the wind and was becalmed in reach of the batteries, and "some of the shots came so near to us that C[aptain] Foley was almost tempted to send us ladies in the Cockpit" (the afterpart of the lowest deck of the ship, where the surgeon's operating table was set up during battle). Naturally, the Wynnes did not want to go there, declaring they were "not in the least alarmed and looked all the time at this famous firework that was quite a new sight for us."

Betsey was much more worried about Captain Foley than she was about the cannon. Foley—whom she called "the old Gentleman" and "the grey headed gallant" despite the fact that he was not yet forty—had fallen madly in love with her, and her parents were in favor of the match.

"I wish I had never never come on board the *Britannia*," she passionately wrote. Reassuringly, however, Sir John Jervis declared that he was in favor of a match with Fremantle. Richard Wynne grumbled that Fremantle "had not what was necessary for the marriage state, any fortune," but Sir John pointed out that Fremantle was in a very good way to get one, meaning that he had a good chance to take enemy ships—or prizes—a proportion of the value of which was divided between captain and crew, with the captain taking the lion's share of three eighths, out of which his flag commander (Sir John himself, in this case) would take the equivalent of one eighth. The reason Sir John was so certain that Fremantle would do well was that he himself had sent the *Inconstant* to patrol an area where there was an excellent chance of finding prizes. Obviously, Fremantle was one of his best-liked commanders—and it paid rich dividends to be a favorite captain of the commander in chief.

Sir William Hamilton, British ambassador to the Court of Naples.

Artist: Ron Druett, after Grignion.

Then, in September, the Wynnes were involved in another mass retreat, for the *Britannia* sailed to Bastia to help in the withdrawal of the British forces. They took refuge on the island of Elba, where the *Inconstant* dropped anchor in October. *"Great was the joy at his arrival!"* wrote Eugenia in her journal. Fremantle himself, while increasingly intrigued with Betsey, was still dithering, dining with Nelson, getting "mortal" drunk, falling asleep at balls, and making "Love to a Miss Watson." On October 18, however, he "went at night to the *Britannia*, where I had much talk with Foley. Find he is violently smitten." Discovering that he had a rival for Betsey's hand spurred him to negotiations with her parents. He wrote on October 20: "Mrs. W. offers 5000 [pounds] or 10 at his death"—this being an attempt at establishing the amount of the dowry.

It wasn't enough, so Fremantle sailed off in pursuit of more prizes. He was in and out of Naples as well, going to the opera and dallying with a dolly named Hannah. Gossip about this got to the ears of Eugenia, who noted in her journal that she believed *"indifference* has taken the place of what he felt *at first."* She also noted that he, like all the men, drank too much, "but you may as soon keep a fish from drinking as a sailor." But still Betsey could see no fault in her hero.

On December 29, Fremantle took the Wynne family to Naples, musing on the thirty-first, "Am amazingly attached to Betsey, but cannot make up my mind to marry. I cannot say I have behaved very well." Next day, Eugenia wrote more or less the same thing. "I believe that B's ascendant over Fremantle continues to be about the same, but he is always undecided, he would and would not, she would, and would heartily, how will it end?"

It ended very happily. Finally, on January 10, 1797, Fremantle "sent a proposal to Mr. Wynne about marrying his daughter. Everything concluded as I could wish. Everything to be finished [signed] on the 12th." Eugenia was more open about the financial side of the transaction. "Fremantle was here both in the morning and evening, he spoke to Papa who behaved very handsomely in granting him my sister and 8000 pounds."

It was a popular match, probably because the British Ambassador to the Court of Naples, Sir William Hamilton, approved of it so highly. "Sir William Hamilton and his Lady came in the morning," wrote Betsey on the eve of the wedding. "It is impossible to say how civil they were, especially Lady Hamilton, she is a charming woman, beautiful and exceedingly good humoured and amiable. She took all the management of the affair, and the wedding is to be tomorrow at her own house."

This is indicative of Betsey's ecstatic frame of mind, for the "beautiful" and "amiable" Lady Hamilton was a controversial figure. Nelson, who met Emma Hamilton in September 1793 during the course of negotiations with the King of Naples, would have agreed with Betsey, for he thought the Ambassador's wife "wonderfully kind and good." Thomas Fremantle, on the other hand, noted that he had to make an effort to "get on tolerably with my lady, whom I dislike."

Born April 26, 1765, and baptized Emy Lyon in May, Emma was the daughter of a Cheshire blacksmith who died before she was two months old. Her mother took her to Hawarden, in Wales, and gave the baby to her mother, Sarah Kidd, to raise—this word being a misnomer, for Emy was allowed to run wild, and was almost illiterate when she first made her name at the age of sixteen by performing an exotic dance routine in flimsy draperies. Her employer was a London quack, James Graham, who guaranteed a successful pregnancy to infertile couples who spent an expensive night in a special bed in his "Temple of Health and Hymen" off the Strand. Emy was one of a cast of beautiful young female assistants advertised as virgins. Their job was to sing and dance while thinly clad, to put the patients in the right mood, as it were.

Emma Hamilton, idealized in one of her famous attitudes.
Artist: Ron Druett, after George Romney.

At this stage, if not earlier, Emma became a dolly. A sea captain, John Willet Payne, is credited with her seduction. Then she became the mistress of Sir Harry Featherstonhaugh, and under his tutelage learned to ride fast horses and dance naked on the dining room table. When she had the bad judgment to become pregnant, however, Sir Harry promptly dropped her. Panic-stricken, Emma turned for help to one of his friends, Charles Greville, a thirty-three-year-old bachelor and member of Parliament. Greville, a shrewd but impecunious man, agreed to support her until after the child was born. In return, he gained a seventeen-year-old mistress and a free housekeeper, for her mother came along too, having mysteriously changed her name to Mrs. Cadogan. Withal, he had made himself a very good bargain. The baby, named Emma Carew, was left behind in Hawarden with Sarah Kidd.

Greville, a connoisseur of art and beauty, taught Emy—now Emma Hart—to read and sing. He also had the excellent judgment to sponsor a relatively unknown artist by the name of George Romney, commissioning him to paint Emma's portrait first in 1782. Romney became besotted with her, portraying her in more than twenty different classical poses. Like Greville's uncle, Sir William Hamilton, he thought Emma one of the most beautiful creatures of the age.

Greville, by contrast, was thoughtfully contemplating the recently wid-owed Sir William, who was in England on holiday. Greville was pretty sure that he was his uncle's heir, but he worried that Sir William might remarry and beget himself another beneficiary. And, as usual, he was strapped for cash to pay his debts. The solution that occurred to him was not particularly gentlemanly. Nonetheless, he set to subtly suggesting that his uncle take over his mistress.

Sir William was slow to pick up the hint, however. By the end of 1784, having got no further than merely flirting with Emma, he was headed back to Naples, having invited both Greville and Emma to visit. In the event, only Emma arrived, her mother in tow. Greville had sent letters ahead that were more open in their urging. After all, the solicitous nephew argued, "at your age a clean and comfortable woman is not su-perfluous." At the age of fifty-five, Sir William was not sure that his viril-ity was up to the challenge. In reply, Greville urged him to experiment. So, in the end, the bargain was concluded. Sir William got a "cleanly and sweet" bedfellow with huge violet eyes, an impressive bust, and auburn hair down to her heels, and Greville got rid of his debts.

Emma was furious. When she arrived in Naples, she'd had no idea of the arrangement. It had been very pleasant to find that she was an instant hit at the Court, her fans including Queen Maria Carolina as well as num-berless gentlemen, but in return she was supposed "to go to bed to him, Sir Wm!" Well, she fumed at the end of this letter to her coldhearted ex-protector, "I will make him marry me." And so she did. She became the mistress of the old knight, but launched a calculated campaign as well. First, she spread the rumor that they were married already. Then, she persuaded Queen Maria Carolina to hint that while Emma Hart, mistress of the British Ambassador, was persona non grata at the Court of Naples, Emma, Lady Hamilton, would certainly be received.

And so, on September 6, 1791, Emma achieved her aim, by becoming Lady Hamilton in a ceremony at Marylebone Church during a visit to London. Sir William was sixty-one, and she was twenty-six. Romney cel-ebrated with another burst of portraits, and Emma astonished society with her statuesque "attitudes," in which she let down her hair, pulled a few shawls about her body, and froze in one classical pose after another while her new husband held up lamps. It was as if Sir William, a noted collector of antiquities, had a whole collection in one woman.

And so it was as the well-established wife of the British Ambassador that Emma Hamilton hosted the wedding of Elizabeth Wynne and Cap-tain Thomas Fremantle, on January 12, 1797. Fremantle recorded, "Was married to Elizabeth Wynne at Sir Wm. Hamilton's, where we dined." His tone was brief and preoccupied, as he had other things on his mind. "Dressed ship and fired 21 guns," he wrote—not to celebrate his wedding, but because it was the birthday of the King of Naples. Betsey had a great deal more to say:

> NAPLES. At one oclock we all went to Lady Hamiltons where the ceremony was performed. . . . What I felt at the wedding is not to be described. Prince Augustus gave me away, Sir Gilbert Elliot, Sir William Hamilton, Mr. Lambton, Colonel Drinkwater were all witnesses. We all dined at Sir Williams, went to the opera in the evening and returned to the Albergo Reale where we intended to be married by a Catholic priest. But we could not persuade the scrupulous Bishop to give us a dispensation. At last we found a priest that gave us his blessing and appeased Mamma's conscience.

There was a proviso attached to this second wedding ceremony—that when a dispensation arrived from Rome, they had to get married again. And so Captain Thomas Fremantle and Elizabeth Wynne were married three times, the third occasion being late in the afternoon two days later, after Betsey's presentation to the Queen. And then, on January 15, 1797, they sailed away.

"I find it quite odd to be alone here," Betsey wrote—and strange indeed it must have seemed, when her family had spent so much time as a large and convivial group on board the frigate *Inconstant*. Nonetheless, it was the start of married life, in the most unlikely confines of a wooden ship of war.

Chapter Fifteen

WOMEN OF WAR

Fremantle is all attention and kindness. I have
got a comfortable little cabin where I can do what
I like.

—Betsey Fremantle,
January 15, 1797,
on board *Inconstant*

B etsey Fremantle was by no means the first or last mariner's wife to live on board a Navy vessel—or on the *Inconstant,* for that matter. As we have seen, in 1791, Mary Ann Parker was sailing the world on HMS *Gorgon.* Both of Jane Austen's admiral brothers took their wives to sea. Captain William Dillon of the *Leopard,* though he was scornful of the captain of the *Camilla* who kept a mistress on board "that did not do much honour to his station," carried both his wife and her daughter, marrying the stepdaughter off to one of his lieutenants.

And it was not just the wives of captains who were accorded the privilege, for the wives of the Boatswain, Gunner, and Carpenter often sailed, too, along with the wives of the Sailmaker, Cooper, Cook, Steward, and Purser. At any given moment on any wooden man-of-war, in fact, it was almost guaranteed that there would be a company of respectable matrons on board, apparently quite undismayed by the prospect of going into battle.

The system started because their husbands were "standing officers," appointed to serve on one particular ship, "standing" by her whether she was laid up or in active service. The ship, in effect, was their lifetime home, for they were "in constant employ" with this one vessel, all the way from her construction until she was broken up or they died, whichever came first. By contrast, all other members of the ship's company held their positions for the duration of a single commission, moving from ship to ship. This was the theory, anyway. In practice, standing officers were regularly promoted from small ships to bigger ones, and those who wanted to go to sea exchanged with those who did not. Still, the current ship was considered home. When the officers changed ships, their wives and families went with them, just like moving from one workplace to another today. These wives and children were supposed to be landed when the ship was commissioned for a voyage, but often they were not, simply because there was nowhere else for them to go. While it was against regulations for petty officers' families to sail, it happened all the time. All that was necessary was for the captain to turn a blind eye.

It was a comprehensive disregard of the rules, and a testament to the women's courage, too. "John Knyveton," a naval surgeon who served during the Seven Years War, was amazed at the gallantry of women who chose to go to sea with their men, "sharing his rotten meat and foul water, the storms and wet, darning his shirts, holding his hand in the black hell of the cockpit; counting all as nothing if they might be beside him to the end."* William Richardson, Gunner of the *Tromp,* related in his memoirs that he did not want his wife to sail in 1800, when the ship was assigned to the West Indies, that station being notorious as a hotbed of fever. She put up a spirited argument, and finally he consented, because "the Captain's, the Master's, the Purser's and the Boatswain's wives were going with them." The Boatswain, as it happened, embarked his whole family, and the captain's wife contributed one more child during the passage, a son.

Giving birth at sea was a natural hazard of the process. "Of all the quaint accidents aboard a ship hard pressed as we are by the elements," wrote "John Knyveton" in December 1756. The "wife of the third Lieutenant, Mr. Preston, was delivered of a fine boy at noon [to]day. Doctor Payne and I to attend her in her stateroom forrard of the mizzen mast, and water running over the floor and more entering under the door, and

---

* *Surgeon's Mate: The Diary of John Knyveton, Surgeon in the British Fleet During the Seven Years War 1756–1762.* Edited and Transcribed by Ernest Gray. London: Robert Hale, 1942. While this journal is fictional, the social details are well founded, the book being based on a "Memoir of my own Life, written in 1779," by Thomas Denman, M.D. (1733–1815), and which was published as an introduction in the seventh edition (London, 1832) of his textbook of obstetrics, *Introduction to Midwifery.*

Aboard a man-of-war. Sketch by Thomas Rowlandson, 1782.

she delivered on blankets which have not been dry this fortnight past.

"But Lord, women be strange creatures," he meditated. Some seamen had been glimpsed lurking in the alley, "to wish her good luck." Her husband "would have kicked them down the length of the main deck," but she sat up, pulled a shawl about her shoulders, and called for a comb and mirror, saying, "let the poor creatures see the baby if they wish":

> and so they crowded into the cabinn, and fingered the infant's hair till it bawled, and she sitting up in her bunk as queenly as Royalty delivered amongst a court; and the Lieutenant muttering they were mutinous hounds and he would flog 'em all, only she frowns at him and lays a finger on her lip for silence; and he bursts into a roar of laughter and cries, "Out upon you you rogue, you have boarded me, have your way" and gets an extra tot of rum served out for all hands to drink the health of young True Blue Jack, as the seamen have nicknamed the babe.

There are several records of births during major battles. "John Knyveton" noted that one of the women on board "grows heavy with child, and is near her time." Five days later the drums were rolling, as the ship was cleared for action, "sailors singing and huzzaing like mad things; even the women helping, and the poor quean so near her time asking for some work." The surgeons set her to tearing up rags for bandages, but within hours she was seized with her pains. "She had insisted on remaining by her man, a stolid fellow one Nat Combes, a shepherd by trade," but the gun-deck being "no lying-in hospital," "Knyveton" insisted she go down into the cockpit, where the surgeons were getting ready to cope with the wounded. She wept and refused, so one of the men picked her up, "and carries her down to the orlop deck, her man holding her hand, and then running back to his station, helped by a whimsical kick from the bosun." Despite the appalling circumstances all went well, and the baby was named "Thunder Dick," in honor of their beloved admiral, "Wry-neck Dick" Boscawen.

A baby born on board the *Tremendous* during the Glorious First of

Frigates battling. Artist: Ron Druett.

June (in 1794) was named Daniel Tremendous Mackenzie. Another little boy was born on board HMS *Romulus* during the Battle of the Nile, on August 1, 1798, and promptly christened Owen Nile Reardon Smith. If it were not for their unusual names, they scarcely would have been noticed, for there were plenty of young boys on board already, in an official capacity. Though often as young as twelve, they were there as apprentices and midshipmen. Because of this, schoolmasters were carried on larger men-of-war. These teachers might allow other children to join their classes, giving them a better education than they would have had on shore. Certainly, the little boys would have skylarked in the rigging with the enlisted boys, unconsciously equipping themselves for a career at sea.

All in all, when on hostile maneuvers a warship must have resembled a country hamlet almost as much as when she was lying in her home port. There were downsides, however. William Richardson's fears about disease in the West Indies were well founded, for yellow fever struck, and very few of the women who sailed on the *Tromp* returned. Commodore Richard Morris was despised by some of those he commanded—not because his wife was there, but because they thought he allowed her to influence his decisions. On board the frigate *New-York* in September 1803, Nancy Staines, the wife of the Quarter Gunner, aborted a fetus, and died of "suppuration of the womb," despite the attendance of Dr. St. Medard, the ship's surgeon. Mrs. Martin, the Boatswain's wife, was the only woman on board during the bloody mutiny on the *Hermione* in September 1797. After her husband's body was heaved into the sea, one of the ringleaders, Redman, broke into the Boatswain's cabin, where—as a crew member, John Jones, noted—he shut himself in "with the Boatswain's wife, and I saw him no more that night."

Seafaring wives, whether the wives of officers or of captains, did not get prizes, or shares of prizes, and were not paid a salary, even though there are many records of women playing their part in battle. During the Battle of the Nile, John Nicol, a seaman on the *Goliath,* related in his journal that when he was stationed in the powder magazine, he got news of how the fight was going from the "women who carried the powder. The women behaved as well as the men and got a present for their bravery from the Grand Signior." This august personage did indeed send a purse of two thousand sequins to Nelson, to be distributed among the wounded, but it is unlikely that any of it got to the women, because their presence was so informal.

Nor did they warrant a pension. "The only female that was at the Battle of Trafalgar, more than 30 years since, is now living at No. 52 John-street, Ordnance-place, Chatham," reported the *Kentish Gazette* in 1836. "She was in the *Euryalus,* now a convict ship at Chatham, which was under a fire of four ships of the line. Admiral Collingwood promised to try to get a pension for her. She has a large family having had 14 children, six of whom are now living." The editor of the *United Service Gazette,* which reprinted this item on September 17, appended the comment, "We would take leave to recommend her case to the noble lord at the head of the Admiralty." Whether this advice was followed is unknown.

Equally unfairly, these women were not eligible for medals. "I was much indebted to the gunner's wife who gave her husband and me a drink of wine every now and then, which lessened our fatigue much," Nicol continued in his account. "There were some of the women wounded, and one woman belonging to Leith died of her wounds and was buried on a small island in the bay." In the recommendation for bravery issued to a man named Alex Browne for valor during the Battle of Lake Champlain in 1814, it was mentioned (but only in passing) that a woman on board HMS *Confiance* was one of those who had died.

There was also the unpleasant fact that these women regularly had to witness brutal punishments being handed out to men who could well be friends and comrades, or even their own husbands. "The weather was bad and in general this a dismal day and unlucky," wrote Betsey Fremantle on January 25, 1797:

Last night the ships company all got drunk and behaved horridly ill. Much flogging this morning which made Fremantle ill and broke my heart. I could distinctly hear the poor wretches cry out for mercy, in the cabin. A man broke his leg. After all this misery I was glad to get out of the Ship and went over to the town.

Thursday Jan. 26th. A Court Martial to try three Mariners of this ship. The weather so bad I could not go on shore, stayed quietly on board. . . .

Saturday Jan. 28. I was quite miserable all the morning as the three Mariners were punished and flogged along side of every ship, some men flogged likewise on board.

Flogging was administered with an instrument known as the cat-o'-nine-tails, because it was made up of nine pieces of rope, attached to a handle that might be made of wood but was more often fashioned of rope, for flexibility and whipping action. If the crime being punished was theft, then the tails were knotted at intervals along their length. First, the whole company was called to witness punishment, and after the thirty-sixth Article of War had been ritually read out, the offender was named, and the nature of the crime described, after which the captain pronounced the sentence and the number of lashes. The victim's back was stripped, and then he was triced up to a wooden grating or the mizzen rigging, his arms stretched upward and outward in a spread-eagle shape. At the captain's order, the Boatswain's mates, under control of the Boatswain, took turns (because they used up so much strength in each blow) carrying out the flogging.

According to one eyewitness account, after two dozen lashes with this horrible tool (a common punishment for drunkenness), "the lacerated back looks inhuman; it resembles roasted meat burnt nearly black before a scorching fire." The tricing up was necessary, for an unrestrained man would have fallen down at the first stroke. In fact, the man who broke his leg was probably injured when the ropes that tied him to the grating gave way. So severe was this punishment that twenty-four lashes could maim a man for life. A flogging around the fleet, where the convicted man was rowed from ship to ship and dealt a dozen strokes beside each one, while the crews looked on and the drums rolled out the Rogue's March, was a virtual death sentence.

This was a brutal age, when hanging was public, gibbets with dangling skeletons in chains were found at major crossroads, and whipping posts and pillories were set up in town squares. In this respect, discipline and punishment at sea were normally no worse than on land. Flogging was not confined to men-of-war, either, being a major means of punishing misdemeanors on merchant ships as well. However, many captains, like Thomas Fremantle, were civilized enough to be "made ill" when forced to hand out such barbaric punishment.

In 1845, Commodore Stockton confided to the Turrill family, when they were taking passage to Honolulu on the frigate U.S. *Congress,* that he "would like to abolish whipping in the Navy." The writer, Consul Turrill's daughter Elizabeth, who was thirteen at the time, recorded that the cabin doors were closed and the blinds put up during the ritual of punishment. "I go in the stateroom, and hold a pillow round my head till they are opened again. Then I feel certain all is over."

Otherwise, there was a lot to commend about this sailing along on wooden men-of-war. While Betsey Fremantle could be sure of good meals, a wife-carrying seaman had to share his rations with his wife and any children, but it is very unlikely that this led to any privation. Indeed, a petty officer's wife could have been much more comfortable than on shore. She had her own space in the ship, along with a certain amount of privacy, its situation and coziness depending on her husband's job and rank. During the day, time would be spent on deck, and in cold weather the wives congregated in the galley to gossip by the cooking fires. An old saying is that a true seaman was "begotten in the galley, born under a gun, every tooth a marlin spike, every finger a fish hook, and his blood right good Stockholm tar"—which broadly hints that the galley might have been a favorite spot for other occupations as well.

There were luxuries, even. The youngest boys were often assigned to the petty officers' wives as servants, doing small jobs for them like cleaning shoes or fetching tidbits from the galley. The arrangement was mutually beneficial, for the wife would knit for the boy, sew his clothes, and perhaps teach him how to read and write, if she was literate. William Richardson recorded that his wife befriended a young stowaway when he was discovered on board the *Tromp,* and was desolate when he was transferred to the flagship to serve the admiral.

And there were many advantages for the husbands, too. Thomas Fremantle was pleasantly surprised at how much he enjoyed married life on board his ship. Betsey played the pianoforte that had been carried on board, and he composed poetry, which he set to music. Together, they dined as guests of the "gentlemen" in the gunroom, and when he got tipsy during a drinking session on the *Minerva,* he was pleased to note, "My Betsey uncommonly good humoured about it." And then, on April 19, they celebrated Betsey's nineteenth birthday.

While these civilized little activities passed the time away on the frigate, things were going badly for the English. "The news very bad, Mantua taken and the french on their march to Rome," wrote Betsey on February 15. "The *Bombay Castle* was lost in entering the Tagus and the *Zealous* so much disabled that she is ordered home. The *Courageous* was also lost a little time ago at Gibraltar." At the end of March, Fremantle was ordered to escort a convoy to Gibraltar, a slow and uncomfortable journey for Betsey. When they finally arrived, "Fremantle went on board with Admiral Nelson and I slept alone in the cabin all night, the first night I have slept alone since I have been married, did not like it."

When he arrived back, it was with more bad news. At home, there had been a "Mutiny that happened in the Fleet at Portsmouth," while closer to hand Captain Oakes of the *Sea Horse* was "very poorly wishes much to get to England, and has wrote to the Admiral about changing with Fremantle." On May 31 it was confirmed. Captain Fremantle was not pleased with the change, but orders were orders, so he and Betsey shifted to the *Sea Horse,* and Oakes took their ship home. A month later Betsey dined

The casualty. Artist: Ron Druett, after a painting by Ward.

on board the *Ville de Paris* and became reacquainted with Sir John Jervis. "Sir John Jervis very gallant as usual, to accommodate me he is going to send this ship home," she wrote. Instead, they were sent to join the blockade of Cadiz.

On July 3, "Admiral Nelson and Captain Martin came on board. Captain Foley dined with us. Fremantle was out all night, he went with Admiral Nelson to bombard the town, much firing all night. I was anxious for Fremantle and did not go to bed until he returned. Spanish gun boats and a barge were taken, many people killed and wounded." Two nights later, Fremantle was in the assault again, "did not return till four oclock in the morning. I was quite unhappy all the time he was away, and sat up till three." On July 6, Admiral Sir John Jervis "wrote that this bombardment must be given over." Betsey added, "Thank God, it was sacrificing men for nothing."

On July 21, however, 350 men from Admiral Nelson's *Theseus* arrived on board the *Sea Horse,* as part of a doomed attempt to capture a Spanish treasure ship from the port of Santa Cruz, Tenerife. Three frigates—*Sea Horse, Theseus,* and *Zealous*—were involved in the attack. As they crept forward in the night toward a hostile coast, Betsey found herself sleeping alone again, so she "had a woman with me the sailmaker's wife"—her first mention of another wife on board.

Nelson "supped with us," Betsey recorded as the frigates lay anchored just out of range of the guns of Santa Cruz; "he then went with Fremantle on their expedition. They are all to land in the Town. As the taking of this place seemed an easy and almost sure thing, I went to bed after they had gone apprehending no danger for Fremantle.

> July 25. The troops landed at two oclock this morning. There was much firing in the Town, but from the ships it seemed as if the English had made themselves masters of it. Great was our misfortune, this proved to be a shocking, unfortunate night. Fremantle returned at 4 this morning wounded in the arm, he was shot through the right arm the moment he had landed, came off in the first boat, and stayed on board the *Zealous* till day light, where his wound was dressed. Thank God as the ball only went through the flesh he will not lose his arm he managed it so well that I was not frightened, but I was not a little distressed and miserable when I heard what it was, and indeed he was in great pain and suffered cruelly all day but it was fortunate that he did get wounded at first, God knows if ever I should have seen him again had he stayed on shore. It was dreadful, poor Captain Bowen killed on

the spot, the Admiral was wounded as he was getting out of the Boat and most unfortunately lost his arm.

Nelson's life was saved by his stepson, Josiah Nisbet, who made a tourniquet of his neckerchief and got him back to the ship. According to legend, Josiah first took Nelson to the *Sea Horse,* but as he did not know whether Fremantle had survived or not, Nelson said, "I will die rather than alarm Mrs. Fremantle by her seeing me in this state when I can give her no tidings of her husband." With daylight, the three frigates were forced to retreat. "A shot went through one of our sails," Betsey related, but she steadfastly refused to go into the cockpit, even though Fleming, the Surgeon of the *Sea Horse,* repeatedly asked her to do so.

This was not an unusual response. As far back as 1690, Anne Chamberlyne, the sister of the captain of the *Griffin,* remained on deck during six hours of fleet action before obeying her brother's orders to go below. Mary Skinner, another captain's sister, sailed on the *Princess Royal,* expecting to meet her fiancé in New York. She and her maid passed away the hours of voyage sewing her wedding dress until the ship was attacked by the French privateer *L'Aventurier.* Then they tore up the gown to make powder bags for the guns, keeping themselves far too busy and useful to hide away in the cockpit.

Betsey's excuse was that she was too busy nursing her husband, who, though he had managed to keep his arm, was not doing as well as Nelson, who, she recorded, "is coming on very well, he wrote me a line with his left hand." Then, on August 6, she "wrote to the Admiral, he answered me a long note, he is astonishingly well."

Meantime, man-of-war life was going on as usual. Having got out of range of the batteries, they chased a ship which turned out to be one of their own—the *Emerald*—and then chased a Portuguese brig and a Genoese ship, despite Fremantle's uncomfortable condition. According to Betsey, "The motion hurts his arm much, and the noise of the guns annoyed us both beyond conception." Finally, on August 16, they rejoined the fleet, and all the captains came on board. "They were uncommonly attentive and kind. We are going to take Admiral Nelson home, which makes Fremantle and myself exceedingly happy."

"I grieve the loss of your arm," wrote Sir John Jervis to Nelson. "I hope you and Fremantle are doing well. The *Sea Horse* shall waft you to England. Give my love to Mrs. Fremantle." Nelson came on board at noon on the twentieth, bringing his own surgeon and sending Dr. Fleming to the *Zealous:* "he is quite stout but I find it looks shocking to be without one arm. He is in great spirits." And so they set sail for England, the ship "worse than a hospital, a number of sick and wounded from the *Theseus,* from morning to night and from night to morning you hear nothing but those unfortunate people groan."

Betsey herself was not at her best. Nelson's surgeon, Eshelby, "seems a sensible young man, he gave me some pills to take, for I am not well at all, but I dont mind as it is easy to guess what is the matter with me." Despite her pregnancy she and the sailmaker's wife nursed the two captains, finding "the Admiral" fretful, "a very bad patient," and Fremantle a constant worry, for though the wounds did not become infected, they would not heal, either—probably because of the lack of fresh fruit and vegetables. Then, at last, on September 1, the Isle of Wight came into view, and the very next day they went on shore at Portsmouth.

Obviously, surgical attention was necessary. Thomas Fremantle gradually mended, though he never regained his full health. Returning to sea, he distinguished himself in command of the *Neptune* at Trafalgar, and was appointed a Lord of the Admiralty. Betsey remained on shore, looking after his mansion in Buckinghamshire, and raising her ten children, whom she christened "the Brattery." Her eldest son became the first Lord Cottesloe, and another—Sir Charles Howe Fremantle—became an admiral.

Finally, after Thomas had been appointed Commander in Chief of the Mediterranean Fleet, Betsey returned to the sea, after a hiatus of twenty-five years. It was fortunate that she did so, for it meant she was with her beloved husband when he passed away. The year was 1819 and, poetically, Naples was the place. Brokenhearted, Betsey returned to England, where she died in 1857.

About the sailmaker's wife, by contrast, absolutely nothing is known.

Chapter Sixteen

NELSON'S WOMEN

*I suppose Ly. Hamilton is now in deep despair, and
I think Ly. Nelson must feel a great deal altho he
behaved unkindly to her.*

—Eugenia Wynne,
November 8, 1805,
after hearing the news of Nelson's death
at the Battle of Trafalgar

Fanny Nisbet Nelson's behavior was exemplary. She did all the right things. She looked after her father-in-law with affectionate attention, paid dutiful calls on her husband's relatives, and worried about Nelson's health and safety. Not quite understanding Nelson's obsessive ambition, she nonetheless did her best to achieve his ends. Though she disliked the vulgarity of such a course, she cultivated influential people such as Lady Spencer, wife of the First Lord of the Admiralty.

Frances, Lady Nelson.
Artist: Ron Druett, after Daniel Orme.

The trouble with Fanny was that she was exactly the kind of woman Horatio Nelson had thought he needed to marry, but all along he had been mistaken. Fanny passed her days like one of Jane Austen's heroines, paying much attention to her dress,

196

Fanny Nelson's social milieu. From a book of design published 1823.

spending the season in London, attending the right parties, writing letters to the right people, paying duty calls on Nelson's relatives, and taking the waters at Bath. In a word, she was unexciting. Compared to the passionate, voluptuous, beautiful Emma Hamilton, she did not have a chance.

And neither, for that matter, did Nelson himself.

He paid his second visit to Naples in September 1798. The port was in a ferment of hysterical delight, for at long last, in one dramatic stroke, it looked as if the fortunes of war were changing. The five years since Nelson's September 1793 visit had not been happy ones. A Jacobin plot had been uncovered. Vesuvius had erupted, losing a ninth of its height. The British fleet had fled from the Mediterranean, leaving the King of Naples to make an uncertain peace with the French, which cost him a great deal of money. Then, came the news of a great English naval victory.

This, Nelson's first command of a fleet action, was fought on August 1, 1798, and has been known ever since as the Battle of the Nile. It was an overwhelming triumph. On September 22 the *Vanguard,* Nelson's ship, hove into sight from the battlements of Naples, and Sir William and Lady Hamilton immediately summoned their barge. Emma had already sent Nelson an overwrought letter which declaimed, "God, what a victory! Never, never has there been anything half so glorious, so compleat. I fainted when I heard the joyfull news, and fell on my side and am hurt, but well of that. I shou'd feil it a glory to die in such a cause. No, I wou'd not like to die till I see and embrace the Victor of the Nile." The actual meeting, therefore, promised all the extravagant passion of an opera.

According to Sir William's secretary, Francis Oliver, as the Hamiltons' barge neared the *Vanguard,* Lady Hamilton "began to rehearse some of her theatrical airs." The captain of the craft was not impressed, voicing the hope that she would get up the side of the ship before she sank his little boat. The barge, however, arrived safely, and with a cry of, "Oh God! Is it possible," Lady Hamilton seized Nelson to her bosom and bore him off to the cabin, trailed by her husband and the rest.

Most laconic sailors would have found this palpitating display embarrassing. Captain Thomas Troubridge, who had come in earlier, escaped the theatrics as soon as he could, to see his ship careened. Nelson, however, saw the performance quite differently, relating in a letter to Fanny that the Ambassador's wife "fell into my arm more dead than alive. Tears however soon set matters to rights. . . . I hope one day to have the pleasure of introducing you to Lady Hamilton," he continued.

> She is one of the very best women in this world. How few could have made the turn she has. She is an honour to her sex and a proof that even reputation may be regained, but I own it requires a great soul. Her kindness with Sir William to me is more than I can express. I am in their house, and I may now tell you it required all the kindness of my

Lady Hamilton in the attitude of Dido bidding farewell to her prince.
Artist: Ron Druett, after James Gillray.

friends to set me up. Her ladyship if Josiah was to stay would make something of him and with all his bluntness I am sure he likes Lady Hamilton more than any female. She would fashion him in 6 months in spite of himself.

As a letter to a proud and devoted wife and mother, this was tactless in the extreme. It would not be at all surprising if Fanny's hackles rose when she read it. However, she might not have seen any real reason for worry. Back in March, Lady Spencer had remarked that Nelson's attentions to his wife "were those of a lover." He had insisted on sitting by Fanny's side at dinner, "saying he was so little with her, that he would not, voluntarily, lose an instant of her society." Fanny knew how important respectability and unblemished honor were to her ambitious husband. It would have seemed unlikely that he would throw all that away for the love of the notorious wife of the British Ambassador.

However, Emma Hamilton was as determined to have the Hero of the Nile as she had been to marry Sir William—and this was a woman who had "art enough to make fools of many wiser than an admiral," as Sir Gilbert Elliot later wrote. To do him justice, Nelson did put up a struggle. When Sir William Hamilton insisted on his staying at their mansion, where "Emma is looking out for the softest pillows to repose the few wearied limbs you have left," Nelson weakly objected, saying, "With your permission and good Lady Hamilton's, I had better be at a hotel."

He wasn't given the choice. By the time he wrote to Fanny, he had been reposing on those pillows for three days, while Emma bathed his battered head, fed him asses' milk (a restorative much in fashion then), and planned a great celebration for his fortieth birthday. "The preparations of Lady Hamilton for celebrating my birthday tomorrow are enough to fill me with vanity." The seventeen hundred guests were given ribbons and buttons with Nelson's name inscribed on them, and the eight hundred who sat down to dine ate from plates with the motto "H. N. Glorious August."

Fanny may have dismissed this, too, for similar celebrations were taking place all over London, where, in a speech to the House of Commons, the Prime Minister described Nelson as "that great commander whose services fill every bosom with rapturous emotion." "Joy, joy, joy to you, brave, gallant immortalised Nelson!" gushed Lady Spencer in a letter to the hero, after conveying the flattering information that her husband had fallen "on the floor insensible" when the news arrived.

Josiah, who was on the spot, knew better. He drank too much during the birthday party, and staggered up to Lady Hamilton to accuse her of trying to supplant his mother in his stepfather's affections. Troubridge and another officer carried him off before too much harm was done, but it seems evident that Emma had mesmerized the Hero of the Nile already. In October, Nelson wrote to Fanny, "My pride is being your husband, the son of my dear father and in having Sir William and Lady Hamilton for my friends. While those approve of my conduct I shall not feel or regard the envy of thousands." This was reassuring enough. At the same time, however, he was writing to Sir John Jervis, burbling, "I am writing opposite Lady Hamilton, therefore you will not be surprised at the glorious jumble of this letter."

When he received this, Jervis felt a stab of apprehension himself, for he dashed off a letter to Lady Hamilton, saying, "Pray, do not let your fascinating Neapolitan Dames approach too near him; for he is made of flesh & Blood & cannot resist their temptation." If Emma understood the underlying message, she paid no attention. The whole of England expected the Hero of the Nile to return, but he did not. The acclaim of the crowds awaited him there, but he preferred to linger with his adoring and very possessive hostess.

"Lord Nelson is gone to Leghorn with the troops of the King of Naples and we expect him soon back," wrote Emma to Fanny in December, in the first of a series of gushing letters that Fanny did not deign to answer, by now recognizing them for what they were, the crowing of a mistress to a wife. As it happens, Emma had promised Nelson to keep quiet about his mission, assuring him, "I would sooner have my flesh torn off by red hot pinchers sooner than betray my trust," but she could not resist the chance to let Nelson's wife know that she was privy to all his secrets. She was even aware of La Correglia, for she sent him strict instructions: "*do not go on shore at Leghorn* their is no comfort their for you."

Josiah, who had been sent away after the fracas at the party, returned to Naples, to provide material for another barbed missive. "We are all delighted with him," wrote Emma to Fanny. "I love him much and although we quarrel sometimes, he loves me and does as I would have him." There was no letter from Josiah himself. Instead, Lady Hamilton passed on the hurtful message that he "desired his duty to your ladyship and says he will write as soon as he has time." Nine days later, back in Naples after taking Leghorn without a shot being fired, Nelson elaborated, "The improvement made in Josiah by Lady Hamilton is wonderful. She seems the only person he minds [though] his faults are not omitted to be told him."

Fanny must have felt mortified, for she scribbled in pencil at the foot of this letter, "My son did not like the Hamiltons and would not dance [to her tune]—No reflections on [my] people are proper." Meanwhile, Josiah lost his temper, objecting strongly to the faultfinding himself. The scene must have been quite spectacular, Nelson writing furiously, "I am sorry to say and with real grief, that [Josiah] has nothing good about him, he must sooner or later be broke." Josiah had been sent off to Constantinople with the Turkish Ambassador. "I have done with the subject it is an ungrateful one."

Since Leghorn nothing had been going well. Neapolitan troops had marched on Rome, despite Sir William's explicit orders from London to discourage any show of arms. King Ferdinand entered the imperial city in triumph on November 29 and fled eight days later, a stout, shabby, hysterical refugee. No sooner had he returned to Naples than the Jacobins took heart from his craven condition and set to plotting a republic again. The Royal family panicked, smuggled their treasures onto Nelson's ships, and retreated to Palermo, Sicily. Then Sir William, who had put his collection on board various

Admiral Horatio Nelson.
Scrimshaw by Robert Weiss.

ships to England, was heartbroken to hear that HMS *Colossus* had gone down off the Scillies, along with his most prized classical vases—a trove that was destined to be known to future generations as the Cuckold's Treasure. One large box had been saved, but on opening it was found to hold the corpse of Admiral Shuldham, which had been shipped home for burial. "Damn his body," wrote Sir William; "it can be of no use but to the Wormes." His digestive system collapsed, and he crawled off to bed—alone.

By this stage, the Nelson-Hamilton *affaire* was common currency. They must have made a bizarre-looking couple. Lady Spencer thought Nelson a "most uncouth creature" with the general appearance "of an idiot," instantly redeemed when he opened his mouth and "his wonderful mind broke forth." He was also very slight, his small body further diminished by the loss of his right arm. Statuesque Emma had become corpulent, though everyone still remarked on the beauty of her face. One cannot help but wonder what Sir William Hamilton thought. However, he had admired Nelson for years. Back in September 1793, Sir William had told Emma that he was going to introduce her to a little man who was not at all handsome, but "will become the greatest man that ever England produced . . . he will one day astonish the world." Being proved so very right could have made him both smug and tolerant.

Meanwhile, the couple had become the focus of much riveted attention. "What a model for a Roman matron!" exclaimed an observer after first meeting Emma. This was a Scotsman, Major Pryse Lockhart Gordon, the traveling companion of Lord Montgomerie, who had also taken refuge in Palermo. According to his description, Emma was in *dishabille*, "her raven tresses floating round her expansive form and full bosom." She was mourning, she told him, for her beloved Naples.

Nelson was busy at a desk, but he left his writing to say to Gordon, "Pray, Sir, have you heard of the battle of the Nile?" No reply was necessary, for Nelson blurted on, "*That* battle, Sir, was the most extraordinary one that was ever fought, and it is *unique*, Sir, for three reasons; first, for its having been fought at night; secondly, for its having been fought at anchor; and thirdly, for its having been gained by an admiral with one arm." Gordon, flabbergasted, commented that if they had been at the dining table, "I should have imagined the hero had imbibed an extra dose of champagne."

Major Gordon and Lord Montgomerie were, indeed, invited to a dinner, to witness an even more remarkable scene, described by Gordon in his memoirs. Another guest was a Turk, who became drunk and boastful:

> "With this weapon," said he . . . drawing his shabola, "I cut off the heads of twenty French prisoners in one day! Look, there is their blood remaining on it." The speech being translated, her Ladyship's eye beamed with delight, and she said, "Oh let me see the sword that did the glorious deed!" It was presented to her; she took it into her fair hand covered with rings, and looking at the encrusted Jacobin blood, kissed it and handed it to the hero of the Nile!

A shocked silence was succeeded by some uneasy laughter and a few cries of "Shame!" and it seems that though various "toad-eaters" applauded, Nelson was very properly embarrassed. Another of Gordon's stories is more amusing. Emma suddenly took it into her head to perform one of her famous attitudes, shaking her hair out of its combs and collapsing into a reclining position on the floor. One of the guests, under the misapprehension that she had fainted, sprinkled her with cold water. Sir William was greatly chagrined, declaring that the blunder had ruined "one of the most perfect attitudes that Emma ever executed."

Throughout, Nelson remained besotted. In February 1799 he was at sea. The cruise was a short one; nonetheless, he was acutely conscious of the gale that was speeding him away from Emma. "I shall run mad . . . ," he wrote.

> Last night I did nothing but dream of you altho' I woke 20 times in the night. In one of my dreams I thought I was at a large table—you was not present—sitting between a Princess, who I detest, and another. They both tried to seduce me and the first wanted to take those liberties with me which no woman in this world but yourself ever did. The consequence was I knocked her down and in the moment of bustle you came in and, taking me to your embrace, whispered, "I love nothing but you, my Nelson." I kissed you fervently and we enjoyed the height of love.

By March 21, Nelson was back in Palermo, writing to Fanny, "Nothing worth relating has occurred since I wrote you last We go dragging an existence from day to day. How matters will end God only knows." Nelson might have been in love, but he was also deeply unhappy, tortured in both body and spirit. Sexual excess must have played a part, along with what surely must have been a guilty conscience where his blameless wife was concerned.

There was also the worry about what was happening in the corridors of power in England. The great victory at the Nile had emboldened the British naval strategists, which made the absence of the hero particularly noticeable. On July 13, 1799, orders arrived from Lord Keith to take his ships to the defense of Minorca. It was a time of emergency. Keith's intelligence had informed him that the enemy was approaching with forty-three sail of the line. Nelson ignored the command and stayed with the King and Queen of Naples. For this, he was forthrightly condemned by not just Lord Keith, but Sir John Jervis and the Admiralty, too. The hero was now the villain of the play, and the love affair was the talk of all London.

* * *

"You, who remember me always laughing and gay," wrote Nelson in despair to a good friend, the wife of Admiral Peter Parker, "would hardly believe the change."

Lady Parker had known Nelson a long time. In fact, she could well have influenced his meteoric career. In 1778, when Nelson was the nineteen-year-old third lieutenant of the *Bristol,* she had made quite a pet of the delicate young man, and family letters indicate that her husband was often apt to take her opinions seriously. Nelson was promoted to the command of the brig *Badger* in December that same year, and then to the rank of post captain in June 1779, in command of the twenty-gun *Hinchingbrooke*—an unusually rapid rise through the ranks, considering that he was untested in battle. When he became very ill with some tropical disease after action in Central America, she nursed him devotedly. Later, Sir Peter Parker became commander in chief at Portsmouth, and Lady Parker forwarded Fanny's letters to Nelson through naval channels so that they would go more quickly and securely.

When the gossip reached Lady Parker's ears, she was greatly distressed. "Sir Peter and Miss Parker called upon us," wrote Fanny to Nelson in December 1799. "Good Lady Parker was ill. I called to see her on Sunday. She was better [but] her spirits was so agitated when she talked of you, that I found it necessary to make my visit short. She tells me she has written two long letters to you endeavouring to point out the necessity of your coming home. I hope she will succeed."

Another admiral's wife who knew both Horatio and Fanny Nelson was Lady Hughes, whose husband was Admiral Sir Richard Hughes. In April 1784, when Nelson was given command of the *Boreas,* his heart had sunk at the news that he was to carry this "fine talkative lady" to Antigua in the West Indies, along with her daughter, Rosy. Not only would he have to listen to her "infernal clack," but Rosy was on the hunt for a husband. The two Hughes women had proved amenable to reason, however. Once Nelson had managed to convey his lack of interest in Rosy in polite but unmistakable terms, mother and daughter had settled down to proving themselves "very pleasant good people," though an awful expense to the ship.

Lady Hughes regarded him with affection right from the start, reminiscing fondly in letters to George Matcham, Nelson's brother-in-law, how kind he was to the "young gentlemen" who were learning seamanship.

> The timid he never rebuked, but always wished to show them he desired nothing of them that he would not instantly do himself: and I

have known him say—"Well, sir, I am going a race to the mast-head and beg I may meet you there." No denial could be given to such a wish and the poor fellow instantly began his march. [When they met at the top, Nelson] began instantly speaking in the most cheerful manner and saying how much a person was to be pitied who could fancy there was any danger, or even anything disagreeable, in the attempt. After this excellent example, I have seen the timid youth lead another and re-hearse his captain's words.

She also recorded how he helped with the lessons in navigation, and kept a sharp eye on their hygiene and diet, particularly as they approached the tropics. When they crossed the equator, he took part in the skylarking. Once on shore, he took the young midshipmen with him to formal occasions, excusing this to his hosts by saying, "I make it a rule to introduce them to all the good company I can as they have few to look up to, beside myself, during the time they are at sea."

So, what did this other admiral's wife think of the goings-on in Naples and Palermo in this strange year of 1799? Lady Hughes could have experienced quite a fellow feeling for Fanny Nelson, having been in much the same position herself. In 1786, when Nelson had been engaged to marry Fanny (and drinking goat's milk and beef tea to build himself up and "make me what I wish to be for your sake" on the wedding night), he had been most derisive about Sir Richard's amorous antics. The reputation of a certain young woman, he wrote to Fanny, had suffered much "from her intimacy with Sir Richard. I should suppose him a bachelor instead of a married man with a family." Confidentially, he went on, "the A[dmiral] makes quite a———of himself in this business." Ironic, indeed.

"The world says [Nelson] is making himself ridiculous with Lady Hamilton and idling his time at Palermo when he *should* have been *else-where*," wrote Admiral Lord Keith to his sister in April. "The extravagant love of [Lord Nelson] has made him the laughing stock of the whole fleet," derided British Consul Charles Lock in June—and all because of a "Dolly Sir William Hamilton married," wrote Lock's mother-in-law, the Duchess of Leinster. "He is now completely managed by Lady Hamilton," wrote Lady Elgin in October. "She is indeed a Whapper! And I think her manner very vulgar. It is really humiliating to see Lord Nelson, he seems quite dying and yet as if he had no other thought than her."

The obvious path to putting the gossip to rest was for Fanny to join Nelson in the Mediterranean. Nelson dismissed the notion out of hand, deriding the very idea of her joining "a wandering sailor." If she came, he said, he would have "struck my flag and carried you back again for it would have been impossible to set up an establishment either at Naples or Palermo." The next idea was for her to travel to Lisbon and meet him there. Her doctors recommended it as a good place to recruit her health. Nonsense, he replied, it was "the most dirty place in Europe." His real reasons are obvious. Not only would it make a difficult situation even more complicated, but Fanny was nursing his father, the Reverend Edmund, a duty that his female relatives—sisters Susannah Bolton and Catherine Matcham, and sister-in-law, Sarah Yonge Nelson—had adroitly avoided.

Meantime, Naples had been recaptured from the city's short spell of democratic republican rule, and Nelson's ships were back in the harbor. The Queen, still in Palermo, sent a letter to Emma directing that the Jacobin leaders must be punished, whatever their sex: "The females who have distinguished themselves in the revolution to be treated the same way and without pity." Thus, on June 29 the city was treated to the horrifying sight, not only of Admiral Prince Caracciolo being hanged from his own yardarm two hours after capture, but of highborn women groveling for mercy at Emma's feet. A shocked young sailor, Midshipman Parsons of Nelson's new flagship, *Foudroyant,* wrote with bitter irony, "I grieve to say that wonderful, talented and graceful beauty, Emma Lady Hamilton, did not sympathise in the manner expected from her generous and noble nature." The women were strung from a great gibbet in the marketplace, executioners pulling on their legs while a dwarf capered about on their shoulders. To do him justice, Sir William Hamilton was appalled.

"The Lyoness," a caricature of Lady Hamilton based on her birth name, Lyon.

Artist: Ron Druett, after James Gillray.

There were lighter moments. When King Ferdinand extended a languid hand for Nelson's servant, Tom Allen, to kiss, Allen shook it instead, barking, "How do you do, Mr. King!" Emma took time off from her duties to organize a celebration for the anniversary of the Battle of the Nile. "In the evening was a general illumination," wrote Nelson to Fanny on 4 August.

> Amongst others, a large vessel was fitted out like a Roman galley. On the oars were fixed lamps and in the centre was erected a rostral column with my name; at the stern, elevated, were two angels supporting my picture. . . . More than 2000 variegated lamps were fixed round the vessel, an orchestra was fitted up and filled with the very best musicians and singers. The piece of music was in a great measure of my praises, describing their distress, but Nelson comes, the invincible Nelson.

There was a ghoulish guest at the party. King Ferdinand was on deck early in the morning when he let out a strangled cry of horror. The corpse of Admiral Prince Caracciolo, which had been heaved overboard after the hanging, had risen to the surface "with his face full upon us, much swollen and discoloured by the water," as Midshipman Parsons described. It was as if the body were standing upright in accusation, for the feet were weighed down with the leg irons. A gaggle of priests was swiftly summoned, to reassure the terrified king that the admiral had risen to beg his forgiveness. Then Nelson ordered the corpse towed to shore.

The grateful Ferdinand made Nelson Duke of Bronte, a 30,000-acre rock-strewn slope of Mount Etna, complete with rickety farmhouse. "The present is magnificent and worthy of a king," Nelson wrote to Fanny, not having inspected this doubtful domain. This, of course, was celebrated with yet another party, at which Nelson wept with weak gratitude. Midshipman Parsons reached into his own pocket, observing that "trusty aide-de-camps could do no less than apply their own handkerchiefs." He pulled out a white silk stocking by mistake, but it didn't really matter, for his own tears stemmed more "from a contrary feeling of mirth" than from any fellow spirit.

And all this time Nelson was supposed to be coming to the aid of the fleet at Minorca. Sir Gilbert Elliot wrote wearily, "He does not seem at all conscious of the sort of discredit he has fallen into, or the cause of it, for he writes still not wisely about Lady Hamilton and all that." In February 1800, Lord Keith, thoroughly tired of Nelson's inactivity, ordered him to Malta with *Foudroyant, Northumberland, Audacious,* and the little frigate *Success.* Partly because of the courage of the captain and crew of the *Success,* they managed to capture one of the two French ships of the line that had escaped at the Battle of the Nile, *Le Généreux*. In March, Sir Edward Berry managed to capture the second, the eighty-gun *Guillaume Tell*, but in the meantime Nelson had got tired of the sea and returned to Emma's arms.

Nelson left Palermo to return to his rightful duty on April 24, but took the Hamiltons with him for "days of ease and nights of pleasure," as the irreverent Midshipman Parsons phrased it. Arriving off Malta, Nelson chose an anchorage beyond the range of the French guns, but, as it turned out, he miscalculated. The French used the ship for target practice. According to Parsons, "Lord Nelson was in a towering passion, and Lady Hamilton's refusal to quit the quarterdeck did not tend to tranquilize him."

Emma demanded that they return to Palermo. The First Lord of the Admiralty Lord Spencer, got wind of it, however, and lost patience. Nelson was ordered home in terms of savage sarcasm: "you will be more likely to recover your health and strength in England than in an inactive situation at a foreign Court, however pleasing the respect and gratitude shown to you for your services may be." Nelson made preparations to return to England in the *Foudroyant,* but Lord Keith soon put a stop to that. "Lady Hamilton," he declared, "has ruled the fleet long enough." They could go to Leghorn in the flagship, but no farther. The journey had to be made overland, despite Bonaparte and his armies.

It was in the nature of a triumphal procession. The peoples of allied Europe were as desperate for a hero as the English, and in Leghorn, Trieste, Vienna, Prague, and Dresden, Nelson was hailed by ecstatic crowds. Otherwise, however, there were annoyances. While it had been flattering to arrive in Prague and find their hotel illuminated, it was irritating to find the cost of the illuminations added to their bill. In Dresden, Emma wished to go to Court. The Electress did not choose to receive her, "on account of her former dissolute life." When they arrived in Hamburg the expected frigate was not there to carry them home. Nelson wrote to the Admiralty, but still none arrived. Finally, on the last day of October 1800, they boarded the mail packet *King George* for Yarmouth.

On November 6, in stormy weather, they arrived. But Fanny Nelson was not there.

Fanny knew that Nelson did not want her to meet the party. In Leghorn, three months earlier, he had written, "I shall come to London or where ever [my father] might be the moment I get out of quarantine therefore I would not have you come to Portsmouth on any account." And so she and his father waited patiently in London. The *Morning Herald* reported on November 11 that "Lord Nelson, the gallant hero of the Nile, on his arrival in town, was met by his venerable father and his amiable lady. The scene which took place was of the most graceful description," the item ran on. On the contrary, the tension must have been palpable. In one of her waspish letters to Nelson's sister-in-law, Emma Hamilton portrayed their meeting as "antipathy not to be described," but it is difficult to imagine that Fanny Nelson did not behave in a reticent and civilized manner.

There was no relief from unpleasantness. Nelson was acclaimed by crowds wherever he went, but his presentation to the King was not a success. He was annoyed because Lady Hamilton had not received an invitation, and the King was irritated because Nelson was festooned with foreign decorations that he had not been given permission to wear. When the First Lord of the Admiralty and Lady Spencer hosted Lord and Lady Nelson to dinner, her ladyship noted with deep disapproval that Nelson treated his wife "with every mark of dislike and even of contempt." It did not help that next day Lady Nelson was presented to the Queen at a Drawing Room, while it had become obvious that Lady Hamilton was to be shunned by the Court.

Fanny did her best to be polite, accompanying the Hamiltons to the theater and inviting them to the house on Dover Street that Nelson had rented. Newspapers avidly followed the progress of the party. "[Lady Nelson's] person is of a very pleasing description: her features are handsome and exceedingly interesting, and her general appearance is at once prepossessing and elegant." Lady Hamilton, by contrast, was "rather *embonpoint*." She fainted on occasion, and during one dinner party Fanny held a basin while her guest was sick into it. The realization that Emma Hamilton was pregnant, and that the sick, elderly Sir William was unlikely to be the father, was inevitable.

Not long after that, the charade was ended. It happened at breakfast. According to Nelson's solicitor, William Haslewood, Fanny stood up and said, "I am sick of hearing of dear Lady Hamilton and am resolved that you shall give up either her or me!" The choice, however, was already made. Nelson made his escape to sea. He sent her a strangely friendly letter from Southampton, addressing it to "My dear Fanny" and signing it, "believe me, your affectionate Nelson." There is also a story that he called on her one morning, and when she stretched out an arm and asked him if she had ever given him cause for complaint, he agreed that she had not. However, the marriage was finished. They never lived together again.

* * *

The Reverend Edmund went to Bath, and Fanny retreated to Brighton. "Let her go," wrote Nelson to Emma. "I care not: she is a great fool and thank God you are not the least like her." He wanted to be rid of her. Not only did she irritate him unbearably, but his mistress was on the verge of giving birth. "I had a letter from that person at Brighton," he wrote to Emma, "saying she had heard from my brother that I was ill and offered to come and nurse me but I have sent such an answer that will convince her she would not be received." Yet he sent Fanny a series of petulant complaints itemizing the unsatisfactory state of his belongings as they arrived on the ship, just as if she were still responsible for his domestic affairs. Perhaps, in the throes of this familiar aggravation, his mind had slipped back into the past.

In fact, it is impossible not to wonder about his mental state throughout. When Nelson had arrived in Naples after the Victory of the Nile he had been weak with recurrent malaria, and very distressed by a splitting headache, the result of a wound on his forehead. It is possible that this hard knock disturbed the equilibrium of his psyche, for so much of what he did from then on was out of character. When Lady Spencer received him in London, she was shocked by the change. "Such a contrast I never beheld!"

His moods swung from irritation, passion, guilt, and pride to piety, for he also became obsessively religious. While he treated Fanny decently as far as financial maintenance was concerned, he became uncharacteristically vindictive. Emma had already embarked on a program of alienating his family from Fanny, succeeding first with Sarah, Nelson's sister-in-law, the wife of his brother, the Reverend William. They exchanged spiteful notes in which Fanny was nicknamed "Tom Tit" because of her bobbing walk. "Tom Tit does not come to town," exulted Emma to Sarah; "she offered to go down but was refused. She only wanted to do mischief to all the *great Jove's* relations. 'Tis now shown, all her ill-treatment and bad heart—*Jove* has found it out." Then, every time Fanny was mentioned in the papers—as she often was, being the rightful Lady Nelson—the malice burgeoned apace.

It had never been in Nelson's character to be small-minded, but now he went along with this, discouraging contact with Fanny so emphatically that first his sisters dropped her, and then his gentle, remorseful father, who owed Fanny so much, found it almost impossible to keep in touch. On November 18, 1801, the Reverend Edmund reluctantly paid a visit to the house that Nelson had bought for Emma, though Emma was reluctant to have him there, fearing him to be the emissary of that "vile Tom Tit" and her "squinting brat." Five months later, when the Reverend Edmund was dying in his apartments at Bath, it was Fanny who made the journey to be with him. Nelson was too "ill" to travel, though in fact he and Emma were celebrating her birthday. After Sir William Hamilton died in the arms of his wife and her lover, in April 1803, Nelson and Emma made no secret of the fact that they wished Fanny would die, their hopes rising with every report that she was ill.

True to her own character, Fanny was both patient and forgiving, writing to congratulate Nelson—whom she still regarded as her husband—after he successfully carried off the Battle of the Baltic, for which he was made a viscount. Perhaps she was simply hoping that he would come to his senses. In December 1801, Fanny—now legally a viscountess, but not caring a whit for that—wrote, "I assure you again I have but one wish in the world, to please you. Let everything be buried in oblivion, it will pass away like a dream. I can only now entreat you to believe I am most sincerely and affectionately your wife, Frances H. Nelson."

The letter was returned, marked "Opened by mistake by Lord Nelson, but not read."

Although Nelson had never adopted Josiah—Fanny's "squinting brat" whom Emma and Sarah Nelson dubbed "the Cub"—he took legal responsibility for "any child [Emma Hamilton] may have in or out of wedlock." In his last Will he wrote a directive saying, "I desire [his illegitimate daughter, Horatia] will use in future the name Nelson." Yet, for a man who declared himself "mad with joy" when he heard the news of the birth, he was remarkably miserable, writing often that he wished himself dead. Despite her hugely increasing girth, Nelson was terrified that Emma would return to her former way of life, having particular nightmares of her being seduced by the Prince of Wales. "Does Sir William want you to be a whore to the rascal?" he demanded in a frantic letter to Emma, penned just days before Horatia's birth. "I see clearly you are on SALE." Because of her own insecurity, Emma deliberately played on this jealousy, hinting at the worst until Nelson was tortured with near-paranoia.

Most illogically, in view of this, he set her on a pedestal of virtue, holding a special divine service on board his ship on the birthday of "my Saint [who] is more adored in this Fleet than all the Saints in the Roman Calendar." This was followed by a banquet where twenty-four captains, including his old friend Thomas Fremantle, were required to drink a toast to

Santa Emma. *Nelson's favorite portrait,
which hung in his cabin.*
Artist: Ron Druett, after Norstri.

Ship of the line Victory.
Scrimshaw by Robert Weiss.

the image of the woman who "has more Divinity about her" than any other living being. "I have no patience with [Lord Nelson] at his age and such a cripple to play the fool with Lady Hamilton," wrote Betsey Fremantle. Her opinion was general. Not only was the little admiral "making himself ridiculous" with another woman, but this time he was the laughingstock of society.

Nelson was in terrible shape physically, too. He was constantly afflicted with drenching cold sweats, undoubtedly due to stress. "I have had a sort of rheumatic fever they tell me," he wrote in 1804 to a doctor; "but I have felt the blood quickening up the left side of my head and the moment it covers my brain I am fast asleep." Only in the urgency of battle was Nelson the genius the world acclaimed.

The rest is history. Nelson was felled by a sharpshooter, in one of Britain's greatest hours. As he had never adopted Josiah, the title descended to his brother, William, who enjoyed it immensely but had never done anything to deserve it. Away from his stepfather's brooding shadow, Josiah left the sea and proved himself successful in business. Emma Hamilton gambled her way into debtors' prison and drank herself to death in 1815. Horatia, who had the misfortune to be her nurse, returned to the Nelson tradition by marrying into the church.

Frances Herbert, Viscountess Nelson, mourned her husband with propriety, in a complete outfit of black purchased from "E. Franks, Milliner & Dress Maker," at a cost of forty-eight pounds, seventeen shillings. After that, she lived quietly, moving from Bath to London and back again according to the season. Finally, she retired to a house overlooking the sea at Exmouth, where she and Horatio had once spent a happy holiday. And there she died, on May 6, 1831, aged seventy-three.

Chapter Seventeen

VOYAGES OF DISCOVERY

*Every particle of fear left me, and I stood quite as
collected as any heroine of former days.*
    —Abby Jane Morrell

It was midnight in the port of Toulon, France, the moon rippling on
the black water. Moored to the dock, the 350-ton, twenty-gun corvette
L'Uranie thrust her three tall masts to the stars, while beyond her the rigging of other ships serried off to the distance. All the windows and
rooftop balconies of the row of high stone buildings along the quay were
dark and silent. Everything was still, save for the slow creaking of ships'
rigging and occasional jingles, as the sentries moved restlessly in the au-
tumn chill. It was September 1817, and although the Napoleonic Wars
were over, still they kept vigilance.

Then—footsteps. Three people came into sight, two men and a slighter
figure, probably a boy, wearing a frock coat with trousers. One was the
captain. The sentinels stamped to attention. The correct password was
called out, but nonetheless a lamp was lit. The boy turned his face away
and was perceptibly trembling. Who was he? The son of the captain's
friend, one said. The sentries saluted and let them pass, and all three went
up the gangway. Only one man came back, but no one seemed to notice.

And so, at 10 A.M. that same day, the corvette *L'Uranie* set sail unhindered, steering for the Cape of Good Hope, Australia, and beyond. It was

the first French discovery expedition since the end of the Napoleonic Wars. The commander was the well-regarded geographer Louis-Claude de Saulces de Freycinet. And there was a cross-dressed stowaway on board.

There are several reasons the 1817–20 voyage of the French discovery ship *L'Uranie* is interesting. It was part of France's attempt to restore her prestige after Napoleon's defeat at Waterloo in 1815, and thus very important to both the nation and the Navy. Be-

Rose de Freycinet. Artist: Ron Druett.

cause of this, the corvette had a handpicked crew, most of them skilled tradesmen. The only civilian officially on board was the expedition's draftsman, Jacques Arago. And there was the illegal presence of the captain's wife—twenty-two-year-old Rose de Freycinet, dressed in coat and trousers and "shaking all over" with fright.

Rose remained hidden in the captain's cabin until the vessel was well out of sight of the French coast. Then, Louis revealed all, by inviting the officers, chaplain, and the expedition artist to a tea party where Rose, still in male attire, presided. According to her, it was a happy occasion. "I received them with a great deal of pleasure and I had a good laugh listening to the various hypotheses which each one had formulated about my identity." And the officers did not seem to mind, either, agreeing one and all that the dainty little lady with the charming manners and very agreeable appearance was a fit companion for her aristocratic husband—though some people said that during mess dinners the conversation at the dining table was more sharp-edged with brilliant wit than it might have been without a woman to impress.

When the news broke in France, reactions varied wildly. On October 4 the editor of the *Monitor Universel* declared, "this example of conjugal devotion deserves to be made public." Reportedly, Louis XVIII was amused.

The British Lieutenant Governor of Gibraltar, the first official to receive visitors from *L'Uranie,* was not, and neither was the French Ministry of the Navy. Women were not supposed to travel in ships of the state, yet Madame was there—in male clothing! It was unsupportable.

One result of this was that every now and then the artists of the expedition painted the same scene twice, one work being true to life, and the other *sans* Madame. This subterfuge was necessary for the official record, *Voyage autour du Monde . . . exécuté sur les corvettes de S. M. L'Uranie et La Physicienne,* which was prepared by de Freycinet and published between 1827 and 1839. Madame herself was embarrassed that her presence was so informal. She was not comfortable in men's clothing. The only time she was glad of it was when the corvette was pursued by an Algerian corsair. The prospect of being enslaved was bad enough, but "the thought of a seraglio evoked even more unpleasant images in my mind, and I hoped to escape that fate thanks to my male disguise." Luckily, the corsair veered off after counting the corvette's cannon, and the possibility of the disguise being penetrated was averted. Then, after a dis-

Baptism of Hawaiian Prime Minister on board L'Uranie. Note the diplomatic omission of Madame from this engraving by Crespin, after the painting by Arago.

astrous meeting with the Governor of Gibraltar, it was decided that she should abandon male dress altogether, to her vast relief.

But then, there was the crew. When Rose arrived on deck the men were deferential, leaving the lee side of the ship so that she could walk in reasonable privacy. They did their best to refrain from swearing too, but inevitably their self-imposed discipline lapsed, a curse slipped out, and Rose was forced to concentrate her troubled gaze on the water. Once noticed, this was considered a very good joke, so from then on the men would swear and sing rude ditties just loud enough for her to hear, while the Boatswain tried to shut them up by making violent signs behind her back.

In the end, Madame was forced to keep out of sight as much as possible. As the *Dictionnaire de Biographie Français* remarked afterwards, this was an admirable display of "moral superiority over the crew," but it did have the disadvantage that it made life on the rolling wave very boring, on the whole—though Rose herself denied this, declaring she was happy enough with her guitar, her journal, and her sewing. At other times, she was terrified to the point of biting her fingers until they bled. Yet, she never regretted her decision to defy the authorities and sail with her beloved husband. She had sailed to be with him, and to care for him when he was sick or weary, and no one could nurse him as she could.

It is a fact that Louis de Freycinet had a delicate constitution. However, what is remarkable is that her decision to go on voyage was considered so strange. Louis XVIII observed that the authorities should regard such an aberration tolerantly because it was so unlikely that other women would follow Madame's example—and yet, as we have seen, in the British Navy women had been sailing with their husbands for several generations. In Mauritius, in May 1818, Rose was delighted to meet one of these ladies, the wife of Captain Purvis of the British man-of-war *Magicienne*. She thought Mrs. Purvis "a charming little woman, very well brought up." Even more delightful was the "pretty little boy" Mrs. Purvis gave birth to soon after the frigate made port, for Rose loved babies and would have adored to have one of her own. In fact, this was probably a major reason she sailed. Though they had been married three years, she and Louis were childless. He was sixteen years older than she, and the voyage was expected to last at least two years—figures that must have preyed on her mind.

"The resemblance between our situations brought us together," Rose commented after meeting Mrs. Purvis, though she had written a little earlier, "But what a difference between Louis' mission and his! He sails the Indian seas to protect the merchants from pirates; at all the stations he finds a house, furnished, and with servants to wait on them. Sometimes he makes short cruises without his wife, so as not to tire her with too much voyaging." This difference between missions is probably very significant. Purvis had the simple brief of cruising about looking for trouble and responding to calls of distress, while Louis de Freycinet had the much more demanding task of accumulating oceanographic data and collecting scientific specimens. Because of this, Rose de Freycinet had less in common with Mrs. Purvis than she did with an American woman, Abby Jane Morrell, who struggled differently, but just as mightily, to sail on another discovery expedition.

The story of the romance of Benjamin and Abby Jane Morrell of Stonington, Connecticut, is quite a contrast to that of Louis and Rose. The de Freycinet marriage was a definite love match, Rose being *bourgeoise*—

Abby Jane Morrell. Artist: Ron Druett.

though intelligent and cultivated—and thus lower on the social ladder than the aristocratic de Freycinets. The Morrells faced a different kind of social impediment. In May 1824, upon arriving back home at the end of his first discovery voyage, Benjamin had learned for the first time that his wife and two children were dead. This kind of tragedy was common enough, just as it was usual for shipmasters to remarry within a remarkably short time, it being considered healthy to find another wife before embarking again. Benjamin left his search until the last moment, however. Just days before he sailed, he still had not found himself a bride . . . though he did have a nice little cousin who liked him a lot. The problem was that Abby Jane was just fifteen, rather too young for marriage.

The voyage was expected to last two years. When he came back, Benjamin meditated, this "opening bud" would be on the verge of bloom, certainly weddable by then. But, he panicked, the "full-blown flower" might have been plucked by another man in the meantime, so he married little Abby Jane in her father's parlor. Then, after committing his "virgin bride to the care of her friends," he sailed off to the Pacific. It was nearly two years before she saw him again. By the time he got back from a third voyage, in 1829, she had completely lost patience and made up her mind to sail. And, like Rose de Freycinet, she planned a campaign.

Where Rose had to counter the French authorities, Abby Jane's opponent was her own husband. First, she tried emotional blackmail. To put it in Benjamin's words, "she assured me that she would not survive another separation." It was a well-chosen argument, Benjamin being both pompous and vain. It didn't work, however, he being scandalized at the very notion of taking his wife to sea, so Abby Jane resorted to relentless nagging, along with frequent bouts of tears. Benjamin pointed out that he had important oceanographic work to do that should and could not be sacrificed to a lady's comfort. "Only take me with you, Benjamin," she obstinately replied, "and I will pledge myself to lighten your cares, instead of adding to their weight." Finally, he agreed, stipulating the following conditions:

> Viz: that she must expect no attentions from me when duty called me on deck; that she must never blame me, if things were not agreeable or pleasant, at all times, during the voyage; and that she must not expect that there would be any extra living on board the *Antarctic* on her account.

While it is obvious that Rose de Freycinet's cross-dressing and stowing away happened with the active cooperation of her husband, she, too, was made acutely aware of the importance of the mission. On September 12, 1819, on departure from Oahu, she noted ruefully that "this part of the voyage will be greatly prolonged." Louis had made the decision "in order to collect data on the magnetic equator. However much I respect science, I am not fond of it," she complained; "nor am I likely to be reconciled to it by Louis' prolonging of the voyage, which holds nothing terribly exciting for me. It is true that this work is one of the main objectives," she allowed, but it was inescapably boring. "If only, like so many travelers, we were fortunate enough to discover some new island."

Louis had promised her that if they did find an unclaimed dot of land, he would name it after her. And lo, two months later, in latitude 14° 32' 42", they did indeed find an atoll that was so insignificant that it did not seem to have a name, so Rose had her wish, even though she was not supposed to be there. "Let's see, what shall we call it?" Arago mused in a letter to a friend, his tongue firmly in his cheek. "Let it be a flowery name. Shall it be Green Island, Red Island, or . . . No, I suppose it will be Rose Island."

Abby Jane had no such luck. Instead, six weeks after departure, she embarrassed Benjamin by falling seriously ill. Eleven of the men were sick, too, and if Abby Jane had not been on board, Captain Morrell would have steered to the nearest port for medical assistance. "But," he wrote, "I reflected that some slanderous tongues might attribute such a deviation from my regular course solely to the fact of my wife's being on board. That idea I could not tamely endure." Because he anticipated "the unfeeling sarcasms of those carpet-knights, on whose delicate frames the winds of heaven are not permitted to blow too roughly," he medicated all the patients himself, with "blisters, friction, and bathing with hot vinegar." Abby Jane was given up for dead several times, and two of the men did expire, but at least Morrell's reputation remained unblemished.

There was a basic difference in the methodology of each mission that affected the two women greatly. Morrell carried out most of his work at sea, charting whaling and sealing grounds and investigating tropical lagoons where *bêche de mer* (sea slugs) grew. De Freycinet and his scientists carried out a lot of time-consuming observations at various landfalls. There is a strange irony in this. Abby Jane, for her part, would have liked to spend a lot more time on land, "to see land, men, shipping, churches, &c.; things I had been accustomed to all my life." Rose, by contrast, found to her dismay that the lengthy spells on shore that were her lot involved all kinds of unexpected hazards, including dirt and boredom.

The first time they dropped anchor in French-held territory was particularly nerve-wracking. This proved to be Bourbon Island (now Réunion), off Mauritius. The only means of getting on shore was by canoe. "I was terrified," Rose frankly admitted. But much worse was the prospect of being forced to leave the expedition. Rose tried to evade Governor Lafitte when she learned that he was visiting the house where she was staying, but he was suddenly ushered into the same room before she had a chance to retreat, so she had "to put a brave face on things.

> I bowed to him as graciously as I could . . . [though] I was shaking with fear; what would become of me far from my family, my friends, in a colony that was so alien to me? But, instead of finding a critic of my conduct determined on repatriating me, all I had to do was to ward off the compliments of someone who was full of admiration for my courage.

What a relief! The authorities in Paris, it seems, had decided—like their British counterparts on many similar occasions—to turn a blind eye to the matter. And appropriately so, for *Madame La Jolie Commandante* was a marvelous ambassador, being most loyally French and a natural diplomat. While her husband navigated his ship at sea and measured eclipses on shore, with equal *élan* she threaded her way through colonial jealousies and strange points of etiquette. When Rose decided not to attend a ball at Government House in Mauritius (because she did not think the expense of a new gown was worth it), she developed a migraine to avoid the social blunder of being seen at a dinner party staged by her host that night. She was equally adept with native peoples. Rose was amused when the Caroline Islanders burst into roars of laughter every time the corvette's officers politely raised their hats to each other—"We must, indeed, appear as strange to the natives as they are to us"—and only a little taken aback when a woman in Guam, after complimenting her on her curly hair, offered to come on board and kill her head lice.

Dietary customs fooled her completely, especially when Moslem guests left the table in horror after pork was served, but a Papuan pirate chief who "became very attached" to her chairs was immediately presented one. Another Papuan inhaled all the pepper on the table, ate all their pickles, and asked for "the plate, the glass and the bottle" he had used. These were gladly given (though she refused him the napkin), for Rose found him such excellent company. She even maintained her poise when some of the Hawaiian men startled her by throwing off all their clothes, layer by layer, as they got hotter and hotter while working their way through enormous meals.

Her letters provide a view of the early-nineteenth-century Pacific that is as feminine as it is French. Only a Frenchwoman, surely, would slyly remark, as Rose did, that a certain Australian was not just "very pretty" but had "a ravishing ankle, or so Louis noticed." And then there was the celestial singing at a religious festival in Rio de Janeiro, in which the voices, "though far too sweet and melodious to belong to men, had a virile force and a vigor which were not characteristic of women's voices. I was overwhelmed," Madame declared, and took the first opportunity to ask details. "The answer"—that the singers were *castrati*—"conjured up a cruelty I could never have imagined before that day!" *Quelle horreur!* What a waste! More amusing were the native girls a party from *L'Uranie* surprised bathing in the Marianas, who screamed with embarrassment and flew to cover themselves, but were more concerned with veiling their backs than their breasts. "Methinks the gentlemen were not tempted to take issue with them on this matter!"

Search as a reader might through Abby Jane Morrell's account of her voyage, it would be impossible to find coquettish little comments like these. In contrast to the vivaciously Gallic Rose, Abby Jane was an unmistakably staid New Englander. For instance, she was very proud that her husband ran a temperance ship, while Rose was rueful that they had not carried enough wine to be properly hospitable. Both were staunchly patriotic, comparing all they saw on shore to the state of things back home, but where Abby Jane was determined to show herself worthy of both her country and her sex, Rose was much more interested in observing the world, commenting on the habits of the people she saw, and deciding which dress would be best.

Ironically, each of the women was faced with a problem that the other could have solved much more easily. Abby Jane's test came in Manila, where the *Antarctic* dropped anchor in March 1830. On shore, she was introduced to the American consul, a gentleman of apparently "respectable acquirements" and "courteous manners," who was extraordinarily attentive. Then, to her horror, Benjamin casually informed her that he was leaving her behind while he sailed off to investigate the *bêche de mer* grounds of Fiji. In his own account, he gave no reason for this, instead ruminating on approvingly about the voluptuously uncorseted dress of Manila females, but he probably had the cannibalistic reputation of Fijians in mind. Abby Jane jumped to quite a different conclusion. To her fevered imagination, it was the consul's fault. He had forbidden Captain Morrell to take her along because he lusted after her precious plump body and wanted her all to himself.

Luckily, perhaps, she didn't confide this to Benjamin, "for fear of the consequences from his quick sense of injury, and his high spirit as a brave man." In a word, she imagined that her short, stout husband would challenge the heavy-breathing consul to a duel. The day before departure, she did her utmost to stow away on the ship (though not to the extent of cross-

Manila, from Le Voyage autour du Monde, *by Dampierre.*

dressing), but this was foiled when Benjamin, along with three visiting captains and the consul, came on board. Abby Jane resorted to her old tactics of fainting and weeping; nonetheless she was firmly returned to shore. Not even taken as far as her boarding place, she was left to stand forlornly on the quay until someone fetched her, while the locals gathered about to stare at this plump little American lady who was so oddly attired in bonnet and voluminous skirts, her middle tightly cramped with her stays.

Abby Jane completely misinterpreted their natural curiosity, jumping to the hysterical conclusion that "the consul had scattered slanders about me and my husband, in order that I might feel myself so shunned and ruined as to fly to him for protection." Instead, she dramatically resolved that she would "die there before I would even speak to him." Meantime Benjamin blithely sailed away, to make the acquaintance of the same bewitching native girls Rose de Freycinet had described—the ones who were abashed about their backs but did not mind showing their breasts— and discover to his pleasure that they had "lips of just the proper thickness for affection's kiss." He did not return for ten weeks, during which time Abby Jane was doing her best to maintain a ladylike pose in Manila, though "frequently annoyed by notes from the consul" which she "never deigned to answer."

High drama indeed, fit for a gaslit stage, even if it did happen mostly in Abby Jane's overheated imagination. It is not a stance that one can picture Rose de Freycinet taking, for with her French sophistication she would have handled the situation with so much more finesse. Poor Abby Jane, who was genuinely scared, would have been the first to concede this, remarking rather wistfully after visiting Bordeaux that there was "such ease in the manners of the French," compared to her own "ruder culture."

There was much that was admirable about Abby Jane. When things went wrong for her, she staunchly reminded herself that "I had embarked at my own solicitation." She forced herself to become brave, declaring that courage was "a virtue which is generally acquired by the necessity of braving dangers." For her, acquiring courage was very necessary, for her husband was far too busy to bother himself with female qualms. And so she developed an insouciance that Benjamin found uncommonly irritating at least once.

It happened on a squally night in a dark, uncharted sea. The schooner was under mainsail, foresail, topgallant sail, square sail, jib, and flying jib, and they were dashing along at the rate of ten knots, when breakers were abruptly sighted dead ahead. For a long ghastly moment, there was nothing to be heard "but the whistling of the winds and the howling of the lofty combers, about one hundred and fifty fathoms under our lee," and then Morrell's orders came thick and fast. "Keep the helm hard a-port! Brace the head-yards aback! Down mainsail! Up head-sails, with sheets to windward!" he cried. The vessel was coming to very fast, she was on the verge of missing stays—and Abby Jane hove onto deck, looked about, and smiled brightly. "Dearest," she inquired, "shouldn't you be wearing a hat?"

"My reply was short and *not* sweet," wrote Morrell. Withal, it is rather nice to learn that after they returned home, and both had written books about their experiences, Abby Jane's book did a lot better than his did.

By contrast, Rose de Freycinet was invariably "shaking with fear" when the weather gusted, in great need of reassurance from her gallant and loving Louis, who was always very happy to oblige her. After two years she confessed that voyaging had altered her nature—that everything she had endured had given her "such a somber outlook on life" that "the gay, wild and scatterbrained Rose has become serious." And so it seems particularly ironic that it was Rose, and not Abby Jane, who was forced to undergo the ordeal of shipwreck.

Departing from Sydney on Christmas Day 1819, the corvette rounded Cape Horn on February 6, 1820, and on the fourteenth struck a submerged rock in the Falkland Islands. As Rose described it, they were sitting at the table when the ship stopped in her wake a moment and then sailed on. The shock was so slight that nothing was upset, but shortly afterward, water started rushing into the holds. The gentle blow was fatal, for a rock had pierced the hull. Pumping madly, they headed for a sandy shore where the ship could be beached and the collections saved before she was a total loss. The operation took ten arduous hours.

Abby Jane, no doubt, would have risen stoutly to the occasion. Poor Rose was abject with terror. She shut herself in her cabin, "overcome by the horror of our situation," and for a while she and the Abbé knelt together in prayer, but then she rallied to help the crew bring all the ship's biscuit to the poop, to save it from being soaked. As Arago put it, *la pauvre petite* "arranged it all with the minutest care." Every now and then she could be seen at her window, vainly searching the faces of passing sailors for a sign of hope. And all the time the men labored at the pump, shouting out crude, wild songs to keep up their strength and spirits. When Rose cried out that they must put their trust in the holy Virgin, Arago retorted, "In the holy pump, Madame!"

Whatever the focus of their prayers, it worked. A faint, kind breeze wafted them up onto a sandy beach at three in the morning. The barren

Sydney, 1823. Contemporary engraving.

sandhills that dawn revealed did not look promising, but the company took the ship's altar ashore and said a *Te Deum*. Then they started the huge task of discharging all the scientific material from the holds and cabins of the corvette, and storing it in tents hastily set up on the beach. With wonderful single-mindedness, the scientists built an observatory in preparation for an eclipse of the sun on 15 March.

It was now that de Freycinet felt very thankful that he had shipped tradesmen for his crew, for he had the necessary carpenters, sailmakers, blacksmiths, and ropemakers to turn the ship's longboat into a seaworthy craft. They called the little vessel *L'Espérance*—Hope. Because they still staunchly believed that they would somehow make the voyage north to Rio, hunting and fishing parties were assembled to go foraging in the hinterland and save as much preserved food as possible. However, fresh provisions soon became scarce. For the hunters to track down a wild horse was an occasion for joy, for otherwise their diet was limited to penguins or seal meat, roasted or stewed in water with biscuit crumbs for thickening. A wild bird was a special treat.

Rose was certainly learning courage. She slept on a plank set on two chairs, wrapped only in a sarong, even when there was ice on the ground in the mornings. Then, as ships and cutters called at the bay, hopes of rescue rose and fell. The captains made promises to take the expedition and their specimens to Rio de Janeiro on the payment of such-and-such a fee, and then changed their minds when Louis de Freycinet agreed, to demand an even higher amount.

Finally, he made an arrangement with the master of the *Mercury*, a leaky old 280-ton tub that had set off to double Cape Horn, who had been forced to take shelter in a hurry to effect some necessary repairs, which the expedition tradesmen promptly did for him. This act of charity did not make Captain Galvin of the *Mercury* any less avaricious. First, he threw a tantrum because some cable he had requested had not arrived on board, and threatened to leave without them. Then, he wanted ten thousand piastres to take them to Buenos Aires, only half the distance they wanted to go.

After another bout of argument, he grudgingly offered to take them to Rio de Janeiro for fifteen thousand, but then abruptly changed his mind, asking eighteen thousand. "This is an enormous price to pay for the minor inconvenience we shall cause him. But he is a rogue who is trying to profit from our present predicament." Meantime, Rose packed boxes, and suffered from the wet and cold, scarcely able to walk because of the agony in her frozen feet.

Finally, after a great deal of insult and shouting, the company was at last on board the *Mercury*, two months to the day since the wreck of the corvette. "*Uranie!* Poor *Uranie!* You who were my abode for so long . . . we must now forsake you for ever!" Rose's cabin on the discovery ship had been small enough, but here she was in a cubbyhole with much of the scientific collection, lit only by a small round of glass in the deck overhead, which went abruptly dark every time someone stepped onto it. Worse still, all her painfully gained courage seemed to be flooding away:

> It deserts me every time I compare our present circumstances with what they were three months ago. Then we were well housed, well fed, about to complete a voyage which up to that point had been entirely successful, and here we are now in a miserable foreign vessel, in a room where we cannot both sit down without touching either the walls or the bed, eating indescribable food with strangers to whom one has to be pleasant and whom I would often like to send packing. . . . I am most distressed to see Louis suffering continually. This saddens me and troubles me so much that I cannot stop crying.

Fate, yet again, was ironic. The commander of the Scottish brig *Jane,* a 120-ton whaler that had been at anchor in Berkeley Sound, not far away, arrived to declare that he would have been glad to rescue them all at no cost. This was Captain James Weddell, a man whose naval career had been interrupted by the end of the Napoleonic Wars, and who went on to become a distinguished Antarctic explorer. He was delighted with the "extreme vivacity" of Madame, "who was young and very agreeable."

Louis presented him with the cutter on which the French seamen had worked so hard, and Weddell christened her *Rose*.

Finally, on April 27, the *Mercury* set sail, still rife with dissension. Galvin kept altering his demands, while first the passengers and then the French company threatened to seize the ship. Finally, the dilemma was settled by buying the ship in the name of the French government, for eighteen thousand piastres, the same amount that had been bargained for the passage to Rio. "All this is preferable to coming to blows," Rose, with French practicality, agreed.

And so the vacillating, blackmailing Galvin and his unpleasant passengers were set ashore at Montevideo with their traps, and the French company sailed on to Rio in their new possession, renamed *Physicienne*. Here, Rose became reacquainted with friends made on the outward passage, listened again to the *castrati* (this time without a tremor), rejoined society, and refurbished her wardrobe. *La Physicienne* was being repaired and refurbished, too, a process that took over two months, and for which Brazil's Minister of Marine would take no payment.

They sailed from Rio at dawn on September 13, 1820. Finally, on November 13, three years and fifty-seven days since the night Rose de Freycinet had crept on board, the expedition anchored in Le Havre. It was a moment that Louis and Rose de Freycinet both welcomed and dreaded, for now they had to face the consequences of their actions.

Louis was, of course, court-martialed for the loss of his ship. The deliberations lasted exactly an hour and a half. Captain Louis-Claude de Saulces de Freycinet was completely exonerated of all blame, the court finding unanimously that he had done all that prudence and honor demanded. Rose's name was not mentioned, her presence tactfully ignored. The ordeal seemed behind them. Rose, who had arrived in Montevideo pale, yellowish, and sunken-eyed, was once again able to dance all night, and Louis, who had been sick and racked with worry and pain, was back to noticing elegant ankles.

The voyage, however, was yet to take its tragic toll. In 1832, when Louis fell ill during a cholera epidemic, Rose was struck down while nursing him and died within hours, at the age of thirty-seven. Heartbroken, Louis survived for another ten years, but, as a friend remarked, it could not be called "living," for "he only languished."

And Abby Jane Morrell? She arrived safely in New York on August 27, 1831, came on shore, and nine days afterward gave birth to a son. This was her first mention of a pregnancy. Rose de Freycinet would have been delirious with delight. Abby Jane merely wrote that "new cares" were now her lot. However, she found time to produce her book.

As for the voyage, it had been a financial failure, though the discoveries of new *bêche de mer* lagoons, made during Abby Jane's nerve-wracking spell in Manila, led to a Salem-based trade that persisted until the Civil War, worth about thirty thousand dollars a year. Otherwise, Benjamin Morrell dropped out of sight, a victim of his own pomposity, his claims about the importance of his voyages being viewed as highly exaggerated.

Chapter Eighteen

TO THE RESCUE!

'Twas on the Longstone lighthouse
There dwelt an English maid
Pure as the air around her
Of danger ne'er afraid.
One morning just at daybreak,
A storm toss'd wreck she spied;
And tho' to try seemed madness,
"I'll save the crew!" she cried

—Popular song

She was born in 1815—an epochal year, the year of the Battle of Waterloo, but without a hint that she would become the icon of her era. In fact, until the age of twenty-two, Grace Horsley Darling passed a thoroughly unexceptionable existence in Longstone Lighthouse in the Farne Islands, a forbidding cluster of rocks off the coast of Northumberland.

The seventh child in a family of eight, Grace was taught by her parents to read (romances, novels, and plays were forbidden), knit, spin, sew, and keep herself and her apartments clean. Like her father, lighthouse keeper William Darling, she studied bird life. And she helped him with the light. This was not at all unusual, for lighthouse keeping was very much a family business. Keepers were allowed to augment their small incomes with salvaging, piloting, and fishing, and their wives and children were expected to maintain the light while they were away. This was officially recognized, though hardly noted at all by the public. But then, at a fateful midnight on September 5, 1838, the 450-ton steamer *Forfarshire* set sail from Hull for Dundee and created history.

The *Forfarshire* might have been small, but by the standards of the time she was very grand, though somewhat suspiciously newfangled, traveling

Advertisement for the Forfarshire.

by steamship being a distinct novelty then. In a drive to get customers, her owners, the Dundee & Hull Steam-Packet Company, advertised her as both "splendid and powerful," and the *Forfarshire* was sumptuous to suit. There were private staterooms and ornately decorated saloons where lavish repasts were served on giltscrolled plates inscribed with a likeness of the vessel. The steam packet *Forfarshire* could be regarded as the *Titanic* of the day.

The starboard boiler began leaking in the morning, while the weather was getting grim. Then, the engines broke down. Instead of turning for port, Captain Humble gave the order for sails to be set—a very bad move, for with their ponderous paddle boxes projecting out to each side, steamboats had very poor sailing qualities. Disaster was imminent and probably inevitable. Shortly before four in the morning of the seventh, the ship ran onto Big Harcar Rock in the Farne Islands, three quarters of a mile from the Longstone lighthouse. Thirty-five people died, nine got away, and nine were stranded on the rock.

> They to the rock were clinging
> A crew of nine all told
> Between them and the lighthouse
> The sea like mountains rolled.
> Said Grace: "Come help me, Father,
> We'll launch that boat," said she.
> Her father cried, " 'Tis madness,
> To face that raging sea."

According to legend, Grace Darling heard the cries of the shipwreck victims from her bed. This was not possible, for the wind was blowing the other way, so it was not until dawn, about three hours later, that she and her father realized that there were people on the rock. The poetic claim that Grace had to urge her father "to face that raging sea" is also sheer fiction—and slanderous, too, for the thought of leaving the poor wretches to their fate never crossed Mr. Darling's

Broadside, "To the Rescue!"

mind. However, he was faced with quite a problem. His only assistant, William Jr., was away with the fishermen in the coastal village of North Sunderland. He had no choice—Grace had to help, and that was that. It was probably not even discussed, being so self-evident. Mrs. Darling (who was in her sixties) helped them shove the lighthouse coble (a sturdy, flat-bottomed rowing boat) into the water, and Grace and her father each took an oar to pull the boat to the nine castaways.

> *They bravely rode the billows*
> *And reached the rock at length:*
> *They saved the storm toss'd sailors*
> *In heaven alone their strength.*
> *Go, tell the wide world over,*
> *What English pluck can do;*
> *And sing of brave Grace Darling,*
> *Who nobly saved the crew!*

The "crew" actually comprised just four sailors, one of them hurt; the rest were passengers, including a woman, Mrs. Dawson, who was in shock, her small children having died in her arms. William Darling jumped onto the rock and helped Mrs. Dawson and the hurt crewman into the boat while Grace held the boat off with the oars. Then he and the three unimpaired seamen rowed the coble back to the lighthouse while Grace sat in the sheets and tended to the hurt man. A second trip was made to pick up the rest of the survivors. The boat was pulled by Mr. Darling and two of the crew while Grace stayed back at the lighthouse to help her mother with the injured man and Mrs. Dawson.

Meantime, Grace's brother, William Jr., had been alerted to the wreck. He and six fishermen set out, but by the time they arrived all the survivors

had been taken off the rock. As the weather was too rough to return to North Sunderland, he and the fishermen made for the lighthouse, which meant that for three days nineteen people were stranded stormbound in the lighthouse keeper's accommodations, a situation that has been memorialized since in countless sentimental engravings.

At first, however, Grace Darling's name was not even mentioned. The earliest report was in the *Dundee Courier,* which noted on September

Grace Darling. Artist: Ron Druett, after C. Cook.

11 that the ship had been wrecked and thirty-five of the crew and passengers had been drowned. According to the Dundee & Hull Steam-Packet Company, eight of the crew and one passenger had got away in the ship's boat, and "2 Firemen; a Carpenter; a Cook; a Woman, and 4 steerage passengers" had been saved by persons unnamed.

Initially, everyone just wanted to know what had caused the disaster. Captain Humble, who had gone down with the ship, was greatly blamed. He had drowned "with his wife in his arms," but that made no difference to editorial severity, for he was definitely guilty of "culpable negligence." However, this was not on the scale of the aspersions cast on the eight crew members—including the mate!—who had got away with the single ship's boat, taking just one passenger and leaving everyone else stranded. Universal condemnation was heaped on the heads of "the false crew," whose conduct was so unlike "that which is a characteristic of British seamen," who, when they found that there was "alas! no boat save one,

> *To that did the false crew hurry,*
> *And of all the passengers was there none*
> *Left to tell the sad mournful story? . . .*
> *A shriek was heard as they sank in the deep,*
> *While away the false crew were gliding!*

And then, like an angel-sent message from heaven, the world found out that goodness still existed, for the story of Grace's role in the rescue hit the papers. One of the earliest to report her deed was the *Warder* of Berwick-on-Tweed, which breathlessly declared that the lighthouse keeper's daughter—though just "twenty-two years of age!"—had displayed a brand of heroism "which in a female transcends all praise." On September 19 the story was taken up by *The Times* of London, which described it as "an instance of heroism and intrepidity on the part of a female unequalled perhaps certainly not surpassed, by any on record. I allude," the reporter trumpeted, "to the heroic conduct of Miss Grace Horsley Darling," the "intrepid daughter" of the lighthouse keeper, who "succeeded after many 'hairbreadth 'scapes' in navigating their frail skiff over the foaming billows." Not just was the boat "kept afloat by the skilfulness and dexterity" of this "noble-minded daughter, who is said to be of slender appearance," but once back at the lighthouse

> the same tender hand that had been so eminently instrumental in preserving them from a watery grave anxiously for three days and nights waited on the sufferers, administered to their wants, and soothed their afflictions. It is impossible to speak in adequate terms of the unparalleled bravery and disinterestedness shown on this occasion by Mr. Darling and his truly heroic daughter, especially so with regard to the latter. Surely such unexampled heroism will not go unrewarded.

"Is there in the whole field of history, or of fiction even, one instance of female heroism to compare for one moment with this?" the writer demanded. The obvious answer is, "Yes, of course," but that made not a jot of difference. The media went mad, producing a torrent of poems, songs, books, and other excessively flowery tributes—and the Darlings nearly went mad, too. It seemed as if the world was calling at their door, the vanguard being no less than twelve artists, all eager to do

MISS GRACE HORSLEY DARLING.

As American readers saw the Heroine.
Detail from *Godey's Lady's Book.*

their portraits. Every post brought a raft of pleas for locks of Grace's hair. Presents arrived, and letters of gratitude had to be written. Boatloads of fans arrived at the lighthouse to tour the apartments and frighten the bird life away.

The Tomb. Contemporary engraving.

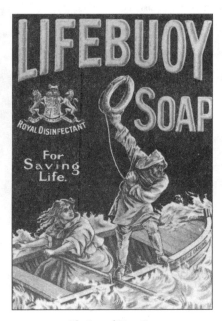

The Legend Lives On.

A hero arrived on the scene, however. With Victorian paternalism, the Duke of Northumberland took a hand. The Duchess, who had been Queen Victoria's governess, received a letter addressed from the Queen to Grace, for safekeeping and proper delivery, and the Duke therewith announced his intention of making the young heroine his ward. He sent for the senior Darlings and their heroic daughter, to explain that he had made the decision to set up a trust fund for all the money that was coming in, and would manage it in Grace Darling's name. Then he sent them off to the servants' quarters (their proper surroundings) for the housekeeper to give them some tea, and after that they were given a tour of the castle by the porter.

And, of course, the Darlings were properly impressed. The Duke remained keenly interested, sending presents at Christmas that had been chosen with their welfare, both corporal and spiritual, in mind—waterproof cloaks for the women, waterproof trousers for Mr. Darling, a silver teapot and tea to go into it, a prayerbook, and a wind-up watch. When Grace became mortally ill of consumption in 1842, the Northumberlands arranged nearby lodgings for her and the attendance of their own physician, the Duchess herself calling on the invalid twice. Nonetheless, Grace died. An elaborate tomb (which kept falling apart) was constructed, Wordsworth wrote a wordy (and very bad) poem, and the gush of romantic adulation continued. All the way into the twentieth century, Grace Darling's deed has been eulogized in girls' magazines without number, her image immortalized on plates, mustard tins, tea canisters, and chocolate boxes, and molded into mugs, jugs, and ornaments. Her picture has even appeared on a bottle of rum. There is a Grace Darling Museum in Bamburgh, Northumberland, her birthplace, and tour boats ply the Rescue Route. As an icon, Grace Darling has startling permanence.

The Lighthouse keeper's Daughter.
From *Harper's Young People*, May 1882.

Yet, other women did as well, and often at greater personal risk. Some were mere teenagers. In September 1814, during the war between the United States and Britain, marines from an English man-of-war landed near the New England coastal town of Scituate. The lighthouse keeper, Simeon Bates, was away on an errand, and his daughters, Rebecca and Abigail, were in charge. Realizing they did not have time to warn the town, the girls grabbed a fife and drum and marched up and down, playing loudly. Like the Welsh women of Fishguard, they fooled the marines into believing that the militia were there, and thus Abigail and Rebecca Bates became quite famous as the "Lighthouse Army of Two."

Fourteen-year-old Maebelle Mason, daughter of the keeper of the Mamajuda Lighthouse in the Detroit River, rowed out into a racing current to save a drowning man, with just her mother to assist. For this, she was awarded a silver (or second-class) lifesaving medal, which she received "with the naïve modesty so charming in a young maiden, believing she had but performed an act of humanity." Kate Moore of Black Rock Light, Connecticut, started trimming the lights at the age of twelve, and remained at her post until 1878, when she was eighty-four years old. In that time she saved at least twenty-one lives, though the lighthouse itself once blew over in a storm.

Another lighthouse keeper's daughter to watch her quarters being wrecked was Abbie Burgess, who began to assist at the Matinicus Rock Light, Maine, at the age of fourteen, and was in charge of the light during a terrible gale at the age of seventeen, in 1856. "You have often expressed a desire to view the sea out upon the ocean when it was angry," she wrote dryly to a friend. "Had you been here on the 19 January, I surmise you would have been satisfied." By the time the storm was over, not one stone of the keeper's house was standing, but throughout it all the lamps had been kept alight.

Kate Walker, who was in her forties when she took over the Robbins Reef Light, New York, in 1894, was just four feet ten inches tall and weighed less than one hundred pounds. Nevertheless, she rescued as many as fifty people who had been blown onto the reef by sudden storms, once rowing out alone to take aboard the five crew of a wrecked schooner. What pleased her most, however, was that she managed to rescue their little Scottie dog, too. She also once retrieved a young woman's reputation. A courting couple were out rowing when their boat was wrecked, and it was so late by the time they were brought to the lighthouse that it was obvious they wouldn't be able to get home that night. So Kate got them to Staten Island, where they were promptly married by a minister. And, after sending off a telegram to the young lady's folks, they commenced a happy honeymoon, secure in the knowledge that the bride's name was safe.

"A great city's water front is rich in romance," observed the *New York Evening Post* after Kate Walker's death in 1931, at the age of eighty-three:

> There is a strangeness about the restless ships that know the other side of the world; there are queer men busy in curious occupations; there are mysteries of sky and sea and weather. There are the queenly liners, the grim battle craft, the countless carriers of commerce that pass in endless procession. And amid all this and in sight of the city of towers and the torch of liberty lived this sturdy little woman, proud of her work and content in it, keeping her lamp alight and her windows clean, so that New York Harbor might be safe for ships that pass in the night.

Another notable saver of lives was Abigail Becker, who was at the other end of the physical scale to tiny Kate Walker, and not even associated with a lighthouse. When the schooner *Conductor* was wrecked on

Long Point, Lake Erie, in a snowstorm on November 23, 1854, Abigail, wife of a local fisherman and trapper, waded out into the icy surf to rescue the seven-strong crew single-handedly. Twenty-three years old, six feet tall, and weighing 215 pounds, she must have been a riveting sight as she plunged in and out of the gusting storm to haul them one by one to shore. No one wrote about her, as they did about Grace Darling, that "down the weather-beaten cheek of one old seaman stole the big round tear when he beheld from the wreck the noble exertions of a young female of slender appearance," but the seamen were undoubtedly grateful. Once they had been dragged to the beach, they thawed out by the fire her children had hastily built. Then, for six stormbound days, Abigail sheltered the men in her driftwood shack, unreservedly sharing her scant provisions.

The owner of the schooner, Captain E. P. Dorr, was so impressed that he rewarded her by sending a boxful of shoes for her and her nine children and stepchildren, along with an inscribed Bible. And he did not neglect to tell the world about it, too. As a result, Abigail became quite famous. The Seamen's Union gave her a dinner in a Buffalo, New York, hotel, and she was presented with a thousand dollars in gold and a medal from the Life-Saving Associates of New York. The Canadian Parliament awarded her a hundred-acre farm in Norfolk County, near Long Point, and Queen Victoria sent her a letter of commendation.

Another such heroine was Idawalley Zorada Lewis, daughter of the keeper of Lime Rock lighthouse in Newport Harbor, Rhode Island. When her father was disabled by a stroke in 1858, Ida took over all of his duties, though she was only just sixteen. That year she single-handedly saved four young men who were clinging to their capsized boat. They were rather shamefaced about it, for they were the "sons of gentlemen," and should not have been playing the silly games that caused their boat to overturn. So they kept quiet about it, and Ida did, too.

Instead of bragging, she

Ida Lewis. Artist: Ron Druett.

kept on rescuing people. One party was a group of soldiers on a spree, who had "borrowed" a boat that was lying about on the shore (and which, incidentally, belonged to Ida's brother) and then had drunkenly broken it. Again, a discreet silence was preserved. Two Irishmen, chasing a sheep that had escaped and was swimming off across the bay, were the next to "borrow" the brother's boat. They, too, wrecked it. Ida rescued them in the lighthouse boat, then rowed out and lassoed the sheep, and towed it to shore as well.

Again, everyone kept their counsel. And so Ida's consistent and matter-of-fact gallantry did not get recognized until 1869, when two soldiers from the garrison at Fort Adams hired a boy to take them out sailing and were wrecked in a storm. With the help of her brother, Ida rowed out and saved the soldiers, though not the boy, who was drowned.

Ida Lewis, cover girl.

It was an exploit reminiscent in style to the Grace Darling feat, something that the papers picked up very quickly. The *New York Herald-Tribune* of April 15, 1869, was the first to laud the courage of "the intrepid daughter" of the lighthouse keeper who "performed a deed that places her side by side, in point of self-sacrificing courage, with the Grace Darling of England." The soldiers, it seemed, had presented her with a gold watch, while "John Carter Brown, esq. of Providence, and John Auchinloss, esq. of New York have each sent her a check for $25." Other tributes flowed from this: The Fifth Regiment of U.S. Artillery collected $218, and the New York Life Saving society gave her a medal just like Abigail Becker's, along with a check for $100. She got a letter of commendation from the Rhode Island General Assembly and a brand-new lifeboat, met President Ulysses Grant, and was the first woman to be awarded the Congressional Medal of Honor.

Public fanhood arrived as well. Young swells wore Ida Lewis hats and ties, and young belles knotted their scarves *"à la Rescue."* Both sexes hopped to the rhythm of the "Ida Lewis Mazurka" and the "Rescue Polka." Hundreds of letters were delivered, along with a multitude of marriage proposals, and people flocked to the lighthouse to laud and explore—nine thousand in just one summer. Like Grace Darling, Ida did not enjoy the adulation. As the *Newport Daily News* phrased it, she could save other folk from drowning but was an abject failure at saving herself from "the impertinent visits of sightseeing jackasses." When the women's rightist Susan Anthony applauded her for advancing the Cause with her deed, Ida remarked tartly that a visit from the formidable Ms. Anthony had been a greater strain on the nerves than the rescue itself.

Ida Lewis, song sheet cover.

However, the nuisance was relatively short-lived. Ida married a sea captain, but they parted after a couple of years. Then she returned to the lighthouse, where she kept the light for the next forty-two years, until the day she died of a heart attack, at the age of sixty-nine. Her last recorded rescue was at the age of sixty-three. A friend who was rowing out to pay a call stood up in her boat to wave, and fell overboard. Ida launched the lighthouse lifeboat and rowed out to the rescue. How did she find the strength? "Don't know," she offhandedly replied. "I ain't particularly strong. The Lord Almighty gives it to me when I need it, that's all."

Like Abigail Becker, Kate Walker, and Grace Darling, she hadn't thought about heroics. She'd simply done what had to be done.

Chapter Nineteen

NORTHWEST PASSAGE

In Baffin's Bay where the whale-fish blow
The fate of Franklin no man may know . . .
Ten thousand pounds I would freely give
To say on earth that my Franklin lives.

—Folk song

Commenting on the ill-fated 1785 discovery voyage of Jean-François de Galaup, Comte de la Pérouse, Abby Jane Morrell observed that the explorer-count's wife was "supposed to have gone in search of her husband." Personally, Mrs. Morrell thought it "sheer fabrication," though, she added, "it would not be unlike a Frenchwoman to do so, if she had an opportunity to indulge her inclinations." However, it was an Englishwoman who turned the world upside down in her quest for a lost husband, in the process making herself an icon and his name the one that will be eternally associated with the Arctic.

Jane Griffin knew she was marrying a man with a vision when she wed John Franklin on December 5, 1828. He was forty-two years old, a veteran of three Arctic expeditions, and a widower. His first marriage, to Eleanor Porden, a poet, was eloquent evidence of his single-mindedness. In 1825, when Eleanor was expiring of consumption, he trotted off regardless on his third Arctic expedition, after taking the precaution of drawing up her will and putting her personal affairs in order before he left. She died six days after his departure, but John did not get the news until he touched base in the heart of British North America. As an ex-

Ship in ice.

plorer, he was a bit of a bungler, too. Constitutionally plump and delicate of health, partially deaf from the roar of broadsides during the Napoleonic Wars, but driven by a hunger for glory, John Franklin pushed on when wiser commanders would have retreated. Ten good men starved to death on his 1819 expedition, and he almost succumbed himself. In England, he was known as the hero who had eaten his boots.

At thirty-six, Jane was old enough to know what she was doing. Highly eligible, she had turned down many other suitors. Attractive and rather rich, she was descended from a prosperous French Huguenot family. It is even likely that she adored Franklin the way that she declared she did. In a letter written before the wedding, she vowed to recognize "the authority which it will be your privilege to use and my duty to yield to."

Lady Jane Franklin. Artist: Ron Druett.

This was stock Victorian phraseology, the recommended stance of a properly demure wife-to-be, but then she added, "But do I speak of *duty*?

> You are of a too manly, too generous, too affectionate a disposition to like the word and God forbid I should ever be the wretched wife who obeyed her husband from a sense of duty alone. [My wedding ring will not be] the badge of slavery, but the cherished link of the purest affection.

However, in John Franklin, who was an easygoing and malleable fellow when not on expeditions, she may well have seen a means of furthering fierce ambitions of her own. Extraordinarily energetic and restless, bilingual and cultured, an inveterate traveler and supporter of good causes, Jane would have aimed for fame herself if she had not been hampered by her sex. Marrying a celebrity was a good alternative. Shortly after the wedding, John was knighted and awarded the gold medal of the Geographical Society of Paris, which she undoubtedly found as gratifying as he did.

Sir John Franklin. Artist: Ron Druett.

Events moved slowly after that, however. The new knight was merely given command of a ship in the Mediterranean. Jane made up for it by plunging into a grand tour of Greece, Asia Minor, and the Holy Land, traveling by every conveyance she could lay hands on, from ship to canal boat to cart and carriage, even trekking by foot when necessary. When Sir John's service in the Mediterranean ended in 1833, Jane was off up the Nile, but that did not deter her from managing his career, for she simply scrawled off a lot of letters. She urged him to ask the First Lord of the Admiralty for a job, and when he replied that he'd been told there was nothing available, she told him to push harder. He should go to the Arctic again and make a great name for himself. What about the Northwest Passage? People had been hunting for years for a trade route from the Atlantic to the Pacific via the waterways of north Canada. Anyone who could find that Passage would be a great hero, and a rich one, too. Why couldn't he persuade the Navy to finance an expedition, and put him in charge of it? After all, he had been knighted for his Arctic exploits, had he not?

Franklin was offered the minor post of Governor of the little island of Antigua, in the Caribbean, and Jane really hit the roof. So the Navy offered Sir John the governorship of Van Diemen's Land—the penal settlement of Tasmania, Australia—and the Franklins accepted. It was a terrible mistake. The unanticipated sight of seventeen thousand wretched convicts boosted Jane's philanthropic instincts to a state of near-frenzy. She was supposed to be a hostess and preside at formal occasions. Instead, she toured prisons, criticized the treatment of female convicts, tried to start a college, and campaigned to make life endurable for the poor wretches. All she accomplished was to make life unendurable for Sir John. He looked like a weakling, and she looked like a meddler, with the result that he was fired in mortifying circumstances in 1844. There was only one way he could retrieve his reputation, and that was by discovering something important. Jane started prodding and pushing about that Northwest Passage again. Sir John was too fat and too old—in his sixtieth year—but that made no difference.

Well, it made no difference to Jane. The Navy thought otherwise, but in the end they organized the most ambitious Arctic expedition to date, outfitting two ships—the 372-ton *Erebus* and the 325-ton *Terror*—that had already proved their worth in the Antarctic, along with a crew of 134 officers and men. And they put Sir John in charge of it, simply because everyone felt so sorry for him. As another Arctic explorer, Sir Edward Parry, wrote to the Admiralty, "If you don't let him go, the man will die of disappointment."

The ships left Greenhithe, in the Thames, on May 19, 1845. The expedition was spoken by the whalers *Enterprise* and *Prince of Wales* in Baffin Bay on July 26, and that was the last of the news. After that, two ships and 129 men (five had left the expedition in Greenland, returning to England on a supply vessel) simply disappeared, just as if absorbed by the Arctic mists.

For two whole years no one seemed very worried, except for a couple of whaling captains. After returning to Peterhead, Scotland, in October 1845, Captain Robert Martin of the *Enterprise,* who had been one of the last to see the Franklin ships, talked about his misgivings to a fellow whaling master, Captain William Penny of the *Saint Andrew.* Consequently, Penny made an attempt to locate the expedition during the next whaling season, completely without success.

Jane, who had been touring the West Indies and the United States, arrived home on the second anniversary of the departure and started to become very concerned, for she thought that she should have had letters by this time, the last she had received from her husband having been from Greenland. In November 1847 she held a meeting at her home, the agenda being a plan to talk the Admiralty into action. The man she chose to lead her proposed expedition was James Clark Ross, a veteran of exploratory voyages to both the Arctic and the Antarctic. Surely, she thought, the Admiralty would be impressed. Instead, the Admiralty turned a deaf ear. So Jane launched a letter-writing campaign that was rewarded with a wave of publicity.

In March 1848 the Admiralty caved in, offering the enormous reward of twenty thousand pounds to anyone who saved the lives of any of the Franklin party, or ten thousand for good information about the fate of the lost expedition. One ship, HMS *Plover,* set off via the Pacific to Bering Strait, where the Passage was supposed to exit in the west, while James Ross and Edward Bird took HMS *Enterprise* and HMS *Investigator* to Lancaster Sound at the eastern end, where Franklin had last been seen. Additionally, an overland party led by John Rae was sent down the Mackenzie River. Jane would have liked to go with Bird and Ross, but did not. She had much more useful work to do, soliciting public sympathy and support.

She was outstandingly successful. By Christmas, prayers were being said in churches. Hundreds of people offered helpful advice, one of them a mystic, the daughter of a Londonderry shipbuilder with the colorful name of Little Wheezy Coppin. More rescue parties set out—two more in 1848, and three in 1849. Jane communicated with all of these and provided funds that she raised from public subscriptions, as well as her own money. A constant stream of letters flowed out from her desk, one of them to the Czar of Russia and another to Zachary Taylor, the new American President, urging him "to join heart and mind in the enterprise of snatching the lost navigators from a dreary grave."

Americans responded immediately, with the result that her mission turned into an international crusade. In 1850 there were ten British ships steering for the Arctic, to be joined by two American Navy vessels, brigs *Advance* and *Rescue,* financed by a New York shipping merchant, Henry Grinnell, helped by Congress. Lady Jane was delighted with the American involvement, writing to Samuel P. Griffin, commander of the *Rescue,* to say how pleased she was to have the assistance of someone with her own maiden name. As a gesture of gallantry all the American officers and men had signed a pledge renouncing any share in the reward if they should be the ones to find out what had happened to Franklin.

Every paper and every magazine ran articles, and books about polar journeys became bestsellers. Talk about the Franklin puzzle dominated clubs and salons. It seemed impossible that two ships and 129 men should disappear so completely, but it had happened. How? It became intensely important that the mystery should be solved and the Franklin party found, and in the throes of it all Lady Jane became a popular heroine.

When she decided that one of the British commanders in the 1850 expeditionary force should be the Scots whaling captain William Penny, who had searched for the *Erebus* and the *Terror* on his own initiative, the

Ships off Greenland, 1850, during the search for Franklin. Illustrated Arctic News.

Admiralty did not agree with her, so she simply announced that she would finance his expedition herself. This led to a public uproar, and the Admiralty yet again caved in, assigning Penny two brigs. The larger, just 201 tons, was christened *Lady Franklin* by Lady Franklin herself. The other, the 109-ton *Sophia,* was named after Sophia Cracroft, Sir John's niece and Lady Jane's devoted friend.

HMS *Lady Franklin,* along with her consort, HMS *Sophia,* entered the Arctic via Lancaster Sound, the same route that Franklin had taken. Thus Penny was with the party that discovered the expedition's winter quarters, on Beechey Island. Chillingly, the base was marked by three graves, the last resting places of three of Franklin's seamen, who had died there in the winter of 1846. There were piles of trash as well—rags, torn-up paper, broken casks, six hundred empty preserved meat cans. Instead of solving the puzzle, however, this merely deepened the mystery. Franklin's party, obviously, had left in a hurry, without time to leave a message. Why? It was unthinkable for the leader of an exploratory expedition not to leave well-marked cairns containing messages, or at least some clue about where he had been and where he was headed. One of the graves was broken open, but no note had been buried with the frozen corpse. Curiosity was at fever pitch. More search expeditions were mounted, two of them financed by Lady Jane herself.

They had as little success as the others, though the Arctic was never so busy. Men were learning how to overwinter in

Graves on Beechey Island. Artist: Ron Druett.

the ice, how to build snow houses, and how to communicate with the natives. Men died, and vessels were abandoned. Commander Robert Mc-Clure and his crew proved the existence of a Northwest Passage by trudging along it while escaping from their iced-in ship, but no more sign of the Franklin party was found. They left huge messages painted on cliffs. Foxes were trapped and released wearing collars with notes tied onto them. Balloons were loosed with more messages, but throughout it all the Arctic kept its silence. One after another the rescue parties were forced to give up, defeated by the huge complexity of the Arctic, the appalling climate, and the ravages of scurvy.

By January 1854, the Admiralty had had enough, and announced that as of March 31, the names of all the men in the Franklin expedition would be struck off the Navy lists, declared dead. Jane was stunned and furious, arguing that the men could not be considered dead when their fate was unknown. She refused to wear mourning and dressed in bright colors. Then John Rae arrived in London with a number of artifacts from the Franklin expedition that some Inuit had sold him—crested forks and spoons, one of Sir John's medals—along with stories of a party of thirty-odd whites who had starved to death. The Admiralty, breathing a corporate sigh of relief, gave Rae and his men the ten-thousand-pound reward, and declared the case closed.

And once again Jane hit the roof. The government should complete the job it had started, "and not leave it to a weak and helpless woman," she exclaimed. The British public applauded wildly, completely ignoring the self-evident fact that she was not weak and helpless at all. By this time she was an adored icon, her fans including such powerful figures as Queen Victoria's husband, Prince Albert.

She wrote more letters, to the Admiralty, to leading men of science, to the papers. Her house on Pall Mall was dubbed "the Battery" because she battered so many important people for support. The general populace was already emphatically on her side. Politicians and monarchs can only dream of the kind of public affection, admiration, and fervent loyalty that Lady Jane inspired. Because of her drive and obsession, the Arctic had been opened up and mapped, and was no longer an unknown quantity. All by herself, Lady Jane Franklin had altered history.

In the middle of this whirl of obsessive activity, she organized an expedition of her own. Spending two thousand pounds of her own money, Jane bought the 170-ton steam yacht *Fox* from the port of Aberdeen and talked a veteran of three previous search attempts, Captain Francis Leopold M'Clintock, into commanding her on an expedition to King

William Island, the one spot in the Arctic where no one had yet searched. The Admiralty, somewhat shamefaced by the bad press they were getting, offered to supply provisions. M'Clintock volunteered to do the job at no pay, calling it a "glorious mission" and "a great national duty," and all the other commissioned officers followed suit. One, Sailing Master Allen Young, even donated five hundred pounds to the cause. On June 30, 1857, the expedition sailed from the Orkneys in a blaze of humanitarian glory.

And Sir John had been dead for exactly ten years.

Lady Jane's orders to M'Clintock were clear and precise. He was to rescue any survivors, recover any documents the expedition had deposited, and prove that Sir John had discovered the Northwest Passage, without unduly endangering his own men. He succeeded in all but the first. After overwintering in Baffin Bay, M'Clintock followed Franklin's trail through Lancaster Sound to Beechey Island, and then turned south to the west coast of Boothia Peninsula and King William Island, where he met a party of Inuit. They had artifacts from the Franklin expedition to trade, along with wooden articles carved from pieces of ships that they said had been crushed and wrecked. There were tales, too, of Englishmen hauling great sledges over the ice toward Great Fish River, who "fell down and died as they walked along," dropping dead in the traces.

It was a grisly trail that M'Clintock followed, marked by scattered skulls and bones. It was also a testament to Victorian pomposity. M'Clintock himself came across one of the Navy sledges, an iron and oak monstrosity with a twenty-eight-foot boat perched on top, the boat itself loaded to the gunwales with silver plate, dinner knives, pocket watches, cookstoves, button polish, scented soap, and religious books—all designed to be hauled by a team of seven men. In among the conglomeration of the kind of luggage that a proper Victorian gentleman thought essential to travel were sprawled two pathetic skeletons.

A ten-ton pile of the same kind of "accumulation of dead weight of little use" was discovered at Victory Point, but here, too, was the evidence that made the M'Clintock expedition worthwhile. Inside a cairn, M'Clintock's first officer, William Robert Hobson, found the only piece of first-hand information that has ever been retrieved from the Franklin disaster.

It was a message dated May 28, 1847, and signed by Lieutenant Graham Gore. The two ships were frozen in off the northern tip of King William Island, he said, but all was well. Everyone was fully confident that they would get out of the ice, come summer. A note with much grimmer tidings, however, had been written about the margins, signed by Franklin's deputies, Lieutenant Francis Crozier and Lieutenant James

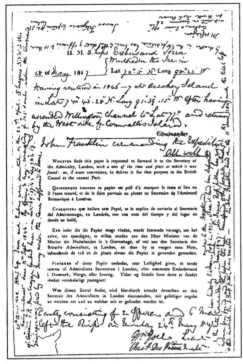

The sole documentary evidence of what happened—the message found in a cairn on the northwest coast of King William Island. The first notation is horizontal and reads: "28 May 1847 H. M. ships Erebus and Terror wintered in the ice in lat. 70 deg 05 min N, long. 98 deg 23 min W. Having wintered, in 1846–7, at Beechey Island, in lat. 74 deg 43 min 28 sec N., long. 91 deg 39 min 15 sec W., after having ascended Wellington Channel to lat. 77 deg, and returned by the west side of Cornwallis Island. All well. Party consisting of two officers and six men left the ships on Monday 24 May 1847." Around the margin, in a different hand, it reads: "April 25th 1848—H. M. ships Terror and Erebus were deserted on the 22nd April, 5 leagues N. N. W. of this having been beset since 12 September 1846. The officers and crews, consisting of 105 souls, under the command of Captain F. R. M. Crozier, landed here in lat. 69 deg 98 min 41 sec. W. Sir John Franklin died on 11 June 1847; and the total loss by deaths in the expedition has been, to this date, nine officers and fifteen men. [signed] F. R. M. Crozier, Captain and Senior Officer. James Fitzjames, Captain of H. M. S. Erebus. And start tomorrow, 26th, for Back's Fish River."

Fitzjames, and dated April 27, 1848. Franklin had died the previous June. Eight officers, including Lieutenant Gore, were dead as well, along with eleven men. The rest had abandoned the iced-in ships, and had begun the impossible mission of dragging the heavily laden sledges toward known fur-trade posts a thousand miles away.

The disaster was total. Not a single member of the expedition had survived. It is probable that the immediate cause of death for most was scurvy, though there is some modern evidence that lead poisoning from poorly soldered preserved meat cans could have played a part, along with starvation, for some of the skeletons show signs of cannibalism. When the ratio of officers to men is considered, however, it seems strange that such a disproportionate number of officers died before the ships were abandoned.

The whole story can never be told, for many mysteries remain. No one knows how Franklin died, or where he is buried. It is impossible to understand why he left no messages, or even signs to mark his route. If he had taken this basic precaution, William Penny would have been able to rescue at least some of the party in 1847. Why did they leave Beechey Island in such a hurry? Only guesses can be made. And had Franklin found the Northwest Passage? Not according to the facts—but, as we shall see, facts can be distorted.

When M'Clintock arrived back in England with his electrifying news, Lady Jane was on a mountaintop in the Pyrenees. She rushed back to London, to find herself more of a popular heroine than ever. Crowds were pushing and shoving to get into the exhibition of expedition artifacts at the United Services Institution. M'Clintock was knighted and given the freedom of the City. Campaigning furiously again, Lady Jane talked Parliament into voting five thousand pounds for the crew of the *Fox*, and they all got the Arctic Medal as well. She herself was the first woman to be awarded the Patron's Medal of the Royal Geographical Society, but to her, that was not what was important.

To her profound satisfaction, at the same time that they gave her the medal, the Society formally testified that Sir John Franklin's expedition had been the first to discover the Northwest Passage. As it happens, Robert McClure had produced the first chart of a Northwest Passage, while in command of a second HMS *Investigator* expedition. But that did not matter. Lady Jane had achieved her ultimate goal, and Sir John Franklin was the undisputed Hero of the Arctic.

Chapter Twenty

ICE QUEENS

Far north, hidden behind a grim barrier of pack ice, are lands that hold one spellbound. . . . The gates swing open, and one enters another world where men are insignificant amid the awesome immensity.

—Louise Arner Boyd

Captain William Penny, the Scots whaling master who was a leader of the party that discovered Franklin's base at Beechey Island, was refused another chance to search in 1852, something which miffed him greatly. He returned to whaling, still with the *Lady Franklin* and *Sophia,* which had been sold into the Aberdeen fleet. Thus, when in 1857 his wife, Margaret, went along with him to spend a long, dark winter iced in at Baffin Island, she sailed in a ship that had already made history.

This was Penny's thirty-fourth voyage to the Arctic, so he knew the area intimately. On the previous expedition with the same two ships, he had also pioneered a method of roofing over the ships to make them habitable while overwintering. It was a very strange existence for Margaret, but for her husband the long, dark months of waiting for spring were well worthwhile, for it meant that the *Lady Franklin* and *Sophia* were ready and waiting for the first migration of whales.

They filled the holds with blubber so quickly, and the news got around so fast, that overwintering became standard Arctic whaling practice. The winters of the last two decades of the nineteenth century regularly discovered a dozen or more whaling vessels snugged up in Pauline Cove at Herschel Island in the western Arctic, all neatly roofed over and with the sides banked up with blocks of snow. Quite a town would be established around these strange residences, for natives, intrigued by the exotic community, built their snow houses nearby on the ice. Inside the ships, it was cozy, and both inside and outside it was sociable.

And Margaret Penny was a trailblazer for her sister sailors as well. It became quite common for whaling captains to expect their wives to come along and preside as hostesses over this strangely domestic scene. In the 1894–95 season there were no fewer than seven European females at Herschel Island—Sophie Porter of the *Jesse H. Freeman* and her daughter, Dorothy, Viola Cook of the *Navarch,* Fanny Weeks of the *Thrasher,* Caroline Sherman of the *Beluga,* Mrs. Green of the *Alexander,* and her niece, Lucy McGuire. It was a strangely formal existence, with dances, whist parties, costume balls, concerts (one concert party being called "The Herschel Island Snowflakes"), and amateur theatricals. Dinner parties were staged, complete with amazing menus. One included "Lobster salad & olives, Oyster Paté with French peas," and "Bartlett Pears, with citron & sponge cake" for dessert. Outside on the ice, there were games and sledding, with boat races once the ice began to melt. The men made up hunting parties and also went in for a great deal of illicit commerce with the natives, trading for furs with rum.

Arctic whaling. Lithograph, Paris, 1860.

The effect of this could be dire. In the spring of 1883 the natives of the northern shore of St. Lawrence Island sold a stockpile of furs for a large quantity of grog. Then they spent the scant summer months carousing instead of collecting food for the oncoming winter. When the Revenue Service cutter *Corwin* arrived on the coast in the spring of 1884, not a single native had survived.

Captain Michael Healy, the commander who reported this calamity, was the most flamboyant law officer of the north. "Roaring Mike," the son of an Irish plantation owner and a mulatto slave, ran away to sea at the age of fifteen and got his first command in 1884 because no one had realized he was black. Mike Healy was tough and fearless, a hard man in a hard trade, a consummate navigator and seaman who rescued innumerable whalemen in distress and arrested countless numbers, too. He was known as "the Ruler of the Arctic Sea." When he was in command of the famous cutter *Bear,* the ship was dubbed "Mike Healy's fire canoe." His word was law, his powers were autocratic—and Mary Jane, his wife, called him hubby.

Captain "Roaring Mike" Healy.
Artist: Ron Druett.

In 1883, Michael was also getting a reputation for hard drinking. Perhaps in order to change this, he asked Mary Jane to come north with their thirteen-year-old son, Fred. They sailed from San Francisco on the steamer *St. Paul* to join him at Kodiak Island. "I am glad of the experience," Mary Jane admitted to her diary; "yet I could not be induced to take another." In May 1884, however, she embarked on the *St. Paul* again, bound for Unalaska to meet hubby again. "I got up to dress," she noted one day out, "but Old Neptune said oh no old lady go back to bed, you must pay me first." Arriving made it all worthwhile, however: "Oh how glad I was to see my hubby and son—In the afternoon hubby and myself went picking wild flowers."

Mary Jane Healy. Artist: Ron Druett.

This time she joined her husband and son on the *Corwin,* venturing into the Arctic. Sailing through heavy ice made her uneasy, for the floes "would shake the vessel as if an earthquake had taken place and strike terror in one's heart." A week later things still looked dire. "We shall have to make a desperate effort to get out," she wrote, "or we will find ourselves here for the winter, not a very pleasant lookout I assure you. We see no loophole for us to get out. My hubby is very much worried."

Despite this, the crew did not seem to be as worried as she was, at one time tying the ship up to an iceberg and climbing out on it to have a snowball fight. Indeed, they were just as interested in finding dead whales as finding a way through the ice. "One of those would give us in bone about $5000 to divide up," and pay the expenses of the trip, she noted with some wonder. "An average whale, oil and bone together, at present prices is worth fully $10,000." Little surprise then, considering the potential profit, that whalemen (and their wives) were willing to spend a winter in these regions. Mary Jane, however, did not want to share their lot, and was understandably relieved when the *Corwin* finally broke through.

In the Bering Strait she had a crowd of visitors on board, all agog to see a woman:

> The women were anxious to see how I dressed. I undid my ulster and they were surprised to see I had a dress under it. Then they wanted me to undo that but I just showed them I had on petticots and liggins but they wanted me to take all off to let them see but I did not gratify their curiosity. I gave them some needles such as we use in sewing. They were much pleased with them and put them through their nose as ornaments. There were some very pretty girls among them. . . . My hair was also a very great curiosity. They would every little while make signs for me to take off my hat and let them see my hair. I gave one of them two hairpins which I took from my hair to let her see I pinned it up. She was delighted and put them in her ears for ornaments.

It was equally delightful to find a thirteen-strong fleet of whaleships off Point Hope. The whalemen gave her a lot of attention and greeted her husband heartily, too, even if he did search their vessels for grog and throw a lot of it overboard. There was a definite love-hate relationship between Roaring Mike and the whaling captains. That year Healy rescued 20 shipwrecked seamen, and in 1888 he saved 110 whose ships had foundered off Point Barrow.

This was a particularly hazardous part of the Arctic Ocean. Mike lobbied the government to build a lifesaving base there, and after they agreed he freighted the building materials and supervised the construc-

Whaling fleet trapped in the ice.
Harper's Weekly, December 1871.

tion. Then, with equal whole-heartedness, he built schools for the natives. All this altruistic energy, however, did not stop people—California's Woman's Christian Temperance Union in particular—from consistently accusing him of drunkenness and brutality, leading to a Board of Inquiry in 1890. The findings cleared Healy, certifying that he had been "a particularly intelligent, zealous and efficient officer in the discharge of his difficult and perilous duties in the Arctic," but the stigma remained, so Mary Jane sailed yet again.

This time, she was on the *Bear*—hubby's "fire canoe." They sailed to Siberia, where she saw reindeer for the first time "and here there were three thousand. It was a never-to-be-forgotten sight." With wonder, she observed the ritual of reindeer-killing, where "the man killing the deer walks towards it, facing the sun; after the knife has been plunged into the heart, the chief's wife inserts her fingers into the wounds and sprinkles the blood around, throwing it first toward the sun."

Mary Jane was on board again the following year when Healy carried sixteen of the animals in pens on the deck, at the start of his mission to save the Eskimos of Arctic America from starvation by introducing domesticated reindeer to Alaska. Again, he searched the whaling fleets for illicit alcohol, throwing eleven barrels of grog and six cases of gin overboard, but the whalemen did not appear to hold any umbrage, dipping their flags in salute as the cutter departed. Then, on the way south, the crew of the *Bear* built more schools for the natives at Cape Prince of Wales and Point Hope, and a storehouse for the whalers at the

Mike Healy's "fire canoe," the revenue cutter Bear.

Point Barrow station that Healy had already established, laboring on through the storms of rain, snow, and hail that Mary Jane described in tones of stalwart endurance. It seems ironic, then, that despite his wife's support and his unstinting efforts on behalf of the whalemen and the natives, in 1895 Healy faced another inquisition, this time a court-martial.

Again, he was charged with intoxication. This time he was found guilty. Captain Michael Healy was suspended from command and kept on waiting orders for four years. In 1900, after a drunken binge, he attempted suicide. Mary Jane wrote sorrowfully, "I am truly brokenhearted." She felt that it would have been better, almost, if he had succeeded in taking his own life: "It is hard to say, but if it was God's will and Michael well prepared, it would be better that He took him, for then we would not dread the future for him."

As it happens, in 1901, Michael Healy was returned to duty after the sudden death of another captain, and in 1902 his rank was restored. His great spirit had been destroyed, however. Roaring Mike Healy died of a heart attack in 1904, and Mary Jane followed him three years later. An era of the Arctic was over.

It was not the end of flamboyancy, however. Mary Jane Healy herself was a distinct character, dressing the captain's parrot (with whom she held long conversations) in a little fur suit. Back in 1891, though, she was amazed when Michael boarded a strange vessel to find it had been chartered by a honeymoon party. The happy couple were from Baltimore, and had come north to shoot polar bears! Captain Healy, much amused, gave the bride a fur coat, and in return she presented Mary Jane with a diamond pin. It was an augury of the future—and extravagant characters like Jo Peary and Louise Arner Boyd.

Jo Peary's married life would have been a lot like Lady Jane Franklin's except that she insisted on going along with her Arctic-explorer husband, Robert E. Peary, the first man to reach the North Pole. In 1900 he left her behind, so Jo arrived unannounced in August, on the *Windward*. Unfortunately, the vessel ran onto the rocks in Smith Sound. Jo was condemned to a winter in the Arctic, while her husband was based at Fort Conger, 250 miles farther north as the snow goose flies. Jo did have a female companion, an Eskimo woman named Allakassingwah—familiarly known as Ally. Embarrassingly, however, Ally was Peary's mistress, and the baby she had with her was his.

Jo, somewhat naturally, was disconcerted and cross. "You will have been surprised, perhaps annoyed, when you hear I came up on a ship," she wrote tartly to Robert; "but believe me had I known how things were with you I should not have come." However, she did admit that she had been warned. Perry had often stated his absolute belief that female companionship was necessary for the contentment of any man. In fact, he openly recommended to his men that they find mistresses among the local women. Jo made the best of it, and in the end got along so well with Ally that by spring the two women were good friends.

Jo had been to the Arctic before, her first expedition being in June 1891, when she overwintered on the Greenland coast. In the summer of 1892 she looked after the base while Peary trekked by sled all over the island, much to the regret of the geologist and surgeon who were with her. The geologist, John Verkoeff, declared, "I will never go home in the same ship with that man and that woman," and walked off, never to be seen again. The surgeon, Frederick Cook, refused to come along on the next expedition, in 1893, somewhat to Jo's chagrin, for she was pregnant. She gave birth to a daughter on September 12, and the natives traveled for miles to view the "Snow Baby."

Louise Arner Boyd, a San Francisco socialite and heiress who led seven expeditions to the Arctic, was notorious for shooting nineteen polar bears in one day—a rumor she denied, saying, "That's a crazy story. I think it was only five or six and that was for food." However, it was widely known that she was a crack shot who could fell a bear from the deck of a moving ship. And this was by no means the end of stories about her. Reputedly, on July 4, 1933, she and six scientists (including the wife of one of them) polished off five pounds of caviar at one sitting.

Becoming the sole inheritor of her father's huge fortune in 1920, Louise could have splashed her money around with ostentatious and immensely vulgar exuberance, like so many of her contemporaries. Instead, she kept firm hold of the helm of the Boyd Investment Company, which her father had formed and taught her to manage. And, she traveled—to Europe first and then, for some reason, to Spitsbergen. And from the first time she glimpsed pack ice, as a tourist in 1924, she was hooked by the Arctic.

She was seen there season after season, striding about tumbling decks in oilskins and hip-high waders, or marching over the ice in hobnailed boots, loaded down with guns and cameras. As well as shooting bears and seals, Louise shot film, accumulating a huge pictorial documentation of Arctic plants, animals, and topography, a heritage that was donated to the American Geographical Society and passed on by them to the University of Wisconsin at Milwaukee in 1978.

Despite all this, she was determinedly feminine. "I have no use for masculine women," she barked at a reporter who had the sauce to hint that she might have liked to be a man. She never went out without a hat, unless it was to the dentist's, and at home she habitually wore a corsage of prize blooms from her extensive greenhouses. She was so well known that she was referred to as merely Miss Boyd. And she would never have dreamed of going off on an expedition without her personal maid.

One of Louise's voyages was an echo of the past. On June 28, 1928, she was in Tromsø on the Norwegian coast, outfitting the sealer MS *Hobby* (the same ship from which she had shot all those polar bears

Louise Arner Boyd. Artist: Ron Druett.

two seasons before) for her second expedition, when she heard that the noted Norwegian explorer Roald Amundsen—the first man to negotiate the Northwest Passage, from 1903 to 1906—was missing. He had flown out of Tromsø that day on a rescue mission, searching by plane for an Italian party that had crashed in a dirigible, *Italia,* somewhere near the North Pole. Within a few hours all communication from his aircraft ceased, and the world swiftly learned that Amundsen was in trouble.

Coincidentally, the *Hobby* had once been Amundsen's own flagship. Louise had never met the explorer; nonetheless she instantly abandoned all her own plans and joined in the hunt. The quest lasted three months and covered ten thousand miles, extending from Spitsbergen to the western Greenland Sea. And Louise paid every penny of the cost, in the spirit of Lady Jane Franklin.

Officially, all hope that Amundsen had survived was abandoned when one of the floats of the plane was found near Tromsø on August 31. In the meantime, however, Louise had taken twenty thousand feet of movie film and several thousand still photographs, creating a remarkably complete pictorial archive of an intensive search in the Arctic. She recorded all the ships involved, as well as the huge area she searched—the Greenland Sea, the Barents Sea, and the Arctic Ocean.

"Four of us stood watch around the clock," she described, in a talk given after being elected to the Society of Woman Geographers. "We would just stand there and look. Ice does such eerie things. There are illusions like mirages, and there were times we clearly could see tents. Then we'd lower boats and go off to investigate. But it always turned out the same—strange formations of the ice, nothing more."

Her search had failed. But, where M'Clintock's last voyage had marked the end of an odyssey for Lady Jane Franklin, for Louise Arner Boyd it was a new beginning. During the quest, she had encountered famous Scandinavian polar explorers such as Lauge Koch and Ejnar Mikkelsen, men who spurred her to explore reaches that had been left uncharted by the Franklin search parties and those since.

Louise started this new project in the summer of 1931. If Lady Jane Franklin had not been so startlingly successful in initiating the comprehensive exploration of the Arctic, who knows what new coasts Louise Arner Boyd might have charted and recorded? As it was, she was the first in the world to make detailed surveys of East Greenland. This was no small proposition. That region of fjords must be the most fractured in the world, often blockaded by impenetrable ice. Louise sailed there in 1931, 1933, 1937, and 1938, in the 125-foot sealer *Veslekari*. She charted and photographed inner reaches that had never been explored. And in recognition of this, the Geodaetizk Institute of Copenhagen named it after her.

They called it "Miss Boyd Land."

Chapter Twenty-one

A WOMAN AT THE HELM

*Periods come in everyone's life when it is struggle
or slip back, fight or go under; these periods are
not incessant in a landman's life; there is an easing
up, a breathing space afforded them when they
can survey their position with a certain amount of
complacency and safety. Those who take the sea for
a career know little of this lull; they admire the sea,
they respect the sea, they like the sea, they love the
sea, but they have to fight her twenty-four hours of
the day.*

—Beatrice Holme Fry

Throughout maritime history, wives and daughters of shipowners have helped out with the bookwork of the business, doing their bit as unofficial (and unpaid) shipping agents. Since before Agnes Cowtie's time they have organized freights, and hired captains and crews. Dealing with chandlers would be just one part of the job of assisting with the details of refitting and provisioning, and as we have seen, there were female ship chandlers and maritime "junk dealers" in abundance. At sea, many a wife wrote reports of the voyage back to the agents and owners of the vessel, many of which were published in the local papers because of public interest—and a lot of that intense interest was felt by other women because they had a personal financial stake in the vessel.

Over the centuries thousands of women, many of them humble housewives, have held shares in the craft, great and small, that plowed the seas of the world. It has been by far the greatest involvement of women with the sea. In the coastal communities of Europe and North America, vessel shares—often as small as a sixty-fourth part of a fishing schooner—were traded as stocks and bonds are today. Ship shares produced an income in the way of dividends, or a capital return when sold. They could be given away as gifts, inherited, or used to pay a debt. It meant that a whole family or an entire community owned a ship instead of just one person.

There were lots of good reasons for dividing a ship into ship shares. Shipping was a hazardous business, and splitting up ownership spread the risk, particularly when insurance was too expensive to afford. If cash was scarce, shares could be given out to shipyard staff and contractors as payment for materials or labor. According to the 1887 records of Bath, Maine, for instance, a sailmaker by the name of William Clifford had shares in thirty-seven vessels, probably part payment for his rope, his canvas, and his work. Builders made a habit of retaining a few shares in vessels they built, perhaps out of pride, perhaps to demonstrate faith in their product.

Similarly, captains were expected to invest in their own ships and voyages, also an act of trust. Often, shares were given to wives and daughters, or female members of the family bought them out of loyalty. And so, within the community, ship shares were spread about widely, and a large percentage of the owners were female.

This was particularly evident in whaling communities. In the little village of Stonington, Connecticut, in 1831, twelve women held shares in whalers, one of them, Malvina Bottum Beebe, owning a total of eleven shares, valued at forty-six hundred dollars.

Whaleship. Artist: Ron Druett.

Whaling ships were very expensive to outfit, for finance had to be found to buy whaling gear such as harpoons and try-pots, as well as provisions for up to five years. Accordingly, investors were actively recruited. Then, as the reports came in of how well or how badly the voyage was going, the shares raced up or down in value, giving opportunity for speculation. Buying shares in a ship with a poor report was risky, even if those shares were very cheap, but sometimes the gamble paid off handsomely. The ship might have a sudden run of luck in catching whales, or the market for oil might dramatically improve.

Women with a little spare money speculated, just like men. In May 1834, in Edgartown, Martha's Vineyard, five months after the whaleship *Champion* had sailed, two women, Harriet Butler and Almira Mayhew, paid $208.56 for one third of a one-sixty-fourth share. Their gamble paid off quite handsomely. When the ship returned in 1837 with a good cargo of 2,100 barrels of spermaceti oil in her holds, the market had leapt to $1.16 per gallon, which meant that the cargo was worth more than $75,000, a good return on a ship that cost one tenth of that amount to fit out.

In 1848, Ruby Mayhew, also of Edgartown, bought a 256th share of the *Champion* before she had left on voyage, paying just $23.43. She would have been quite pleased with the return on even this tiny part-ownership, for in 1851 the ship returned with a cargo worth about $60,000. Sophrona Fellows, on the other hand, must have kicked herself when the same ship came in from yet another voyage, in April 1864. In November 1860, exactly one month after the ship had sailed, she sold her sixty-fourth share for $50, perhaps because reports of whaleships being seized and burned by Confederate raiders had made her nervous. The *Champion* survived unscathed, with a cargo worth more than $80,000 in the war-inflated market.

Whaling was certainly not the only branch of the trade to attract this kind of wheeling and dealing. A cursory glance at shipping records in any maritime locale is sufficient proof of a brisk trade in ship shares, Maine being a very good example. In Bath, in 1887, there were 378 owners of ship shares. Of these, 73 were women, some with substantial portfolios. Mary F. Campbell, widow of Charles R. Campbell, for instance, owned shares in fifteen vessels, ranging from a thirty-second share of the large ship *James Drummond* to one sixteenth of the small schooner *George W. Jewett.*

Her neighbor, Ellen M Adams, had shares in six, worth $1,299. Another Bath resident, Lilly Crooker, acquired one sixteenth of the schooner *O. N. Merritt* in 1869, and was so pleased with her business acumen that she continued buying shares, despite the loss of her second investment, schooner *Mary E. Douglas.* Lilly ended up with interest in eleven vessels, holding shares with a total worth of $6,215 in 1887. At the other extreme was Emma E. Alvord, who in 1882 acquired one sixty-fourth of just one vessel, schooner *Alice Montgomery,* which was lost, wiping out an investment of $200.

There were many more women like Emma Alvord than there were like Lilly Crooker, naturally. However, it was not unusual for women to do very well indeed. One such was Maria Tibbetts of Camden, Maine, who, in just one day in 1881 (September 30), bought shares in fourteen ships, writing out a check for $10,528.27—an enormous amount at the time. The largest investment was $2,074.07, in the 1,737-ton *Wandering Jew,* and the smallest $22, in the little 46-ton schooner *Arcade.* As well as that, she took over shares in three ships at the token payment of one dollar each. On April 2, 1883, she took over shares in no fewer than twelve ships, each for that symbolic dollar. The dutiable value of just one of these—a mere one 128th share of the bark *Adolph Obrig*—was $3,539.91. Almost as an afterthought, on that day Maria bought shares in three more ships, spending a mere $680.44.

These were sums that most women could only dream of, so how did Maria Tibbetts do it? Easily—by being born into the right family. In 1881

Wandering Jew. Artist: Ron Druett.

she was executing her father's will, and in 1883 she was settling her mother's estate. That valuable one-128th share of the 1,448-ton bark *Adolph Obrig* was passed on to her according to "the last will and testament of Harriet M.A. Norwood, late of Camden," and the amount of $3,539.91 was the rebate of duties according to Section 2513 of the "Revised Statutes."

Maria already owned two 128ths of this vessel, which had a remarkable ratio of female ownership, two substantial owners being Adilia C. Talpey of Boston and Harriet T. Parsons of "Neworleans," each of whom owned twenty-four 128ths. Naturally, the dollar paid over for each share she inherited from her mother did not reflect the real commercial value. It was a tax-avoidance measure, which demonstrates that Maria had inherited a good head for business, along with all those shares. Her father was Joshua G. Norwood, partner in the firm Carleton & Norwood, shipbuilders, lime manufacturers, and traders of Rockport, Maine, the original founders of the community's prosperity. By the day he died, May 9, 1876, forty-five

Carleton-Norwood vessels, many of them large ships, had made the firm's name a familiar one in ports all over the world. By holding on to all the shares, Maria kept her hand firmly on the financial helm, not allowing her sex to make any difference when it came to the inheritance of ships and the business of running them. A kindred spirit was Mrs. Charles Seal (Christian name unknown), of Hobart, Tasmania, Australia, who inherited her husband's fleet when he died in 1852. His rivals assumed they could easily take it over; instead, Mrs. Seal held on to control, buying more ships and extending the original operation.

A contemporary of Maria Tibbetts held shares on an even more magnificent scale—and spent them all, in the name of family loyalty. This was Miss Jennie Rodbird Morse, a "music teacher" of Bath, Maine. Jennie's first investment was made in August 1873, when she bought two sixty-fourth shares of the 513-ton schooner *Uriah B. Fisk* from Daniel Blaisdell of Bath, for the sum of $800, but her subsequent lively trading in vessel shares was certainly not limited to her local area. Pendleton Brothers, the ship brokers and commission merchants at 430–432 Pearl Street, acted as her agents in New York, sending her regular dividends on her investments, and she had

Carleton-Norwood shipyard, Rockport, Maine.
Artist: Ron Druett.

ship investments with Morse & Co. in that city as well, her dividends on eight of their schooners totaling $283.40 in December 1892.

Her financial activity was not confined to ship shares, either. "I went to the bank, took account of my stocks," she wrote on January 6, 1909, in her diary. A decade earlier, Jennie had invested heavily in the Hudson Navigation Company, as well as in the New Jersey Ice Company, and she also owned speculative shares in companies such as Butterick, Campbell Wallpaper, Standard Oil, and American Electric Heating, as well as in financial institutions such as Garfield Bank, the Bank of North America, and the People's Trust Company. On that day she "took account" of her stocks, her holdings totaled just over one million dollars.

Jennie's father, the original source of all this wealth, was Benjamin Wyman Morse, an energetic entrepreneur in the shipping trade. Benjamin started out as a tugboat operator, but had the good fortune to marry an heiress, Anna Eliza Jane Rodbird, known as Annie, who was reputedly worth $750,000 in her own right at the time of her death in 1898. Benjamin was one of the founders of the Knickerbocker Steam Towage Company, which quickly grew to monopolize the towing business on the Kennebec River. He was also heavily involved in the ice-shipping trade,

Jennie Rodbird Morse. Artist: Ron Druett.

first cutting ice in Georgetown, Maine, in 1876, and shipping it to icehouses in the South, often on old cut-down square-riggers to save the cost of transportation. At the time of his death, in 1887, he was a millionaire.

Jennie, born October 1, 1854, had only one sibling, a brother, Charles Wyman Morse, who was her junior by two years. She never married, but she did have parental responsibilities, for she raised Charles's four children—Benjamin, Erwin, Harry, and Anna—after his wife, Hattie Bishop Hussey Morse, died of tuberculosis in 1897, shortly after giving birth

to Anna. This was a responsibility that must have been eased by Jennie's large income, which was reported at $60,000 per year in 1900.

Her home in Bath was palatial, thanks to brother Charlie, who bought her a large brick mansion on Washington Street. There were four grand pianos in the house, so that she and her friends could play quartets, and another in the barn for her nephews to use in their minstrel shows. She also had her own box at the Metropolitan Opera in New York City—Grand Tier box number 27—paid for her by Charlie, who funded jaunts to Europe as well. Jennie's lifestyle was certainly enviable, characterized as it was by a mix of music, lavish entertainments, constant visits with a host of friends (many of whom invested in ship shares, too), sleighing parties, and leisurely evenings of bridge, but she did not seem to inspire jealousy. Instead, held in great esteem, she was called Aunt Jennie by just about the whole of Bath.

Jennie's brother, by contrast, was the cause of a great deal of acrimonious gossip in New York, though he seems to have been held in affectionate regard in Bath. Charles Wyman Morse was an even more opportunistic businessman than his father, setting up as a speculator in shares in New York City about 1880, at the age of twenty-four. Although J. P. Morgan and J. D. Rockefeller dismissed him as a country upstart, he nonetheless managed to make $50,000 in his very first year. It was a record he improved on with energy, ambition, and nerve, so by the age of fifty Charles Wyman Morse was exactly where he wanted to be—at the top of the City's financial world, and in control of $334 millions' worth of assets, including the virtual monopoly of coastal shipping from Bangor, Maine, to Galveston, Texas, which earned him the nickname "Admiral of the Atlantic Coast."

Charlie's methods were not always nice. In 1902, for instance, he withdrew a great deal of money from the Ice Securities holding company he himself had formed, just before the price of ice fell dramatically. In 1908 he was arraigned for bank fraud after the collapse of his shipping and banking empire in the Panic of 1907. Jennie immediately authorized her agents to pay all expenses in connection with the case, which was the reason she "took account" of all her stocks on January 6, 1909.

The rest of her 1909 diary documents an exceedingly frugal household budget, which exceeded $30 a month only when she went to New York. Despite the money she lavished on lawyers, however, Charlie was convicted and sentenced for a term of fifteen years. He—and her money—still had clout, however, for he served only a few months before being pardoned by President William Taft for medical reasons, after making a promise that he would stay out of banking. Jennie exulted in her diary, "Charlie set free from the tomb," believing that she had finally achieved what she had ardently desired, "the vindication of the good name" of her brother. Her loyalty had cost her dearly, however. When Jennie passed away in 1927, her four heirs—Charlie's children—received little more than $10,000 each.

Meantime, however, she had demonstrated an interesting dichotomy, personifying the two basic female roles in the business of ships and shipping. Independent, spirited, and intelligent, Jennie Rodbird Morse had used inherited money to build a huge fortune of her own, despite the disadvantage of her sex. But then, in response to the demands of domestic loyalty, in the spirit of Lady Jane Franklin and other heroic predecessors, Jennie Rodbird Morse had squandered the lot. Queen Victoria would have been proud of her.

*   *   *

Equally privileged in the business of ships was a young Scotswoman named Betsey Miller, whose somewhat eccentric involvement with her father's shipping business came to public attention in the March 13, 1852, issue of *The Times* of London. There, an editor reported that he had discovered an item in the *Glasgow Post* that was fascinating enough to be well worth reprinting.

"A Female Ship Captain," the headline exclaimed.

> Amongst the fleet lately windbound in Lamlash not the least but perhaps the greatest wonder was the good old brig *Cloetus* of Saltcoats, which for more than twenty years has been commanded by an heroic and exceedingly clever young lady, Miss Betsy Miller, daughter of the late Mr. W. Miller, shipowner and wood merchant of that Town. He was concerned with vessels both in the American and the coasting trade. Miss Betsy before she went to sea acted as a "ship's husband" to her father : and seeing how the captains in many cases behaved her romantic and adventurous spirit impelled her to go to sea herself. Her father gratified her caprice, and gave her command of the *Cloetus,* which she holds to this present day, and she has weathered the storms of the deep when many commanders of the other sex have been driven to pieces on the rocks. The *Cloetus* is well known in the ports of Belfast, Dublin, Cork, etc.

Like Maria Tibbetts and Jennie Morse, Betsey was able to do what she did because she was born into a shipowning family—and had an uncommonly tolerant father to boot. For surely it was highly unusual for a young woman to become so impatient with the captains the family hired that she took over the helm of one of the ships herself. It is easy to picture the editor who reprinted the item shaking his head in admiring wonder at this strong-minded young female.

Other similarly strong-minded women had to resort to strange stratagems to do anything of the kind—and one of the most remarkable was also one of the last to be forced to battle the constraints of her sex to take charge of the ship. This was Beatrice Holme Sumner Fry, who gained virtual control of the lives of hundreds of young seamen in a highly sensational manner.

Born in 1862 of aristocratic but impoverished parents, "Beatie" was a headstrong, precocious girl who spent her time in the stables and the hunt instead of at lessons. At the age of fifteen she was seduced by an extremely rich merchant banker, Charles Hoare, who was exactly twice her age. They met on the hunting field and plunged headlong into an affair. Charles was caught in Beatie's bedroom with no satisfactory excuse, and when Beatie had a minor hunting accident, her injuries were exaggerated so she could live with Hoare and his wife in a strange *ménage à trois* for four months. Meantime, Charles placated her family by making them large "loans."

By the end of 1884 their first illegitimate child was born, and Beatie and Charles were openly living together. Today, it is hard to comprehend why this was considered so depraved (though one feels the same natural sympathy for Hoare's blameless wife, Margaret, that one felt for Fanny Nelson), particularly as Beatie was over twenty-one by then. By Victorian standards, though, it was an even more monumental scandal than it had been in Nelson's time. Banned from the Hunt Club that had been his passion, beleaguered by a sensational court case because of his seduction of a minor—and a blue-blooded one at that—Charles took measures to restore his reputation. He bought a bark he found at the London Docks called *Illovo,* converted her into a replica of a man-of-war, renamed her TS (Training Ship) *Mercury,* and set her up as a school ship for "street arabs of fourteen or fifteen years of age who have vouched for themselves that they are willing to enter the Royal Navy." It was designed to save boys picked up from the slums of London "from temporal and eternal ruin." Then—though neither of them had ever been to school or even on any voyage of significance—Beatie and Charles set to running the strange establishment.

Beatie threw herself into the task with huge energy and enthusiasm. Wearing trousers and shirt, she learned to run the rigging and sail a boat so quickly that before long she was leading the boys aloft—in bare feet, every morning, winter and summer—and teaching them the tricks of tacking, gybing, and running before the wind. Gradually, as Charles became embroiled in court cases again, and his own bank requested his resignation as senior partner because of the scandal, Beatie took over most of the management of the ship. Starting in 1898, the aging Charles gradually retired from the scene, appointing a famous sportsman, Charles Burgess Fry, to the captaincy after arranging Fry's marriage of convenience to his mistress.

Beatie was thirty-six and the mother of Hoare's two illegitimate children, and Fry was ten years her junior. "C.B."—as he was affectionately known throughout England—had had a distinguished academic and sporting career at Oxford, winning "blues" in athletics, cricket, and soccer, and fully justifying the scholarships that had supported him. Despite all this he was an impoverished and reluctant schoolmaster when Hoare came along with his proposition. It was an offer C.B. could not refuse. In return for giving Beatie respectability (along with three more children), he attained the monied leisure that allowed him to devote his entire time and energy to the sports that were his passion.

Beatie Fry. Artist: Ron Druett.

While Fry played cricket and soccer at first-class level, Beatie looked after the ship, and Charles kept a grandfatherly eye on the boys. Then, in 1908, Charles passed away. C.B. became Captain-Superintendent, but the person who was now in charge of the entire operation was Beatie. Charles had even allowed for this in his will, in which one of the directives to the trustees was that Beatrice Holme Sumner Fry should be "manager" of "the said training ship." It was a role she retained until the day that she died, in her eighties.

These are the notorious years. Under Hoare, the school had been like an extended family, strict but kind. Under Beatie's sole charge, it became an institution. Even the ship itself changed. The aging *Illovo/Mercury* was sold as a coal hulk and replaced by the ship *President,* once the sloop-of-war HMS *Gannet,* now renamed *Mercury.* The daily affairs of the school were run by so-called Watch Officers, who were ex–petty officers of the Royal Navy, the "hard men of the lower deck," and it all happened under the unflinching eye of Mrs. Fry, who was universally feared.

At Saturday inspections she wore a "uniform" of navy blue double-breasted jacket, ankle-length skirt, thick woolen stockings, and brightly polished black shoes with silver buckles. The boys had a superstition that if the stockings were red she was in a bad mood, and yellow if she was not; they were usually red. And the consequences of any lapses could be awful, for she would not hesitate to order a flogging. One boy died, while others were removed by their parents, but the boys who graduated and went on into the Navy distinguished themselves, one and all.

Feared and hated as she may have been, though, Mrs. Fry was universally respected. No one ever thought of her as a man—she was known to all as Madame—but she successfully fulfilled a man's role, at times in man's dress. She was a walking testimony to the fact that a woman could do as much as a man, given the skills. Yet, it was evidently impossible for her to command the ship under her own name, as the enterprising Betsey Miller had done. Charles Hoare knew perfectly well that Beatie was capable of taking over the helm, but still felt that he had to organize a marriage of convenience for reasons of appearance.

Beatie was definitely the last of her era. Just a generation later she could have crewed or commanded ships freely, taken part in cross-ocean races, become a pilot or a ferry master, owned and managed tourist operations or fishing fleets, been the first female to sail solo around the world. As it was, she was trapped in her time, her social class—and her lover's dinosaur thinking.

EDITORIAL NOTE

Naturally, with a topic that is as far-reaching as the seven seas themselves, many books had to be read, articles perused, and people consulted. A single bibliography was going to prove both unwieldy and confusing, so I have written a series of chapter commentaries here. Hopefully, despite the absence of footnoting, this will assist anyone who chooses to read further on any individual topic. The many helpful experts I consulted for each chapter are listed here, too. This book would not have been possible without them.

SOURCES

INTRODUCTION

The story of Queen Tomyris comes from *Herodotus,* trans. A. D. Godley (London: William Heinemann, 1925), 1. 205, 206, 212–14. Biographical and background details were found in John Gould's *Herodotus* (London: Weidenfeld & Nicolson, 1989).

More feel of the time and setting was gleaned from three wonderfully illustrated books: Tim Severin's *The Ulysses Voyage—Sea Search for the Odyssey* (London: Hutchinson, 1987); Bernard Ashmore's *Architect & Sculptor in Classical Greece* (London: Phaedon, 1972); and Bedrich Forman's *Borobudur—The Buddhist Legend in Stone,* trans. Till Gottheinerová (London: Octopus, 1980).

I thank Somasiri Devendra of Sri Lanka for the charming story of Princess Sanghamitta, and his helpfulness in the face of my constant questions. The story of Tokoyo, originally published by Eric Protter and Nancy Protter in *Folk and Fairy Tales of Far-Off Lands,* trans. Robert Egan (New York: Duell, Sloan and Pearce, 1965), was found in the excellent collection *Fearless Girls, Wise Women & Beloved Sisters—Heroines in Folktales from Around the World,* ed. Kathleen Ragan (New York: Norton, 1998), pp. 199–202. The foreword, by Jane Yolen, was very inspiring.

1. The Warrior-Queens

Herodotus also provides the story of Queen Artemisia, 7.99; 8.68, 87, 101–103. Greek female spies and the Battle of Salamis are described in Anton Powell's *The Greek World* (London: Kingfisher Books, 1987). The story of Queen Teuta came from Polybius, *The Histories of Polybius*, trans. Evelyn S. Shuckburgh from the text by F. Hultsch. 2 vols. (London: Macmillan, 1889) 2.4, 6, 8, 9, 11, 12. Also Ralph T. Ward's *Pirates in History* (Baltimore, Md.: York, 1974).

Helpful discussion of the Cleopatra story is in *100 Great Kings, Queens and Rulers of The World*, ed. John Canning (London: Oldham's, 1967). The relevant contributory essay is by Robert Greacen. The Hatshepsut account was extracted from Rupert Matthews's collection *Power Brokers: Kingmakers & Usurpers Throughout History* (Oxford, England: Facts on File, 1989). Ship details came from Lionel Casson's *The Ancient Mariners: Seafarers and Sea Fighters of the Mediterranean in Ancient Times* (London: Gollancz, 1959). Also William McDowell's *The Shape of Ships* (London: Hutchinson, 1950), chap. 1.

The details of ships and battles in classical times would not have been possible without the expertise of Lincoln Paine, Steve Alvin, Frank Young, Gerard Mittelstaedt, Marc James Small, and Iiro Hyrsky. I also thank Christine Lampe, David Meagher, John Macek, and Elisabeth Shure for information on Queen Teuta and early Mediterranean pirates, and Lincoln Paine for suggesting the remarkable Queen Hatshepsut.

2. The Valkyria

Beowulf. Saga. Lines 1905–1909 are quoted at the end.

Ellms, Charles. *The Pirates Own Book, or Authentic Narratives of the Lives, Exploits, and Executions of the Most Celebrated Sea Robbers* (Boston: Sanborn & Carter, 1837).

McDowell, William. *The Shape of Ships* (London: Hutchinson, 1950), chap. 3.

Olaus Magnus. *Historia de Gentibus Septentrionalibus* ("History of the Northern Peoples"), 1555. Reprinted by the Hakluyt Society as vols. 182 (1996), 188 (1998), and 189 (1998). Alvild's story is in book 5.

Rodger, N.A.M. *The Safeguard of the Sea: A Naval History of Britain*, vol. 1, *660–1649* (London: HarperCollins, 1998), chap. 1.

Saxo Grammaticus. *The First Nine Books of the Danish History of Saxo Grammaticus*, trans. Oliver Elton, introduction by Frederick York Powell (London: David Nutt, for the Folk-lore Society as no. 33 [1893]). I have amended the Saxo translation very slightly, replacing the word "amazon" with the more appropriate term "Valkyrie." The introduction by F. Y. Powell proved both useful and illuminating.

Stanley, Jo. "Warrior Women in Command," in *Bold in Her Breeches: Women Pirates Across the Ages*, ed. Jo Stanley (London: Pandora, 1995), pp. 63–92.

Villiers, Alan, et al. *Men, Ships and the Sea* (Washington, D.C.: National Geographic Society, n.d.).

I am very grateful to Edwin King for his advice and help, particularly with Olaus Magnus. I also thank Lars Bruzelius for his help with the background of Saxo Grammaticus. Anthony Clover provided interesting comments on Viking migrations. There is an excellent website on early English documents, including *The Anglo-Saxon Chronicle*, on *http://library.byu.edu/~rdh/eurodocs/uk.htm*. I thank Royston Palmer for introducing me to this. Lars Bruzelius recommended a site on Nordic neo-Latin literature: *http://www.uib.no/cgi-bin/neol/neol.pl.*

3. Mistress Cowtie and the Pirates

Anonymous (probably John Oakes). *A True Relation, of the Lives and Deaths of the Two Most Famous English Pyrats, Purser, and Clinton Who Lived in the Reigne of Queene Elizabeth* (London: Io. Okes, 1639).

Bingham, Madeleine. *Scotland Under Mary Stuart: An Account of Everyday Life* (London: Allen & Unwin, 1971).

Boyd, William K., ed. *Calendar for State Papers Relating to Scotland and Mary, Queen of Scots* (Edinburgh: H. M. General Registry House, 1910).

Calendar of Scottish Papers, 1583: items 380 (James VI to Elizabeth), 429 (Bailies to Walsingham), 445 (deposition of "Scottish ambassadours"), 465 ("Minute of some particular piracies"), 726 (note of "Redress desired by the Scottish Ambassadors").

Calendar of State Papers, Domestic, Elizabeth, 1578–1583, vol. 156 (December 1582), p. 7 (Francis Hawley's deposition; complaint of the merchants of Southampton); 160 (May 1583), p. 55 (deposition against Clinton).

Dyer, Florence E., "A Woman Shipowner," *Mariner's Mirror* 36 (1950), pp. 134–38.

———. "Reprisals in the Sixteenth Century," *Mariner's Mirror* XXI (1935), pp. 187–97.

Ewen, C. L'Estrange. "Organized Piracy Round England in the Sixteenth Century," *Mariner's Mirror* 35 (1949), pp. 29–42.

Lucie-Smith, Edward. *Outcasts of the Sea—Pirates and Piracy* (New York and London: Paddington, 1978). A good general background text on pirates.

Mowat, Susan. "Shipping and Trade in Scotland 1556–1830," *Mariner's Mirror* 83:1 (February 1997), pp. 14–20, esp. p. 19.

Whall, W. B. *Sea Songs and Shanties* (Glasgow: Brown, Son & Ferguson, 1910).

Williams, Neville. *The Sea Dogs: Privateers, Plunder & Piracy in the Elizabethan Age* (London: Weidenfeld & Nicolson, 1975).

Searching Agnes Cowtie's story would not have been possible without the active help and interest of Edwin King and Alan O. Watkins. Michelle Gait and Myrtle Anderson-Smith of the University of Aberdeen provided considerable help in understanding the social background of the time. Janet West kindly confirmed the maiden name issue. Those who were very helpful with background details of Elizabethan pirates were Aaron Miedema, David Meagher, Donald Markstein, John Richard Stephens, Ken Kinkor, Lars Bruzelius, John Bethell, and last but certainly not least, Richard Pennell. The voyages of the *Grace of God* (unfortunately a very common ship's name) can be traced through the excellent website of the Tayside Maritime History Project, *http://www.dmcsoft.com/tamh/* I thank Douglas MacKenzie for introducing me to this, and Ian Flett, Dundee archivist, for his interest. For information about Campveere, I am indebted to Bill Bedford, Peter McCracken, Martin Navarro, and Alistair Deayton.

4. Pirate Queens

Berckman, Evelyn. *Victims of Piracy: The Admiralty Court, 1575–1678* (London: Hamish Hamilton, 1979). Case histories, interpreted with lively expertise.

Chambers, Anne. *Granuaile: The Life and Times of Grace O'Malley, c1530–1603* (Dublin: Wolfhound, 1979; rev. 1998).

———. "The Pirate Queen of Ireland: Grace O'Malley." In *Bold in Her Breeches: Women Pirates Across the Ages,* ed. Jo Stanley (London: Pandora, 1995), pp. 93–108.

Cordingly, David. *Under the Black Flag: The Romance and the Reality of Life Among the Pirates* (New York: Harcourt Brace, 1995), pp. 72–78.

FitzGibbon, Constantine. *The Irish in Ireland* (New York: Norton, 1983).

Frank, Stuart. *The Book of Pirate Songs.* (Sharon, Mass.: Kendall Whaling Museum, 1998).

Glasspoole, Richard. *Mr. Glasspoole and the Chinese Pirates, Being the Narrative of Mr. Richard Glasspoole of the Ship* Marquis of Ely; *Describing his Captivity of Eleven Weeks and Three Days Whilst Held for Ransom by the Villainous Ladrones of the China Sea in 1809; Together with Extracts from the China Records and the Log of the* Marquis of Ely; *and Some Remarks on Chinese Pirates, Ancient and Modern,* ed. Owen Rutter (London: Golden Cockerel, 1935). This account is an elaboration upon a report Glasspoole wrote to the president of the East India Company's factory, dated December 8, 1809, which is reproduced, with many editorial comments, in John Richard Stephens, ed., *Captured by Pirates* (Cambria Pines by the Sea, Calif.: Fern Canyon Press, 1996) pp. 292–318.

Gosse, Philip. *The History of Piracy* (New York: Longmans, Green, 1932; repr., Glorieta, N.M.: Rio Grande Press, 1995). Dated, badly sourced, but still useful account.

Grehan, Ida. *Irish Family Names—Highlights of 50 Family Histories* (London: Johnston & Bacon, 1973).

MacDermott, A. "A Most Famous Sea Captain Called Gráinne O'Malley," *Mariner's Mirror* 46 (1960), pp. 133–41.

Murray, Dian. "Cheng I Sao in Fact and Fiction." In *Bold in Her Breeches,* pp. 205–33.

————. "Chinese Pirates." In *Pirates: Terror on the High Seas—from the Caribbean to the South China Sea,* ed. David Cordingly (London: Salamander Press, 1998; North Dighton, Mass.: JG Press, 1998), pp. 212–35.

A decision had to be made about which spelling to use for Grace O'Malley—"Grace O'Malley" being a modern version of her name, one that she herself never heard. When they were being polite, her contemporaries referred to her variously as Grany Imallye, Granie ny Maille, and Grainy O'Maly; at other times they were much more apt to call her pirate, rebel, murderer, or "notable traitor." She herself spelled her name "Grany ny Mally." Since then, scholars have spelled her name Grania, or Gráinne. Chroniclers, however, prefer to call her by the affectionate nickname Granuaile—yet another name she is unlikely to have used. According to one of the many legends about this Irish female pirate, Granuaile means "the bald Grania," and refers to her hair, which was cropped like a boy's. However, it is probably just a contraction of her first name and her patronymic or clan name. I chose to use Grania, the form of her name used by Irish genealogists. I am very grateful to Dian Murray for her interest and help with Cheng I Sao. Thanks also to Paulo Edson.

Website: *www.maths.tcd.ie/~jaymin/sca/Granuail.htm*

5. CAPTURED BY CORSAIRS

Baker, Thomas. *Piracy and Diplomacy in Seventeenth Century North Africa: The Journal of Thomas Baker, English Consul in Tripoli, 1677–1685,* ed. C. R. Pennell (Rutherford, N.J.: Fairleigh Dickinson University Press and Associated University Presses, 1989).

Bradley, Eliza. *An Authentic Narrative of the Shipwreck and Sufferings of Mrs. Eliza Bradley, Wife of Captain James Bradley of Liverpool* (Boston: James Wald, 1821).

Brooks, Francis. *Barbarian Cruelty: Being a True History of the Distressed Condition of the Christian Captives Under the Tyranny of Mully Ishmael, Emperor of Morocco* (London, 1693). Wing Collection of Early English books on microfilm, reel 84:10.

Clissold, Stephen. *The Barbary Slaves* (London: Elek, 1977).

Coxere, Edward. *Adventures by Sea of Edward Coxere,* ed. E. H. W. Meyerstein (London: Oxford University Press, 1946).

de Paul, Vincent. Account of his slavery, from an extract in the anthology *Captured by Pirates,* ed. John Richard Stephens (Cambria Pines by the Sea, Calif.: Fern Canyon Press, 1996), pp. 331–36. De Paul went on to found organizations to help the slaves, including the Daughters of Charity. For this, he was canonized in 1737.

Pennell, C. R. "Piracy Off the North Moroccan Coast in the First Half of the Nineteenth Century," *Journal of the Society for Moroccan Studies* 1 (1991), pp. 69–78.

Phelps, Thomas. *A True Account of the Captivity of Thomas Phelps at Machaness in Barbary and His Strange Escape* (London: Joseph Hindmarsh, 1685).

Platt, Richard. "Corsairs of the Mediterranean." In *Pirates: Terror on the High Seas—from the Caribbean to the South China Sea,* ed. David Cordingly (London: Salamander Press, 1998; North Dighton, Mass.: JG Press, 1998), pp. 76–99.

Rodger, N.A.M. *The Safeguard of the Sea: A Naval History of Britain,* vol. 1, 660–1649 (London: HarperCollins, 1998), chaps. 23, 24, 26.

Senior, Clive. *A Nation of Pirates: English Piracy in Its Heyday* (New York: Crane, Russack, 1976).

Tully, Miss. *Letters Written During a Ten Years' Residence at the Court of Tripoli, Published from The Originals in the Possession of the Family of the late Richard Tully, Esq., the British Consul* (London, 1816). A limited (thousand-copy) edition edited and introduced by Seton Deardon was published in London by Arthur Barker, 1957. The exact identity of "Miss Tully" is unknown, but she was the companion of Richard Tully's wife.

I am greatly indebted to Richard Pennell for his active help and knowledgeable advice.

6. The Widows

Brooks, Graham, ed. *Trial of Captain Kidd* (Edinburgh: William Hodge, 1930).

Cordingly, David. *Under the Black Flag: The Romance and the Reality of Life Among the Pirates* (New York: Harcourt Brace, 1995).

Earle, Peter. *The Wreck of the* Almiranta: *Sir William Phips and the Hispaniola Treasure* (London: Macmillan, 1979). The complete story of the wreck of the *Nuestra Señora de la Concepción* and the expeditions to recover the treasure, told in entertaining and well-founded detail.

Edwards, Everett, and Jeannette Edwards Rattray. *Whale Off* (New York: Coward-McCann, 1926). The story of Long Island offshore whaling.

Laing, Alexander. *The American Heritage History of Seafaring America* (New York: McGraw-Hill for American Heritage, 1974). A shorter version of the Phips story.

Overton, Jacqueline. *Long Island's Story* (New York: Doubleday, Doran, 1929).

Rediker, Marcus. *Between the Devil and the Deep Blue Sea—Merchant Seamen, Pirates, and the Anglo-American Maritime World, 1700–1750* (Cambridge, England: Cambridge University Press, 1987).

———. "Libertalia: The Pirates' Utopia." In *Pirates: Terror on the High Seas—from the Caribbean to the South China Sea,* ed. David Cordingly (London: Salamander Press, 1998; North Dighton, Mass.: JG Press, 1998), pp. 124–39.

Ritchie, Robert C. *Captain Kidd and the War Against the Pirates* (Cambridge, Mass.: Harvard University Press, 1986).

Thank you to the Mattamuskeet Foundation for information about William and Sarah Kidd, and a rousing toast to the host of interested and enthusiastic commentators on Tony Malesic's pirate discussion list.

7. Bonny & Read

Anonymous. *The Tryals of Captain John Rackham and Other Pirates . . . Also, the Tryals of Mary Read and Anne Bonny, Alias Boon, on Monday the 28th Day of the said Month of November, at St. Jago de la Vega* (Jamaica: Robert Baldwin, 1721).

Dow, George Francis, and John Henry Edmonds. *The Pirates of the New England Coast, 1630–1730.* (repr., New York: Dover, 1996), chap. 1 (from which the quotation from Captain John Smith's *Admiral of New England* is taken); chap. 5.

Johnson, Captain Charles. *A General History of the Robberies and Murders of the Most Notorious Pyrates* (London, 1724). Some of the numerous editions of this book have the simpler title *A General History of the Pyrates,* and in several, also, the author is given as Daniel Defoe.

Kinkor, Kenneth J. "Black Men Under the Black Flag," 1998. An excellent discussion of democracy on pirate ships and motives for joining a crew.

Marx, Jenifer G. "The Golden Age of Piracy." In *Pirates: Terror on the High Seas— from the Caribbean to the South China Sea,* ed. David Cordingly (London: Salamander Press, 1998; North Dighton, Mass.: JG Press, 1998), pp. 100–123.

Rediker, Marcus. "Liberty Beneath the Jolly Roger: The Lives of Anne Bonny and Mary Read, Pirates." In *Iron Men, Wooden Women: Gender and Seafaring in the Atlantic World, 1700–1920,* ed. Margaret S. Creighton and Lisa Norling (Baltimore, Md.: Johns Hopkins University Press, 1996), pp. 1–33.

Wheelwright, Julie. "Tars, Tarts and Swashbucklers." In *Bold in Her Breeches: Women Pirates Across the Ages,* ed. Jo Stanley (London: Pandora, 1995), pp. 176–200.

Websites which provide excellent evidence of the enduring popularity of the legend:
http://www.powerup.com.au/~glen/anne.htm
http://www2.waikato.ac.nz/education/edstudies/0085204/ammm6'bonny.htm
http://www.geocities.com/CollegePark/4704/annebonny.html
http://www.discovery.com/DCO/doc/1012/world/history/2pirates/2pirates.html

I am grateful to Gillian Smythe for her enthusiasm in searching these out for me. Tony Malesic's pirate discussion list *pirates@listbox.com* also made the research for this chapter a lot of fun.

8. "THE NAKED TRUTH"

"Lucy Brewer." *The Female Marine,* etc. (New York: Luther Wales [actually Boston: N. Coverly Jr.], 1815). Published in *The Female Marine and Related Words: Narratives of Cross-dressing and Urban Vice in America's Early Republic,* ed. Daniel A. Cohen, who also wrote the excellent introduction (Boston: University of Massachusetts Press, 1997).

de Pauw, Linda Grant. *Seafaring Women* (Boston: Houghton Mifflin, 1982), chap. 2. Professor de Pauw's citation for the story of Rachel Wall is Edward R. Snow's *Women and the Sea* (New York: Dodd, Mead, 1962).

Fernández-Armesto, Felipe. *Columbus and the Conquest of the Impossible* (New York: Saturday Review Press, 1974).

Johnson, Captain Charles. *A General History of the Robberies and Murders of the Most Notorious Pyrates* (London, 1724).

Paine, Lincoln P. *Ships of the World: An Historical Encyclopedia* (Boston: Houghton Mifflin, 1997). I am grateful to Lincoln for pointing out the aptness of de Barreto's story.

Pennell, C. R. ("Richard"). "Who Needs Pirate Heroes?" Paper in preparation for publication. I am grateful to Richard Pennell for sharing this with me.

Rogozinski, Jan. *Pirates! An A–Z Encyclopedia—Brigands, Buccaneers, and Privateers in Fact, Fiction, and Legend* (New York: De Capo, 1996). Not entirely reliable, but a useful and entertaining resource if taken with a grain of salt.

Schweikart, Larry, and B. R. Burg. "Stand by to Repel Historians: Modern Scholarship and Caribbean Pirates, 1650–1725," *The Historian,* 46:2 (1984), pp. 219–34. A very pertinent overview of publications about pirates. Attributes *A General History* to Defoe.

Stairs, Captain John. Testimony in the Jordan trial, Court of Admiralty, Halifax, November 16, 1809. Reprinted, with commentary, in *Captured by Pirates,* ed. John Richard Stephens (Cambria Pines by the Sea, Calif.: Fern Canyon Press, 1996), pp. 337–42.

Stark, Suzanne J. *Female Tars: Women Aboard Ship in the Age of Sail* (Annapolis, Md.: Naval Institute Press, 1996), chap. 3. Ms. Stark's masterly analysis of the Mary Anne Talbot story is on pp. 107–10 under the heading "The Spurious Autobiography of Mary Anne Talbot." It must be noted that most historians accept the Talbot account as fact, but I find Ms. Stark's arguments and documentation convincing.

Verrill, A. Hyatt. *The Real Story of the Pirate* (New York and London: Appleton, 1923; facs., Glorieta, N.Mex.: Rio Grande Press, 1989). Enjoyable, but to be taken with a grain of salt. Yet another version of the Mary Read appearance—this time in dress coat and breeches.

Wheelwright, Julie. "Tars, Tarts and Swashbucklers." In *Bold in Her Breeches: Women Pirates Across the Ages,* ed. Jo Stanley (London: Pandora, 1995), pp. 176–200.

"Woman Privateer Captain," Stamford [Lincolnshire] *Mercury and Philadelphia Press.* Reprinted in *Mariner's Mirror* 79: 4 (November 1993), pp. 471–72.

The account of Mary Harvey comes from the Proceedings of the Court of Admiralty in Virginia, HCA 1/99 fols. 2–8, quoted in Peter Wilson Coldham, *English Convicts in America,* vol. 1, *1617–1775* (New Orleans: Polyanthos, 1974), pp. 67, 123; also see H. R. McIlwaine, *Executive Journals of the Council of Colonial Virginia* 4:149 (Richmond: Virginia State Library, 1930); and Donald G. Shomette, *Pirates on the Chesapeake: Being a True History of Pirates, Picaroons, and Raiders on Chesapeake Bay, 1610–1807* (Centreville, Md.: Tidewater, 1985), pp. 240–41. I am grateful to Ken Kinkor for drawing this to my attention. I also thank John Richard Stephens for the copy of the entry in the London *Times.*

9. Ship's Business

Berckman, Evelyn. *Victims of Piracy: The Admiralty Court, 1575–1678* (London: Hamish Hamilton, 1979).

Burford, E. J. *Queen of the Bawds* (London: Spearman, 1973). The rousing story of Madam Elizabeth Holland, taken from her biography, *Madame Britannica Hollandia* (London: Richard Barnes, 1632).

Busch, Briton Cooper. *The War Against the Seals: A History of the North American Seal Fishery* (Kingston and Montreal: McGill-Queen's University Press, 1985).

Evenden, Doreen A. "Mary Rose of Portsmouth: A Seventeenth Century Physician and Surgeon," *Mariner's Mirror* 79:3 (August 1993), pp. 333–34.

Jones, A.G.E. *Ships Employed in the South Seas Trade, 1775–1861* (Canberra: Roebuck Society Publication #36, 1986).

Laing, Alexander. *The American Heritage History of Seafaring America* (New York: McGraw-Hill for American Heritage, 1974).

Linklater, Elizabeth. *Child Under Sail* (London: Jonathan Cape, 1938), introduction.

Mowat, Susan. "Shipping and Trade in Scotland, 1556–1830," *Mariner's Mirror* 83:1 (February 1997), pp. 14–20.

Parish, Rev. W. D. *A Dictionary of the Sussex Dialect and Collection of Provincialisms. Together with Some Sussex Sayings and Crafts* (Lewes, Sussex: Farncombe, 1875).

Richards, Rhys. *Into the South Seas: The Southern Whale Fishery Comes of Age on the Brazil Banks, 1765 to 1812* (Paremata, New Zealand: author, 1993).

Stark, Suzanne J. *Female Tars: Women Aboard Ship in the Age of Sail* (Annapolis, Md.: Naval Institute Press, 1996), chap. 4. Here, Ms. Stark weaves the story of Mary Lacy through comprehensive quotations from her book.

Waugh, Mary. *Smuggling in Kent & Sussex, 1700–1840* (Newbury, Berkshire: Countryside Books, 1985). One of a series of books on English smuggling, all recommended.

A great deal of valuable information was received from the members of "marhst-1," a maritime history internet discussion list sponsored by the Museum of the Great Lakes at Kingston, Ontario, with the support of Queen's University. I thank Michael Wenzel and Robert Parthesius for the stories of Anne Wyatt and Geert Jans. For background details of the frigate *Delaware,* I am grateful to John Snyder, Steve McLaughlin, Keith E. Allen, Paul "Stormy Weather," Peter Beeston, Scott Peterson, Marc Bartolomeo, Lars Bruzelius, David Meagher, and Craig O'Donnell.

10. Fatal Shores

Bateson, Charles. *The Convict Ships, 1787–1868* (New South Wales: A. H. & A. W. Reed, 1974).

Cook, Judith. *To Brave Every Danger: The Epic Life of Mary Bryant* (London: Macmillan, 1993). The definitive account.

Hughes, Robert. *The Fatal Shore: A History of the Transportation of Convicts to Australia, 1787–1868* (London: Collins Harvill, 1987).

Mayhew, Henry. *Mayhew's London, Being Selections from "London Labour and the London Poor,"* ed. and introduced by Peter Quennell (London, 1851; London: Spring Books, n.d.).

Paine, Lincoln P. *Ships of the World: An Historical Encyclopedia.* (Boston: Houghton Mifflin, 1997).

Parker, Mary Ann. *A Voyage Round the World* (London, 1795; facs. with a commentary by Gavin Fry, published by Hordern House for the Australian National Maritime Museum, 1991).

Robinson, William. *Nautical Economy* (London: author, 1836). Memoir of "Jack Nastyface." Reprinted as *Jack Nastyface: Memoirs of a Seaman* (Annapolis, Md.: Naval Institute Press, 1973).

Stark, Suzanne J. *Female Tars: Women Aboard Ship in the Age of Sail* (Annapolis, Md.: Naval Institute Press, 1996), chap. 1.

11. Fatal Impact

Cameron, Ian. *Lost Paradise—The Exploration of the Pacific* (Topsfield, Mass.: Salem House, 1987).

Dauphin rhyming log, Nicholson Whaling Room, Providence Public Library, Providence, Rhode Island.

Dening, Greg. *Islands and Beaches: A Discourse on a Silent Land, Marquesas 1774–1880* (Melbourne: Melbourne University Press, 1980).

Forster, Honoré. "Paradise & Noble Savages," *National Library of Australia News* 9:4 (January 1999), pp. 3–8.

Grayland, Eugene. *Coasts of Treachery* (Wellington, New Zealand: A. H. & A. W. Reed, 1963).

Jones, Richard M. "Stonington Borough: A Connecticut Seaport in the Nineteenth Century." Ph.D. diss., City University of New York, 1976. The *Cavalier* reference is taken from here.

Lawson, Will. *Blue Gum Clippers and Whale Ships of Tasmania* (Tasmania, Australia: The Shiplovers' Society, 1949; repr. 1986).

Moorehead, Alan. *The Fatal Impact: An Account of the Invasion of the South Pacific, 1767–1840* (New York: Penguin, 1966; repr. 1985).

Rhodes, Captain W. B. *The Whaling Journal of Captain W. B. Rhodes, 1836–1838,* ed. C. R. Straubel (Christchurch, New Zealand: Whitcombe & Tombs, 1954).

Simpson, Tony. *Art & Massacre: Documentary Racism in "The Burning of the Boyd"* (New Zealand: Cultural Construction Company, 1993). Interpretation of Walter Wright's 1908 painting *The Burning of the* Boyd, now held by the Auckland City Art Gallery

12. THE DECEIT OF DRESS

Dugaw, Dianne. "Female Sailors Bold: Transvestite Heroines and the Markers of Gender and Class." In *Iron Men, Wooden Women: Gender and Seafaring in the Atlantic World, 1700–1920,* ed. Margaret S. Creighton and Lisa Norling (Baltimore, Md.: Johns Hopkins University Press, 1996), pp 34–54.

Knowsley, Jo. "Beware, Big Welsh Girls in High Hats," *Daily Telegraph,* February 1997.

O'Neill, Sean. "How Welsh Women Turned the Tide on French Invasion," *Daily Telegraph,* February 1997.

Pipe, Daphne. "Spinster Sailor," *Mariner's Mirror* 64:3 (August 1978), p. 275. Story of Ann Jane Thornton.

Stark, Suzanne J. *Female Tars: Women Aboard Ship in the Age of Sail* (Annapolis, Md.: Naval Institute Press, 1996), chap. 3.

Thompson, Edgar K. "Spinster Sailor," *Mariner's Mirror* 63:4 (November 1977), p. 334. Story of Elizabeth Stephens.

"Women as Sailors," *Mariner's Mirror* 3 (1913), pp. 352 (Bowling), 381 (Bowden).

I am very grateful to Edwin King for forwarding the news items.

13. DECENTLY SKIRTED

Dow, George F. *Slave Ships and Slaving* (Salem, Mass.: Marine Research Society, 1927).

Fraser, Antonia. *Mary Queen of Scots* (New York: Delacorte, 1969).

Haley, Nelson Cole. *Whale Hunt* (London: Travel Book Club, 1951). Memoir by the boatsteerer on the *Charles W. Morgan.*

Heffernan, Thomas Farel. "Eonism on the *Town-Ho:* Or, What *Did* Steelkit Say?" *Melville Society Extracts,* no. 83 (November 1990), pp. 10–12. Amusing discussion of the *Lalla Rookh* pamphlet and the E. C. Hine novel, from which the quotations are taken.

Howland, Ellis L. "Romance on a Whaleship. America's Murderous Mutineer Proved to Be a Woman in Disguise," *The Evening Standard,* n.d., save for pencil on clipping, 1903.

Little, Elizabeth A. "The Female Sailor on the *Christopher Mitchell:* Fact and Fantasy." I thank Dr. Little for sending me a copy of this useful and interesting article.

Ryan, William Redmond. *Personal Adventures in Upper and Lower California in 1848–9* (1850; repr., New York: Arno, 1973). Californian cross-dressers.

Stark, Suzanne J. "The Adventures of Two Women Whalers," *American Neptune,* 44:1 (winter 1984), pp. 22–24.

———. *Female Tars: Women Aboard Ship in the Age of Sail* (Annapolis, Md.: Naval Institute Press, 1996)

"Woman Shipped on a Whaler as a Man," *New Bedford Sunday Standard,* April 1, 1917. Another version of the Weldon story.

"Women as Sailors," *Mariner's Mirror* 4 (1914), p. 30 (female on *Boudeuse*).

Wynne, Elizabeth. *The Wynne Diaries,* ed. Anne Fremantle. Vol. 1, *1789–1794* (London: Oxford University Press, Humphrey Milford, 1935).

I thank Catherine Mayhew and the Martha's Vineyard Historical Society for searching out all the Georgiana Leonard material from their archives.

14. WAR BRIDE

Austen, Jane. *Persuasion.* 1818.

Fraser, Flora. *Beloved Emma: The Life of Emma Lady Hamilton* (London: Weidenfeld and Nicolson, 1986).

Naish, G. P. B. *Nelson's Letters to His Wife and Other Documents, 1785–1831* (London: Routledge and Kegan Paul, with the Navy Records Society, 1958).

Pocock, Tom. *Horatio Nelson* (London: Bodley Head, 1987).

Russell, Jack. *Nelson and the Hamiltons* (London: Blond, 1969).

Wynne, Elizabeth. *The Wynne Diaries,* ed. Anne Fremantle. Vol. 2, *1794–1798.* (London: Oxford University Press, Humphrey Milford, 1937).

I am particularly grateful to Lincoln Paine for his help and interest, and also thank Jane Buchman and Trevor Kenchington for their advice.

15. WOMEN OF WAR

Estes, J. Worth. *Naval Surgeon: Life and Death at Sea in the Age of Sail* (Canton, Mass.: Science History Publications, 1998). A particularly useful insight into life on a man-of-war.

Fitchett, W. H. *Nelson and His Captains* (London: Bell, 1902).

Lewis, Michael. *A Social History of the Navy, 1793–1815* (London: Allen & Unwin, 1960).

Lloyd, Christopher. *The British Seaman* (London: Collins, 1968).

Masefield, John. *Sea Life in Nelson's Time* (London: Conway Maritime Press, 1971).

Nicol, John. *The Life and Adventures of John Nicol, Mariner,* ed. John Howell (Edinburgh, 1822; repr., New York: Farrar & Rinehart, 1936).

Pope, Dudley. *The Black Ship.* (New York: Holt, 1998; repr. of 1963 edition). The story of the *Hermione* mutiny.

Richardson, William. *A Mariner of England: An Account of the Career of William Richardson . . . as Told by Himself,* ed. Spencer Childers (London: Conway Maritime Press, 1970).

Rodger, N. A. M. *The Wooden World: An Anatomy of the Georgian Navy* (London: Collins, 1986).

Stark, Suzanne J. *Female Tars: Women Aboard Ship in the Age of Sail* (Annapolis, Md.: Naval Institute Press, 1996), chap. 2.

Van Denburgh, Elizabeth Douglas. *My Voyage in the United States Frigate "Congress"* (New York: Desmond FitzGerald, 1913). The story of the Turrill family on passage to the U.S. consul's post in Honolulu.

Wilks, Brian. *Jane Austen* (London: Hamlyn, 1978).

"Woman in HMS *Euryalus* at Trafalgar." Reprinted from *Kentish Gazette* and *United Service Gazette. Mariner's Mirror* 76:1 (February 1990), p. 76.

Wynne, Elizabeth, et al. *The Wynne Diaries,* ed. Anne Fremantle. Vol. 2, *1794–1798* (London: Oxford University Press, Humphrey Milford, 1937).

16. NELSON'S WOMEN

Fraser, Flora. *Beloved Emma: The Life of Emma Lady Hamilton* (London: Weidenfeld and Nicolson, 1986).

Hibbert, Christopher. *Nelson: A Personal History* (London: Viking, 1994).

Naish, G. P. B. *Nelson's Letters to His Wife and Other Documents, 1785–1831* (London: Routledge and Kegan Paul, with the Navy Records Society, 1958).

Pocock, Tom. *Horatio Nelson* (London: Bodley Head, 1987).

———. *Nelson and His World* (London: Thames and Hudson, 1968).

———. *Nelson's Women* (London: Andre Deutsch, 1999).

Russell, Jack. *Nelson and the Hamiltons* (London: Blond, 1969).

White, Colin. *The Nelson Companion* (Annapolis, Md.: Naval Institute Press, 1995).

17. VOYAGES OF DISCOVERY

Bassett, Marnie. *Realms and Islands: The World Voyage of Rose de Freycinet in the Corvette* Uranie, *1817–1820* (London: Oxford University Press, 1962).

Cameron, Ian. *Lost Paradise—The Exploration of the Pacific* (Topsfield, Mass.: Salem House, 1987).

Dunmore, John. *French Explorers in the Pacific* (Oxford: Clarendon, 1969).

de Freycinet, Rose. *A Woman of Courage: The Journal of Rose de Freycinet on her Voyage around the World, 1817–1820,* trans. and ed. Marc Serge Rivière (Canberra: National Library of Australia, 1996). The first complete translation of Rose de Freycinet's writings. Informatively introduced; a beautiful publication, lavishly illustrated.

Morrell, Abby Jane. *Narrative of a Voyage to the Ethiopic and South Atlantic Ocean, Indian Ocean, Chinese Sea, North and South Pacific Ocean* (1833; repr., Upper Saddle River, N.J.: Gregg, 1970).

Morrell, Benjamin. *A Narrative of Four Voyages to the South Seas, North and South Pacific Ocean, Chinese Sea, Ethiopic and Southern Atlantic Ocean, Indian and Antarctic Ocean from the Year 1822 to 1831* (New York: J. & J. Harper, 1832).

Paine, Lincoln P. *Ships of the World: An Historical Encyclopedia* (Boston: Houghton Mifflin, 1997).

18. TO THE RESCUE!

Armstrong, Richard. *Grace Darling, Maid and Myth* (London: Dent, 1965). An effort to debunk the myth; it gives the facts but is more amusing than convincing.

Clifford, J. Candace, and Mary Louise Clifford. *Women Who Kept the Lights: An Illustrated History of Female Lighthouse Keepers* (Williamsburg, Va.: Cypress Communications, 1993). An excellent study of these American women by two dedicated researchers. Contains the stories of Kate Walker, Abbie Burgess, and Kate Moore.

Mitford, Jessica. *Grace Had an English Heart* (London: Viking, 1988). An entertaining and extremely well-illustrated account that includes the story of Ida Lewis.

Paine, Lincoln P. *Ships of the World: An Historical Encyclopedia* (Boston: Houghton Mifflin, 1997). Entry on the *Forfarshire.*

Stonehouse, Fred. *Maritime Women on the Great Lakes* (forthcoming). I am very grateful to Fred for his interest and assistance, and the stories of Abigail Becker and Maebelle Mason.

Website: *http://www.tiac.net/users/buster/shiningsea/scituate/scituate.html*

I am grateful to Frank Young, John B. Hunter, Craig O'Donnell, Andrew Toppan, and Jeffrey B. Smith for help with the story of the Bates "Army of Two."

19. NORTHWEST PASSAGE

Beattie, Owen, and John Geiger. *Frozen in Time: The Fate of the Franklin Expedition* (London: Bloomsbury, 1987).

Berton, Pierre. *The Arctic Grail* (New York: Viking, 1988).

———. *Jane Franklin's Obsession* (Toronto: McClelland & Stewart, 1992).

Lubbock, Basil. *The Arctic Whalers* (Glasgow: Brown, Son & Ferguson, 1937).

Neatby, Leslie H. *Search for Franklin: The Story of One of the Great Dramas of Polar Exploration* (London: Arthur Barker, 1970). An excellent account of the various search attempts of the Franklin party, using primary material that brings the protagonists to life.

Paine, Lincoln P. *Ships of the World: An Historical Encyclopedia* (Boston: Houghton Mifflin, 1997).

Parker, Franklin. "George Peabody and the Search for Sir John Franklin, 1852–1854." *American Neptune* 20:2 (April 1960), pp. 104–11.

Ross, W. Gillies. *Arctic Whalers, Icy Seas* (Toronto: Irwin, 1985).

———. "William Penny (1809–1892)," *Arctic* 36:4 (1983), pp. 380–81.

I am indebted to Walter Lewis, who posted a long and fascinating account of the search on "marhst-l," the maritime history discussion group administered from Kingston, Ontario. A comprehensive history can be found on the website compiled by Michael Phillips and Dave Mullington, *http://www.cronab.demon.co.uk/frank.htm.* I am also very grateful to Martin Evans, who pointed out many good sources, particularly in reference to the ships *Lady Franklin* and *Sophia.*

20. ICE QUEENS

Apostol, Jane. "Sailing with the Ruler of the Arctic Sea," *Pacific North West Quarterly* 72:4 (October 1981), pp. 146–56. I am grateful to The Huntington Library for permission to quote from Mary Jane Healy's diaries.

Berton, Pierre. *The Arctic Grail* (New York: Viking, 1988).

Bockstoce, John. *Whales, Ice, & Men: The History of Whaling in the Western Arctic* (Seattle: University of Washington Press in association with the New Bedford [Massachusetts] Whaling Museum, 1986).

Hare, Lloyd Custer Mayhew. *Salted Tories: The Story of the Whaling Fleets of San Francisco* (Mystic, Ct.: Mystic Seaport Museum Publications, 1960).

Olds, Elizabeth Fagg. *Women of the Four Winds: The Adventures of Four of America's First Four Women Explorers* (Boston: Houghton Mifflin, 1985). Part 4, Louise Arner Boyd.

Ross, W. Gillies. *This Distant and Unsurveyed Country: A Woman's Winter at Baffin Island, 1857–1858* (Montreal: McGill-Queens Nature and Northern States), p. 15.

I thank Bill Wells for sending me information about Mary Jane Healy, and Gillian Smythe for sending an image of the cutter *Bear*.

21. A Woman at the Helm

Bath records, 1887 (Maine Maritime Museum), MS-46.

Camden-Rockport Bicentennial publication (Camden, Maine: W. Douglas Hall, Publisher, The Camden Herald Pub. Co., 1969).

Champion, whaleship, bills of sale. Martha's Vineyard Historical Society, Edgartown, Massachusetts.

Eaton, Cyrus. *Annals of Warren* (Warren, Maine, 1877; facs. ed., Warren Historical Society, 1968).

Grindle, Roger L. *Quarry and Kiln: The Story of Maine's Lime Industry* (Rockland, Maine: Courier-Gazette, 1971).

Jones, Richard M. "Stonington Borough: A Connecticut Seaport in the Nineteenth Century," Ph.D. diss., City University of New York, 1976.

Locke, John L. *Sketches of the History of the Town of Camden, Maine, 1605–1859* (Hallowell, Maine: Masters, Smith, 1859).

Maria Tibbetts Papers, Manuscripts Collection, coll. 99, G. W. Blunt White Library, Mystic Seaport Museum, Mystic, Connecticut.

Morris, Ronald. *The Captain's Lady* (London: Chatto & Windus, 1985). The full and fascinating story of Charles Hoare and Beatrice Holme Sumner Fry.

Morse, Charles Wyman, in Morse family papers, Maine Maritime Museum. MS coll. 47.

Overlock, Leland. *Windships of Warren, Maine: Being a Collation of Records of Shipbuilding, 1770–1867* (Brewer, Maine: author, 1988).

Owen, Henry William. *History of Bath* (Bath, Maine: Times Company, 1936).

Robinson, R. *History of Camden and Rockport Maine* (Camden, Maine: Camden Publishing Co., 1907).

"Women as Sailors," *Mariner's Mirror* 4 (1914), p. 91. The report of the enterprising Betsey Miller, reprinted.

For offering comments and information about the training ship *Mercury,* I wish to thank Lars Bruzelius, John Guard, Lyn Morris, Andrew Sellon, Pat Barnhouse, Alistair Deayton, and John Harland. Lincoln Paine, yet again, has been extremely helpful, in this instance having a lot of fun with the ship-shares figures that I gave him. I thank Catherine Mayhew and the Martha's Vineyard Historical Society, Edgartown, Massachusetts, for the *Champion* material. In this regard, I also thank Kelly Drake and other Mystic Seaport Museum G. W. Blunt White Library staff, and particularly Nathan Lipfert of the Maine Maritime Museum at Bath.

Websites on women and the sea
enthusiastically searched out by Gillian Smythe:

http://www.simmons.edu/~hollistj/history.html
http://www.simmons.edu/~hollistj/women.html
http://www.simmons.edu/~hollistj/biblio.html
http://www.simmons.edu/~hollistj/maritime.html
http://www.literascape.com/Readers/Reader/1996Summer/smith.html
http://www.rmm.ac.uk/rcs/women/index.html

INDEX

Index

Index

Index